Repressed Memories

Repressed Memories

Can You Trust Them?

Dr. Arlys Norcross McDonald

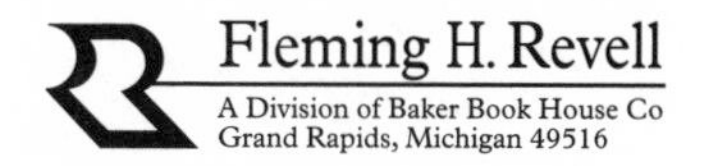
Fleming H. Revell
A Division of Baker Book House Co
Grand Rapids, Michigan 49516

Published by Fleming H. Revell
a division of Baker Book House Company
P.O. Box 6287, Grand Rapids, MI 49516-6287

Printed in the United States of America

Library of Congress Cataloging-in-Publication Data

McDonald, Arlys Norcross, 1943–
Repressed memories : can you trust them? / Arlys Norcross McDonald.
p. cm.
Includes bibliographical references.
ISBN 0-8007-1715-5
1. Adult child abuse victims. 2. Recovered memory. 3. False memory syndrome. I. Title.
RC569.5.C55M385 1995
616.85'82239—dc20 95-021481

Names and details of the case studies used in this book have been changed to protect the confidentiality of those involved.

To my friends and clients,
who have so courageously faced their own traumas,
and diligently pursued the truth of these memories.
Thank you for allowing me to take this journey with you.

Contents

Acknowledgments

I wish to express my deepest appreciation and thankfulness to:

My family, Gary, Brian, and Carmen for your love and patience during my preoccupation with the writing of this book. Gary, your legal expertise gave me a different and valuable perspective, and you assisted me in so many different ways. Brian, thanks for teaching me to use the computer, especially "save." Carmen, your smiles and laughter brought light into the dark, dreary moments.

Marita Littauer for your advice, direction, and enthusiasm in both organizing and writing, and for your negotiations with the publishers. Thanks for believing in this book and in my ability to write it.

Marsha Williams, my assistant, for countless hours in word processing, locating the research, and numerous other tasks necessary for completing the manuscript and organizing my life and business. You always did it with an amazing cheerfulness and enthusiasm.

Marilyn Murray, for your time and willingness to be involved in this book, for your openness about your own trauma and search for truth, for your reading and recommendations, and for continually encouraging me to begin and complete this book. Thanks for your exuberance and your friendship.

Les Eddington, dean and biology professor at Azusa Pacific University (and my brother-in-law), for your assistance in research and writing about the functioning of the brain.

Lana Jones, for bringing fun and laughter into my life. You were always there when I needed you.

My friends, especially Renee Goodrich and Wendy Hancock. You listened and encouraged me, read the manuscript, and gave such excellent input.

Other family members, Lyla, Terresa, Tracie, and Randy, for your assistance in searching for those elusive journals and books.

My mentors and professors, especially Dr. Logan Wright, Dr. Joseph Reyher, and Dr. Carl Kadlub, for believing in and encouraging me.

Robert Solso and Dr. Bruce Narramore for your roles in getting me into the field of psychology. Without either of you, I would not be a psychologist today.

The staff at Baker Book House/Revell Books for your assistance in the publication of this book, especially Randy Petersen, Becky Van Arragon, and the other editors, and Karen Steele in publicity.

Most of all, I thank God, for wisdom, direction, love, and acceptance, and for the gifts he has given to me through my life. SOLI DEO GLORIA.

Introduction

Major controversy exists in the psychology community, on radio and television, and among the general public concerning the truth of memories. What is this all about? Why is this topic so controversial and so emotionally charged?

On one hand are those who adamantly support the belief that all childhood memories are true, including those memories that have been partially or totally blocked out of conscious awareness, often called *repressed* or *recovered* memories. The belief is that children do not lie about such issues as abuse. Nor would an adult make up such a story because of the shame, guilt, and humiliation associated with any victimization, especially sexual abuse. Many therapists tell of their experiences with clients and the convincing emotions accompanying their stories of abuse. They observe present-day difficulties that seem directly related to the type and severity of abuse described by the client and they see the healing that occurs when the memories are resolved. Many clients are very hurt when they describe their painful, frightening experiences of abuse and are not believed.

On the other hand are people who claim to be accused of abuse that never occurred. Some believe therapists are introducing these ideas to the alleged victims. Those who have been falsely accused have suffered extreme pain, especially when the accusations come from their own children, whom they have spent years loving and nurturing. They believe their children's damage is the result of therapy that has created lies. These parents become the targets of their children's anger and revenge. They lose contact with their children and grandchildren, suffer public humiliation, and sometimes face lawsuits and financial ruin, all for something they claim they never did.

> The False Memory Syndrome Foundation was established in 1992 by Pamela and Peter Freyd after their daughter Jennifer, now a professor of psychology at the University of Oregon, publicly confronted them with accusations of sexual abuse by her father—an allegation they have energetically disputed. Many of these families blame zealous therapists and popular self-help books for encouraging their children's "fake memories."[1]

There is a third group involved, the many therapists who are expressing fear, hurt, and anger for being accused of implanting these memories. They have done in therapy what they were taught to do. They have given enormous amounts of time and emotional support, sometimes without pay, to deeply hurting individuals. Instead of appreciation, they are receiving threats of lawsuits and suspension of their licenses, ruining their livelihood and reputation, for actions they believe they have not committed.

The intensity of the conflict appears to be fueled by the move toward confrontation and lawsuits against alleged perpetrators, and breaking all contact with accused families.

My husband, Gary, an attorney, has provided for me the understanding of important distinctions between the way a therapist looks at memory, and the high level of proof or evidence the law requires. Our whole legal system is based on the fact that we are presumed innocent until proven guilty, and that must apply to those accused of child abuse.

Therapists, on the other hand, have generally accepted a client's truth as whatever he or she presents, unless the client is obviously psychotic or out of touch with reality. The crossover from therapy to a legal suit cannot and must not be taken without compelling corroboration.

And yet:

> Lawsuits filed by adults who claim to have recovered memories of childhood sexual abuse have mushroomed in the past few years. Since 1989, a total of 19 states have passed legislation allowing people to sue for recovery of damages for injury suffered as a result of childhood sexual abuse remembered for the first time during adulthood. Other states are contemplating similar laws. No exact numbers exist, but at least 300 lawsuits involving formerly repressed memories—mainly of sexual abuse—have been filed. This rush to legal judgment has created an intense desire for

> scientific certitude about how people recall past sexual abuse. For now, however, anecdotes and animosity far outpace relevant data in these highly publicized legal confrontations.[2]

The November 1993 *Monitor*, published by the American Psychological Association (APA), briefly discusses some of the conflict as well as the plans to study this topic. The APA has appointed a task force called the "Working Group on Investigation of Memories of Childhood Abuse." They are charged with "examining what is currently known about memory and suggestibility in adults who claim they were abused as children." In their first meeting, they reached a consensus that "both ends of the continuum" on people's memories of abuse are possible. They also agreed "it is possible that, under some cue conditions, early memories may be retrievable. At the other extreme, it is possible under some conditions, for memories to be implanted or embedded."[3]

In December 1994, the *Monitor* reported the release of the task force's interim report: "The report, which is the work of a cross-disciplinary panel . . . acknowledges both the possibility of remembering long-forgotten memories of abuse and of constructing convincing pseudo-memories for events that never occurred."[4]

The *Monitor* also summarizes the conclusions of the report as follows:

- Controversies about adult recollections should not obscure the fact that child sexual abuse is a complex, pervasive problem in America that has historically been unacknowledged.
- Most people who were sexually abused as children remember all or part of what happened to them.
- It is possible for memories of abuse that have been forgotten for a long time to be remembered, although the mechanisms by which this might happen are not well understood.
- It is possible to construct convincing pseudo-memories for events that never occurred, although the mechanisms by which this occurs are not well understood.
- There are gaps in knowledge about the processes that lead to accurate or inaccurate recollection of childhood sexual abuse.[5]

The American Medical Association (AMA) recently made the following policy statement: "The use of recovered memories is fraught with problems of potential misapplication. . . . Few cases in which adults make accusations of childhood sexual abuse based on recovered memories can be proved or disproved. . . . It is not yet known how to distinguish true memories from imagined events in these cases. . . ."[6] The council urged therapists to address their clients' emotional and mental needs apart from the truth or falsity of their claims.

At the 1993 convention of the APA in Toronto, intense feelings and reactions were expressed over this topic, dividing the members into two opposing camps. Two recognized experts debated the issue. Dr. Elizabeth Loftus, a research psychologist from the University of Washington, specializes in the area of the unreliability of eyewitness reports and is a frequent expert testifying for the defense. She questions the accuracy of memories, and even the existence of repression of psychologically traumatic events. Dr. John Briere, from the University of Southern California, is a recognized expert therapist in treating trauma patients. He presented the view of many therapists who find repression of traumatic events common in their practices.

Frank Farley, former president of the APA, says he never has seen an issue in which "you have science and (therapeutic) practice coming into such conflict." The American Psychiatric Association issued a four-page statement urging its members to maintain neutrality about their patients' recovered memories.[7]

My interest in childhood memories and reports of child abuse began in the '60s at Michigan State University, where I was completing my Ph.D. in clinical psychology with a minor in child development. I pursued additional training in repressed trauma. Since that time, I have continued a full-time clinical practice, with part-time teaching in assessment and child development. Especially in the '70s, there were few professionals who worked with blocked memories. As I became a psychologist who specialized in this area, other professionals requested treatment of their patients diagnosed with repressed trauma. I have worked in both inpatient and outpatient settings.

I am currently the owner-director of McDonald Therapy Center in Vista, California, which specializes in the treatment of childhood and adult trauma. Over the past twenty-five years, we have treated men, women, and children of all ages. Their abuse has occurred as long ago as fifty years and as recently as a few days before entering therapy. Memories have been repressed, partially remembered, or totally remembered by one or more people. We also have seen admitted perpetrators, those claiming false accusations, people questioning their memories, and families seeking reconciliation after true and after false accusations.

Through extensive personal therapy, I have experienced and recovered from my own repressed trauma. After prayerful consideration and investigation, I have come to believe that some of my memories are true, some are false, some are symbolic of my childhood view of events, and many are a mixture of facts and fears. Only as I have been able to examine the reality of my memories, being open to all options, have I been able to leave the past behind me.

I also have faced false accusations. The incredible pain, fear, confusion, and disbelief have provided great empathy for those who are not guilty, but who are faced with the difficult task of proving innocence. I have experienced the necessary steps of restoration, finding hope and faith in God when there was none in the circumstances. I survived, and learned how to forgive and rebuild shattered relationships.

Facing all sides of this controversy—as a survivor of repressed memories, as a therapist specializing in trauma, and as a falsely accused parent—I have been highly motivated to thoroughly study memory. With a clearer understanding of our legal system, I have come to understand the seriousness of establishing the truth. As a result, I have prayerfully searched for the truth as I have studied extensively over the past few years.

I have spoken frequently on this topic on radio and television, at professional conferences, recovery conferences and groups, and at schools and churches.

All this history is to say that I do not approach the writing of this book without intense feelings, extensive research, personal involvement, time, and experience. As I have seen the controversy over repressed memories escalate, I have had varying opinions of my own. We live in a time where it is finally acceptable to openly talk about child abuse. As a result, people who have kept this secret for years are now revealing it. We are shocked and horrified at the details and the frequency of abuse to young children. It feels like an epidemic. We have fifty to sixty years of backlog, and we live in a very sexualized society where the media repeatedly depicts sexuality in all forms. At the same time, people all across the world are proclaiming their innocence of the abuse of which they have been accused. Some are denying their guilt, but many are truly innocent and have had their lives destroyed by a lie. This, too, seems to be hitting epidemic proportions.

Many of my colleagues and former clients have urged me to put my ideas in writing, in a form that is easily understood by the general public. They have had difficulty finding information that considers all sides of the argument. Thus, this book was created.

I hope you can read it with an open mind. Especially seek understanding for the side that is opposite your current point of view. There is truth on all sides of the debate, and deep pain caused for every side when the truth does not prevail. We would all love simple, black-and-white answers; however, they do not exist. We cannot assume that all accusations of abuse are true or that all are false. We cannot defend or accuse all therapists. And we must not convict all accused perpetrators or believe all claims of innocence.

Our search for truth in each individual situation is paramount for healing and restoration. Admitting the truth demands incredible courage and a willingness to face ourselves, our God, and our victims—whether of abuse, false accusations, or improper therapy.

1

Should We Always Believe Our Memories?

A man sat in our counseling center sobbing. He had the build of a bodyguard, and he had closely guarded his memories and emotions for years. Now he was hunched over in his chair, the tears rolling freely down his face. The floodgates had opened. He hadn't let himself cry since grade school.

Beatings. He described childhood beatings by his father and mother. Between sobs, he told of feeling terrified, alone, and completely helpless.

It was anxiety, not repressed memories, that brought Greg to our counseling center. Despite his muscular build and six-foot stature, he lived in fear of violence. When any anger or irritation would surface with his wife or with others, Greg would just leave. He never learned to resolve conflicts, and so he allowed them to continue unresolved for years. His method of coping with unmet needs was to withdraw and look elsewhere rather than to risk confrontation. When his marriage grew unsatisfying he began an affair with another woman. Greg came for counseling shortly after his wife, Melissa, learned of his affair.

He was terrified by Melissa's occasional outbursts of anger, although his description of them sounded very mild for the circumstances—mostly she cried and withdrew into depression. After a few months of counseling, he ended the affair and began marriage counseling, both of which stabilized his life. Yet, because he continued to feel so anxious, he requested a week of intensive therapy to try to regroup and regain his ability to function.

During that week of intensive therapy, he stayed at the center all day so that his therapy process wouldn't be interrupted by family and work responsibilities. Greg began to describe scenes that came to his mind from his childhood. And that was when he began to weep. The deep sobs and feelings of fear continued throughout most of the day. Slowly, he was able to become comfortable with the frightened and hurt feelings that he had blocked for so long. By the end of the day, he was very tired, yet he felt relieved and peaceful. He learned he could survive fear, pain, and sadness, and even feel good after their release.

Later in the week he also experienced anger, the other emotion he had so frantically avoided. He found a safe place and a safe method of release for the childlike rage. Previously he feared that if he ever got angry, he would explode, breaking and destroying everything within reach. It was a relief for Greg to feel the limited extent of his anger, and to realize that he could choose a nondestructive method of release. It did not overwhelm him, as he had anticipated. He had broken through his childhood fears and now he could relate to others in new, healthy ways.

Similar stories occur in therapy all the time. It's almost a cliché now to say that people get in touch with their adult feelings by dealing with childhood memories. People often recall scenes of physical, sexual, or emotional abuse from their younger years. Accusations fly. Some are urged to confront their abusers, some to detach from them, and some to bring lawsuits. And those accused of abuse often challenge the accuracy of the memories and sometimes even present evidence to debunk them. What do you do with these memories? Can we trust them?

In Greg's case, did this childhood abuse really happen? At this point of the story, *it really doesn't matter.* Of course, in many legal, social, and moral ways, it matters very much whether a child is abused. But to a therapist trying to help Greg pull his life together, his memory of childhood abuse may or may not be true. The value of the memory is in the release of feelings that Greg has feared for so many years: sadness, fear, and anger. This release dramatically changes his current relationships.

As he sits in therapy, Greg is not at a point to know the facts of the events he remembers. Later, we'll investigate Greg's story—and those of his wife and children—as we discuss ways of evaluating the accuracy of memories. At this point, any attempt to focus on that will interfere with Greg's healing process. But he definitely should *not* confront his parents. This is an internal processing time, and should be completed as quickly as possible. This experience opened the door to Greg's feelings. Some of those feelings may belong to the past with his parents or other people, and some may be connected to his unexpressed and previously unrecognized feelings toward Melissa or to other current relationships. Greg is no longer so terrified of feelings, and is at the beginning stages of sorting them out. If we immediately begin a frenzy of fact-finding, we would confuse the issue. Greg needs to accept his feelings and explore them further.

Memories and Healing

It may surprise you to consider that memories may not always be accurate representations of what happened. We tend to assume that our eyewitness accounts of past events are true as we remember them. But have you ever compared notes with a friend or relative about an event you both witnessed, only to find that your stories differed substantially? Who's right and who's wrong? It's hard to say. We remember things differently, depending on our preconceptions, our vantage points, and our feelings at the time of the event.

So what are memories? How do our brains store information from the past? This is a topic of current research, interest, and debate. The full answer is not known even after many years of research. What we do know is that *we never have a guarantee that any memory is perfectly accurate.*

The field of clinical psychology has traditionally viewed memories as perceptions to be processed, evaluated, and healed. Childhood memories are considered especially important because they seem to lie behind many adult misperceptions and irrational fears. For example, an adult who experienced childhood physical abuse may feel that the world is a frightening place, full of people who may try to hurt him. This was Greg's situation, and it's fairly common. Such people make generalizations about their adult lives from the emotional wounds of their childhood.

How do you heal such emotional wounds? By going back to the specific source of the abuse. "Why were you afraid as a child? Oh, you had good reason to be afraid then. But what has changed? You were small and helpless then, but now you're stronger, all grown up. You have new options available to you as an adult." The memories are validated, but "that was then, this is now." Healing occurs when we stop applying those childhood fears to our adult lives, where they are no longer relevant.

And what about the remembered events that caused the emotional wounding—the beatings, for instance. Did these really occur? We don't always know. But we do know that there is an emotional wound that came from somewhere. Whether or not the memory is accurate, the wound is very real, and must be healed.

Memories and Emotion

Memories Express Emotion

Events observed or reported while experiencing intense emotions are not to be viewed as factual information, but as expressions of feelings. We need to view our childhood memories as we would view a very emotional story told by our own children. The final picture will often look different than initially reported.

As we continued in family therapy, Greg's wife, Melissa, described an incident with Tim, their oldest son. A quiet, reserved child, Tim was a first-grader at the time and Melissa picked him up after school one day. He was very upset, refusing to talk. She described her fear as she imagined what horrors must have happened to him. When safely in the car and away from the school, he began to cry, a reaction fairly unusual for him. She heard his hurt, bewilderment, and anger mixed together with his story that nobody would play with him, and no one believed anything he said. His emotional outpouring continued for three or four minutes. He stopped and said he was done. Then he calmly talked about what had happened.

As the story unfolded, it changed a bit. It took on more reasonable proportions. Tim said that one child would not play with him during the last recess and one teacher did not believe him when he tried to retrieve his class ball. That obviously was different, and much milder, than the initial story, although the central theme was the same. But until the feelings were released, he could only tell a story that fit the strength of his feelings.

Melissa would have been wrong to question his reality during the emotional intensity. He first needed a safe place to feel. Then he changed the story himself. It was clear that something upsetting had happened. That was all that she knew initially. It was time to listen and time to provide support and caring. It was also essential that she allow him to change his story, without condemning him or calling him a liar.

This is what needs to happen in the therapeutic process. We need a place to express feelings such as hurt, fear, anger, and confusion. The therapist's role is not one of fact-finding, but one of support and encouragement. The search for truth rarely precedes the feelings, at least the initial expression of feelings. At the point of strong emotion, we are not rational enough even to see the facts, let alone to discuss them or to solve the problems they raise.

Emotions Don't Prove Memories Are True

The intensity of a feeling does not necessarily indicate the true content of the memory. Many parents have been terrified by their children's screams, assuming the damage must be severe. But for many infants and young children, differing degrees of pain result in similar screams or emotional reactions. For more serious injuries, the screams last longer, but they might sound alike at the beginning. Each child is unique in his or her response to pain. Some children are close to panic at any sign of pain, physical or emotional. At the other extreme are the children with high pain tolerance.

Jenny, the youngest child of Melissa and Greg, often cried intensely over even minor hurts.

Tim, on the other hand, rarely cried as an infant, even with severe ear infections, cuts, and bruises. He handled emotional pain similarly. Knowing that, Melissa made an immediate trip to the doctor following a recent injury. Although he didn't say much, he did say he was hurting, and he seemed very quiet and withdrawn. As it turned out, two bones were broken, each in two places. Other children might have screamed in pain over the same experience. Certainly Jenny would have.

Tad, the middle child, handled pain by getting angry and blaming something or someone. The responses to pain, both emotional and physical, may be different. We need to understand and respect each individual's method of expression. Yet sometimes a child like Tad needs to learn a more socially acceptable way of expressing pain.

Many adults who are processing childhood pain expect to have the reaction an adult would have in the same situation. Often this is not the case. A child's experience is different. Children may overreact or underreact. A little boy may be terrified by his mother's anger, as Greg had been. She might have done nothing more than yell at him in an angry moment, but that would be enough to terrify this impressionable boy. From an adult perspective, little Greg may have overreacted—but that is how he felt at the time. The adult Greg remembers those intense feelings and struggles to find a reason for them. So, quite innocently, he constructs the memory of terrible beatings that would match the intensity of his childhood fears.

Later, we will look more closely at Greg's story, to see how a childhood overreaction may have caused his adult mind to distort his memories.

On the other hand, a child may underreact, not understanding the future pain or consequences. For example, a child may not feel very strongly about a molest from someone who is kind and gentle and does not physically hurt him or her. This was Cindy's experience.

As a teen and young adult Cindy was very promiscuous. She did not seek out men, but if they initiated anything sexual she went along with their requests. After she married she really wanted to be faithful to her husband, but she could not say no to another man's approaches. Instead she *dissociated,* meaning she lost conscious awareness of her behavior, and another part of her took over and agreed to the sexual involvement. Her husband was unaware but suspicious of her activities. He decided to follow her and, to his amazement, discovered she had another life, unknown to the woman he loved and married. He brought her into marriage counseling as the last option before divorce.

Cindy's first memories were of an unknown stranger sneaking into the house and into her bedroom. He wore all black, so she "knew he was bad." He came often, talking softly, telling her he loved her, and touching her for long periods of time, some of the touches being sexual. Sometimes he would crawl into bed and sleep all night with her, but would be gone in the morning. In her memory, Cindy's feelings were confused. It seemed like she wanted him there and loved him. But that couldn't be true, because she didn't know him and she seemed to understand that he was bad. As she sorted it out, she found it difficult to believe that some stranger had access to her on any regular basis, especially involving long periods of time.

Through her prayerful search for truth, Cindy came to suspect that it was no stranger in black. It was probably her grandfather who often came to stay with her family. She dearly loved him and often slept with him when she was very little (her mother confirmed this). He did come to bed after she was asleep and he got up earlier than she did in the morning. Grandfather is still the most loved person in Cindy's life, and she really doubts that he could have ever done anything bad. The molest by Grandpa might be true and it might not be true.

But somehow Cindy had learned that anyone who wanted sex from her had that right. As the truth came to light, it was her loving grandfather who had taught her to have no boundaries or limits. As a child, she didn't understand sexuality and the ways in which she had been violated. Young Cindy had underreacted to the threat against her. For the adult Cindy, the process of therapy involved facing the pain that her grandfather had brought into her teen years and the disastrous effects it was having on her marriage. She needed to react properly, as an adult, to her victimization. It required anger, the type of anger that would mobilize her power to protect herself from further pain.

How we loved the old westerns where the good guys wore white and the bad guys wore black. Then we knew whom to trust. It's upsetting and shocking when good people do bad things. It's also upsetting to us when bad people do good things, because we don't want to like or trust them in any area. We'd all like clear villains and clean heroes. We want to know who is trustworthy. But life isn't like that. Those we have idealized will soon show their weaknesses as we get to know them.

Cindy's grandfather is a good, kind man in almost every way, but he has very deviant sexual behavior. His daughter, Cindy's aunt, acknowledged that he had repeatedly molested her as she was growing up. Children, in their concrete manner of thinking, often conclude that there really are good guys and bad guys. So Cindy believed that everything Grandpa did was good. This is why she had no internal morality against sexuality outside of marriage, even though that was the teaching of her church and her parents. She handled the conflict and her early frightening experiences by splitting and dissociating. Cindy had part of her who was the good one, who had no awareness of sexual behavior except with her husband. She was very responsible, controlled, intelligent, and acceptable. But another part of her loved the attention and touching by her grandfather and other men, resulting in her promiscuous behavior. Another part carried all the feelings of hurt and fear, and often felt like a terrified little child. A fourth part had all the anger at men and anyone else who betrayed her. Cindy accepted the morality she had been taught, and blocked all awareness of the molest. So she struggled with the truth about Grandpa.

She wanted to believe that he loved her and had not done anything to molest her. Yet part of her felt that Grandpa molested her because she was bad and deserved it. The angry part of her believed that Grandpa didn't love her. And yet another part of her believed that some unknown bad guy in black did the bad things. She remembered all these truths—that Grandpa loved her; that he molested her; that it was at times terrifying; and that it was her fault. Cindy's brain considered all of this and said, "This does not compute." (Cindy's story will continue to unfold in later chapters.)

This type of abuse from a trusted, loving caretaker is often the cause of repression or dissociation. A child cannot make any sense of it. The more dissonant a behavior is, challenging a child's beliefs, the more likely it is to be discarded as untrue, or to be blocked as never having happened. The most commonly found reasons that children fail to report abuse are: (1) they believe that the abusive behavior is deserved punishment; (2) they try to ignore or forget or block out what's happening and just look at the positive; (3) they feel embarrassed; and (4) they want to protect their parents.[1]

For these reasons, children may fail to report when abuse has taken place. The memory may be blocked or changed to alleviate the mental contradictions, or to overcome one of these problems.

As the stories of both Greg and Cindy will demonstrate, we cannot expect a direct correlation between our adult feelings and the events of our childhood. Even the most intense memories can be distorted.

How we all would love a definitive answer concerning memories. We would like to know that all our memories are true or that all our memories are false. But there are no black-and-white answers here.

At least we'd like to know that *certain* memories are totally true or totally false. But even that is rarely the case. Often, there is partial truth to even seemingly unlikely memories, and some distortions to memories that are mostly accurate.

With that in mind, any childhood memories can be explored. They must not be written in indelible ink. Memories may, and often do, change during the therapeutic process. Feelings can be released and healed. Beliefs can be identified and modified. A therapist will probably never know the truth about a client's memories. That is for each client to find, if possible. The purpose of therapy is to allow all feelings to surface in a safe place.

Symptoms May Not Correlate with Abuse

Symptoms do not necessarily identify childhood abuse. There are several books and pamphlets that present lists of symptoms that purport to identify childhood abuse. They may be helpful, but are not a definitive answer to the type of abuse, or even a reliable indicator that the problem stems from childhood.

Like a fever, psychological symptoms do warn of emotional damage that has occurred. But the same symptoms can be present for different reasons. For example, I can recall four women who were all experiencing sexual problems in their marriages. All of them became anxious when they were even touched by their husbands. But the causes were different. One woman had been sexually abused and one had been physically abused. Both had learned that touches hurt, and immediately became frightened even of the touch from a loving person. The third wife was neglected as a child, and rarely touched. For her, touch was unfamiliar and thus very uncomfortable. The fourth woman disliked her husband and did not want any form of intimacy with him. This was a marriage problem. Because of their symptoms, all the women might have assumed they had been sexually abused. Three of the four would have created false beliefs by only looking at the symptoms.

Truth Is the Goal

Our goal is truth, freedom, and health. Believing a lie leads to destruction. Sometimes one of the obvious tests of truth is the effect it has on our mental and emotional health. If the wrong disease is treated, we will not recover. We may instead get worse. If we are staying in a place of destruction, our memories could be false, or we might not have the correct program or treatment for our recovery.

We cannot confirm or deny another person's reality if we were not there. In this stage of exploration, confrontation should not occur. (We will discuss confrontation more thoroughly in a later chapter.)

2

Could I Have Repressed Memories?

A former Miss America, Marilyn Van Derbur Atler, told *People* magazine about the incest in her childhood. She had repressed or dissociated these memories for thirteen years. "We had all the trappings of a perfect family, . . . wealth, social status, a handsome father and a lovely mother. . . . In order to survive, I split into a day child who giggled and smiled, and a night child, who lay awake in a fetal position, only to be pried apart from my father. Until I was 24, the day child had no conscious knowledge of the night child."[1]

Skeptics might question her recovered memories. There's nothing odd about sleeping in a fetal position, and a "night child" might be deeply influenced by dreams.

But Marilyn says she confronted her father, "and my father didn't deny anything." Her mother wouldn't believe her at first, but "it was only after my sister Gwen said, 'me too,' that my mother acknowledged the truth."[2]

This case had some corroborating evidence. Does that mean *every* claimed memory of childhood abuse is accurate? No, of course not. But Marilyn's case and those of countless others confirm that, at least *some of the time,* these memories are accurately stored, repressed, and recalled with some precision years later.

The debate over the accuracy of repressed and recovered memories is intense and heated. Both sides quote experts and give examples of cases that support their positions. Marilyn's case could be answered by others in which the memories were proven to be false. For the person seeking an unbiased opinion, the whole matter can be confusing.

Part of the problem for the scientific community is that researchers are limited in their ability to experiment with repressed memories. They can't go into the lab, cause trauma in a person, and then observe it scientifically. It would be ethically preposterous even if such an experiment could be designed.

And in the case of childhood abuse we are further hampered by the cloak of secrecy over the traumatic events. It is hard to establish with certainty, legally or scientifically, what really happened when one of the two witnesses isn't talking.

Most of our understanding of amnesia, repression, and dissociation comes from the clinical experience of psychologists, especially those who see the victims of trauma. Most of our evidence is anecdotal—from the stories of the clients we serve. It's hard to test new theories, but we keep collecting the stories and building our understanding of this phenomenon.

Adding to the difficulties is the emotional (and political) heat generated in the debate over memories of childhood abuse. There's more at stake than scientific theories—we're dealing with people's emotional health and their reputations. Thus people interpret and present the evidence in completely different ways, further muddying the waters.

I have found in my practice that both sides of the debate have validity. Our clinic has seen clients with inaccurate memories and other clients with memories that have proven accurate. As we will see in later chapters, it is possible for people to distort their memories or misperceive the original events. But that does not mean that all repressed memories are false. In fact, there is strong evidence for the existence of traumatic memories outside of our conscious awareness.

What Is Repression?

Part of the problem in the debate is finding agreement on definitions. What does it mean to *repress* a memory? In recent years, psychologists have developed broad, diverse definitions of repression, including the lack of conscious memory of a traumatic event or a lack of awareness of appropriate feelings in response to a traumatic event. It is distinguished from *forgetting* by the nature of the event—trauma—and by the resulting psychiatric and physical symptoms that accompany repression. It is often related to *dissociation,* in which part of one's consciousness breaks away and functions as a separate unit.

Dr. Elizabeth Loftus, a research psychologist from the University of Washington, has written and testified widely about the *un*reliability of eyewitness reports. Though she questions the existence of repression of repeated trauma, she also states,

> I wouldn't doubt that there's such a thing as repression, depending on how you define it. If repression is really just pushing something unpleasant or traumatic out of your mind and then, later, something can trigger a memory for it, no one would deny that kind of thing happens. What there is not cogent, scientific support for is the idea that you can totally push into a corner of the unconscious a traumatic memory that's completely walled off, almost in a walnut shell from the rest of mental life and that it can return decades later in some pristine, accurate form that you can rely on.[3]

Can we be sure that a long-repressed memory will be recovered accurately? The experts disagree. Still, while differing on the details, the psychological community has gained a broad understanding of what repression and dissociation are, why they occur, and some of the mechanisms they use.

What Causes Us to Block Memories?

We Don't Want It to Be True

The first cause of amnesia is *the desire for the trauma to be false or unreal.* Almost everyone who goes through any trauma, even in adulthood, experiences some form of splitting or blocking at the time of the trauma. It is God's method of helping us to cope with pain by giving us a temporary numbness. I have experienced the unexpected, shocking death of loved ones and less severe traumas such as car accidents and illnesses. I have also observed other people, both clients and friends, as they have experienced trauma. For almost everyone, our initial reaction is *denial.* "NO! This can't be happening!" We can't take it in. We don't want it to be true.

"If there is a 'universal' response," writes Charles R. Figley, "it is the denial or numbing during the trauma for days or weeks . . . or years or decades . . . in chronic or delayed cases."[4]

Generally, as soon as someone is there to assist us and do whatever is necessary to help us cope, the denial begins to lift. Even then, the denial may come and go as needed for coping. If there is not anyone to assist us, we may stay in the denial. In most cases, people are unable to function normally while facing trauma. But if, for some reason, we're required to act as if nothing occurred, we tend to put the memory away and pretend it never happened. This is usually not a conscious decision. We hide it even from ourselves (or from a part of us, in the case of dissociative disorders).

It Doesn't Make Sense

A second cause of blocked memories is that *it doesn't make sense,* we cannot fit this incident into our view of life, people, or ourselves. If we see the cow jumping over the moon, we laugh and know it is a fantasy. It doesn't fit with our knowledge that cows don't fly. A child who experiences abuse that is contrary to previous experiences will often decide that it didn't happen. This is especially true when a loving, kind adult, whom the child usually enjoys, is also abusive, as in the case of Cindy and her grandfather.

It Overwhelms Us

The third cause of blocking memories is *the overwhelming nature of an event.* Any abuse, physical or emotional, is difficult to endure, especially for a child. After the denial lifts, other intense feelings follow. The sadness and grief will come through deep sobs and tears. The anger will occur and may be directed toward anyone we might be able to blame, including ourselves and God. The loneliness and reality of loss will at times be overwhelming, even for someone surrounded by loving friends and family. The fear and anxiety surface, along with depression, confusion, helplessness, despair, hopelessness. It is not an integrated, rational reaction. The various feelings may come in any order, for unpredictable lengths of time. They may occur once, for minor incidents, or numerous times for severe trauma.

In the early stages, usually for a month or more with severe trauma, it is too overwhelming to experience all feelings at the same time. So we split in some way, and each of the feelings may occur intermittently. We could describe it as putting feelings in different boxes, and taking them out one at a time as we are able to cope with them. This is not usually a conscious choice.

Elisabeth Kübler-Ross has written several books about her extensive work with people who are dying. She talks of the stages of dealing with that kind of trauma:

1. Denial and isolation
2. Anger
3. Bargaining to delay death
4. Depression, including sadness and facing the reality of the loss
5. Acceptance[5]

Dr. Mark Stern and Virginia Stern present the stages they observe for traumatized patients:

1. Dissociation and personal depreciation
2. Increasing terror
3. Resigned dread and depression
4. Acceptance[6]

Threats of the Abuser, Dependency of the Child

Although facing death is certainly traumatic, a trauma that includes threats and physical pain also elicits great intensity of feelings, and thus may be even more overwhelming. In one study of childhood sexual abuse, 47 percent of the children were abused by a family member, 42 percent by an acquaintance, and only 8 percent by a stranger.[7]

This means that almost half of these sexually abused children continued to live with the abuser. About 75 percent of this abuse by a family member is from a father or stepfather, a person the child must depend upon. The younger the children, the greater the dependency and inability to care for themselves. Therefore, they must find some way to cope with living with their abuser. Their lives literally depend upon it.

Because young children have less ability to cope with trauma, they are more likely to repress it, according to Dr. Lenore Terr, a child psychiatrist at the University of California, San Francisco. She has studied more than four hundred traumatized children and has written extensively of her findings. Her work will be referred to throughout this book, since she is one of the recognized authorities in the field of childhood trauma.

For their own emotional survival, Dr. Terr notes, children will often *idealize* the parents or caretakers who abuse them, blocking the truth out of their conscious awareness.[8]

Dr. Arthur Green, clinical professor of psychiatry at Columbia University, describes children's "desperate need to protect themselves from the terrifying awareness of the parent's destructive impulses toward them," which results in "denial, projection, and splitting. . . . to maintain the fantasy of having a 'good parent.'" Dr. Green found the splitting "more frequently and dramatically . . . in those children whose abusive parents were their sole caretakers."[9]

As children are overwhelmed by any trauma, they often block out either the events or the accompanying feelings, or both. Even adults who live with abusive mates often deny the reality of the abuse, or the resulting pain, focusing on the good qualities of their abusers, and ignoring the obvious physical bruises and damage to property, as well as the emotional devastation.

Abusers of children are usually aware of the need for silence. In order to prevent criminal prosecution and incarceration, social reprisals, and to maintain access to the child, they often make threats to keep the abused children quiet.

- Most often they threaten pain or the loss of something that is very important to the child.
- Sometimes they raise fears that, if the secret gets out, the family will break up, and there won't be anyone to care for the child.
- Abusers also warn their victims that, if they tell, no one will believe them and that people will know it's their own fault—that the *child* is the bad one.

Every abuser who is a relative, friend, or family member knows the child well enough to perceive what threat will work with that particular child, just as we parents know what unique discipline is effective for each of our children. If children cannot physically escape from their abusers, repression or dissociation allows them a way to escape *emotionally.*

These threats, explicit or implied, along with the dependent needs of the child, are a fourth cause of blocking out memories in childhood. If we have no one to tell and no way to escape, the denial part takes over, and says that nothing happened. It's the way we cope with such situations on our own without outside help.

This denial makes recovered memories confusing to both clients and therapists. As a memory returns, there will be a part of us that denies it even when it is verified. We even find denial in adults who come into counseling with documented trauma that has just occurred.

So when is the denial a part of the splitting and coping, and when is it denial because the event never occurred? This is the very question that makes it difficult to assess the accuracy of the stories our clients tell.

The Process of Repression and Dissociation

There is usually *splitting* each time a trauma occurs. If we have the assistance and support we need, we will release these separated feelings, and *integrate* by the normal process of talking and grieving.

You are probably well aware of how painful and chaotic the normal grieving process is for an adult. But imagine that you are a little child and nobody else knows what has happened. You feel it's your fault in some way. You have no way to release any of the feelings, you have no assistance, and you've been threatened with terrifying consequences if you tell. Furthermore, you are dependent on your abuser for your very existence.

When we feel totally helpless and powerless, we give up or surrender. We freeze, like an animal that is trapped or captured. Many people have described this numbness and freezing during a trauma. It often includes a detached state of awareness or consciousness. Some people describe the experience as if they are watching the trauma happen to someone else. The greatest fear of anyone who has experienced a trauma is that it will happen again. If it does reoccur, the feelings of helplessness, hopelessness, and despair are overwhelming. Repetitive abuse is even more likely to be repressed than one-time abuse.

We could either go crazy and live in a world of unreality, or put it away in a box (repression, dissociation, or amnesia) where it can't affect us. What a conflict! We either feel crazy because we deny reality or we accept a reality that seems to be more painful than we can bear. If it were a minor incident, we might find some way to work it out by ourselves or to ignore it. People who have experienced a trauma and have not repressed it, but have not talked to anyone about it either, are sometimes very controlled, attempting to keep a tight rein on the feelings that threaten to be overwhelming.

When a trauma occurs in a group that continues to discuss the event (such as natural disaster, war, concentration camp, and so forth), it is much less likely to be blocked from awareness than trauma that we endure alone with no one to verify or validate the experience. When we hear the trauma repeatedly discussed, denial is more difficult. Blocking can occur with traumatic events experienced by a group, but it is more likely that we will block a specific aspect of the trauma or the feelings associated with it, rather than the complete event.

I vividly recall the unexpected death of my father. I was fifteen. I immediately isolated myself and I felt numb. When I was asked to baby-sit that evening, I agreed, not saying that my father had just died. I wanted everything to be the same, to be normal. But when the children were in bed and I was alone, I felt like I was going crazy. I was starting to thaw out, and my feelings of grief were threatening to come out.

Fortunately, I wasn't allowed to stay in the denial. I had to attend the funeral and face my dad's death and the feelings associated with it. Our family had to live each day after that without his presence and its impact. We all were forced to grieve in our own ways. Yes, it was difficult to adjust, but if I had stayed in the denial or the emotional numbness there would have been a time bomb within me waiting to explode.

This is a normal process of coping with a traumatic event. But many people get stuck somewhere in the process. In the case of childhood abuse many get stuck at the point of denial. Their brains do extraordinary things to hide these memories, to wall them off. The rest of the healing process can't continue until those walls are broken down.

3

How Does the Brain Remember?

There is probably nothing more complicated than the human brain. After decades of scientific study, we still don't know exactly how it functions, especially regarding memory.

Let's say you look up a phone number in your Rolodex and then pick up your phone and push the appropriate numbers. For those few seconds, you memorize the number. But that's *short-term memory,* which can hold a limited amount of information, about five to nine items, for a very short time. Two minutes later, the number is forgotten—unless you decide to place it in *long-term memory.* Then, usually by rehearsing the number, you learn it.

How does the brain record things in long-term memory?

Three Steps of Long-Term Memory

The memory process has three distinct steps: *sensing or perceiving, storing,* and *recalling.*

When you experience something, the input from your senses—what you see, hear, smell, taste, or touch—goes to sensory areas of your brain first, and then on to a part of the brain called the *hippocampus.* Here, the experience is divided up and parceled out for storage in different parts of the brain. There's really a rather elaborate filing system at work. The different pieces of a memory remain connected by the *corpus callosum,* a bundle of fibers, running between the right and left hemispheres of the brain, that act like telephone cables.

Researchers believe they have identified a neurochemical process that creates a memory trace in the brain, called an *engram*. You might consider the engram a code or label identifying a particular piece of memory. When you recall something, your memory system quickly hunts for the proper engrams and joins the pieces of the memory back together.

Dr. Mortimer Mishkin, chief of the neuropsychology laboratory of the National Institutes of Health, says,

> momentous events make a biochemical impression in . . . the hippocampus. To file them away permanently, it shunts the elements of the experience—the sounds, smells, and sights—through a network of nerve cells to different areas of the brain. It's a whole cascade of processes, physiological and chemical, that sensitizes the neurons to transmit messages. The proper stimulus, say, a whiff of a perfume or a glimpse of a familiar place, trips the relay, firing the neurons and bringing a past event to consciousness.[1]

You may have had the experience of recalling an event in bits and pieces. You remember a place, a face, a feeling. Slowly the pieces come together as you try hard to remember. Essentially, that's your hippocampus searching through the files of your brain for the right engrams. One piece connects to the next, which connects with the next, until the memory is reassembled.

Recall is often triggered, however, by cues in your environment. You hear a familiar song and your hippocampus quickly assembles the memory of the moment you first heard that song. The more closely the circumstances of initial learning can be replicated, the more likely the recall of the event.

Scott Wetzler, Ph.D., chief of psychology at Albert Einstein College of Medicine at Montefiore Medical Center in New York City, says, "When forgotten memories poke their way into our awareness, it's usually the result of strong sensory cues: the smell of a particular perfume, the sound of foghorns, a visit to the old neighborhood. Of all the senses, smell is the most directly linked to memory because the brain's limbic system, where scent perceptions are recorded, is also where emotions are stored."[2]

If a client is struggling to bring back a blocked memory, a therapist will often suggest that the client visit the site of the incident, if this is possible. The setting itself may fire up some long-dormant engrams and may help to pull the memory together.

Three Theories of Memory

There are currently three views of memory. One theory is that the mind functions like a *video camera*. It takes in information from all of the senses, then decides either to erase it because it is unimportant, forgetting it, or to store it in memory for retrieval at some later date—much like you would decide either to record over a favorite TV show you've taped or save it for later viewing. This theory proposes that retrieval may at times be difficult, but not impossible, and the memory will be an accurate replay of the event.

The second view of memory is that it is *reconstructive*. Again, the mind takes in information from all of the senses. It forgets the unimportant and stores the important data. As time passes the mind adds new information to these "open files," changing and modifying the initial information. Retrieval then produces memories that are a combination of the old and the new—including facts, fears, and fantasies, as well as stories heard. This view is currently accepted by the scientific community, but ongoing research in the laboratory continues to explore and understand the brain's memory processes.

The third view is a *combination*. Proponents say that most of the time memory is reconstructive—the mind is adding new information to the old; yet some intensely emotional experiences are burned into the mind exactly as they happened—only minimally contaminated or modified by new experiences.

Traumatic Memories Are Different

Have you ever said or heard, "I'll never forget the day my father died"? Or, "I remember that accident like it was yesterday"? Or, "I know exactly what I was doing when the earthquake hit"? Such traumatic events seem to be etched in the consciousness. This also applies to positive events, such as weddings, the births of children, first love, graduation. How many Americans know exactly where they were when they learned that John F. Kennedy was shot, or when they saw the first steps on the moon, or when they watched the Challenger tragedy?

Dr. Francine Shapiro's work with trauma victims seems to support this third view of memory. She is a California psychologist who discovered and developed Eye Movement Desensitization and Reprocessing (EMDR). She has observed the "intrusive thoughts, flashbacks, and nightmares" among Vietnam veterans and other victims of post-traumatic stress disorder (PTSD). She states that traumatic incidents disturb "the excitatory/inhibitory balance" of the brain. As a result, one part of the brain might be overexcited, and this would change the normal way of processing memories. Shapiro suggests that this condition "freezes" the information "in its original anxiety-producing form, complete with the original image, negative self-assessment, and affect." In other words, our everyday memories may shift and alter over time, but traumatic events get frozen in our memories and they can later come back in crisp detail, even when we don't want them.[3]

Robert Jay Lifton studied survivors of Hiroshima, civilian disasters, and combat. He explains traumatic memory as "an indelible image or . . . imprint."[4] This highly visual and behavioral form of memory, which is typical for young children, seems to also occur for adults in times of trauma.

Separate Storage

The May 1994 issue of *Discover* magazine presents an interesting article entitled, "Flights of Memory." The authors are Minouche Kandel, an attorney, and her father, Eric Kandel, the recipient of many awards, including the National Medal of Science. The article reviews the current understanding of memory storage, and tries to explain how we repress and retrieve traumatic memories. The Kandels suggest that the conscious recollection of an emotionally charged event and the feelings associated with this event are stored in separate systems of the brain. That may be why you sometimes remember a certain action or feeling without recalling all the details of when you acted or felt that way.

Self-Sedation

According to recent research, the brain may secrete opiates to dull the senses during traumatic events. That is, *the brain sedates itself in times of high emotion.*[5] The Kandels note this and suggest that "if an incident is so distressing that the brain makes opiates to dull the pain, the opiates may interfere with the memory-storing process."

When we receive traumatic information, the Kandels are saying, our brains may drug themselves to cope with it, and then file the information in perfect detail, but in various parts of the brain.

"Furthermore," the Kandels say, "some studies show that a weakly stored memory can be enhanced by injecting a stimulant drug like adrenaline."[6] But we don't have to be injected with adrenaline—we make our own adrenaline during times of stress. That may explain why flashbacks of repressed memories tend to happen at these times.

Along the same lines, Dr. James Dobson, founder and director of Focus on the Family, says the past is there, "locked into the brain. With the proper stimulation, you can pull it up." He discusses the research by two surgeons who are specialists in brain neurophysiology, Dr. Penfield and Dr. Rasmussen. During certain surgeries that required patients to be conscious or semiconscious, they were able to touch electrodes to various parts of the brain, and the person would "experience and remember, in vivid detail and in full color, the complete complexity of an experience that they'd had in the early part of their lives. Direct electrical stimulation to that part of the brain brought back the memory which is locked there."

Dr. Dobson went on to express his view that this is why it is so important to pay attention to a child's experiences, because they "are being stored and will have some influence. . . . We are a product of the inner child of the past, because those experiences are there. They're recorded. We can't pull them up. We don't have instant access to them all. But under the right stimulation, they are there, and occasionally, they pop into your conscious mind."[7]

Why Do We Forget?

Why, then, do we forget things? If our memories are locked in our brains, why can't you remember the name of your third-grade teacher?

Disuse

There are different theories concerning *forgetting*. One is that it occurs with disuse. The neural engram (the memory trace in the brain) gradually decays or loses its clarity. It's like a file folder with a label that has yellowed to the point of illegibility. According to this theory, the file may be still there, but you can't find it when you need it because the label has worn away.

Interference

A second theory is called the Phenomena of Interference. In this case, new learning interferes with the retention of the old, or old learning interferes with the new. For example, you may have learned to play tennis on your own, developing ways to hold the racket, hit the ball, stand, and so forth. Then, you decide to take lessons. At first it would be very difficult, because your previous learning would interfere. After repeated practice, however, you would break the old habits, and the new learning would predominate. As you continue to play in the new way, eventually you would forget your old way of playing. Even if you were asked to demonstrate your pre-lesson form, you would not be able to recall it.

Repression: Something Different

But repression of memory is something else entirely. It's not the loss of a memory, as we know from those unwelcome flashbacks. It seems to be a blockage of some kind. But how and when does this occur?

Self-Censorship

In *Health* magazine, psychologist J. R. Goldberg says that the blocking happens right away, before a memory even gets stored.

> Recent data suggests that the human brain is organized to promote self-deception in certain anxiety-arousing situations. In the tenth of a second it takes for information to enter our awareness, the brain acts as a censor.
>
> On the right side of our brains are centers of negative emotions. On the left side are centers of speech. The two sides are connected by the corpus callosum, a band of fibers that unites the brain's hemispheres. Sometimes

> information may get lost or confused traveling from one side of the brain to the other, much the way messages are garbled when relayed in the children's game of telephone. For example, our brains might rapidly register the information that a loved one is seriously ill, but this information might not enter the consciousness immediately. Denial can be helpful if it doesn't go on too long. It allows a person time to reorganize, to pull his or her resources together.[8]

In other words, denial allows some time to find a way to cope with trauma.

Changes in the Brain

Other research promotes the idea that repressed memories may be more than information mismanagement. Traumatic events may actually change a person's brain. In a review of the literature on post-traumatic stress disorder, the *Journal of the American Medical Association (JAMA)* says that trauma "produces not only adverse psychological effects, but also potentially long-term neurobiological changes in the brain."[9]

If this is true for adults, like Vietnam vets, it may be even more significant for young victims of abuse. Psychiatrist John H. Krystal of the Yale University School of Medicine refers to a theory (as yet untested) that "early traumatic stress alters a child's brain development in important ways."[10] Dr. Krystal describes the infant's reaction to trauma as becoming "overwhelmed or flooded with intolerable and excessive emotions."[11] Does this overload affect the way the memories are stored? Do they perhaps even change the way all future memories will be stored?

The *Family Therapy Networker* presents the ideas of Harvard Medical School research psychiatrist Dr. Bessel Van der Kolk in the article "Trauma and Memory."

> [Dr. Van der Kolk] maintains that chronic, severe childhood trauma may permanently alter the neurobiology that integrate cognitive memory and emotional arousal in normal people. . . . The emotional sensations related to trauma are remembered *through a different memory*, either as bodily sensations or visual images. At subsequent moments of very high arousal, the trauma comes back—not as words, not as memories—but as a flashback or nightmare or visual image, and the person experiences it again; but the words are simply not there because it has not been integrated into

> the totality of his or her experience. . . . In other words, when a child is continually exposed to trauma, the operation of the limbic system—a group of structures located below the brain's cortex that filter and help integrate emotion, sensation, experience, and memory—is sharply and chronically disrupted. The brain is so overwhelmed, so many times, by negative stimulation and arousal that it cannot accommodate and integrate all the information it is receiving. Memory and emotions are, in effect, severed. This helps explain the phenomena of flashbacks and body memories in the absence of conscious recollections, which skeptics find so hard to believe.[12]

His biological model for trauma is based upon what happens to animals who face repetitive "inescapable shock."[13]

Dr. Van der Kolk treated Boston-area children who had seen the murders of their parents. "These are our most extreme cases. We look at how kids process these memories. They act it out with their muscles or have burned-in images in the mind. The images can be dreams that occur during different stages of sleep when ordinarily dreams do not occur. Or something suddenly triggers a flashback of these images and they experience body sensations."[14]

It seems clear from these findings that traumatic memories are very different from normal memories. The brain's biochemical response to the trauma somehow creates new pathways for the information. Thus the memories may come back in unusual ways.

There is much information about the functioning of the human brain that we cannot even begin to consider here. Each of the various models of memory—video camera, reconstructive, and combination—has a different way of explaining how memories are blocked and later triggered. These explanations are beyond the scope of this book. Other sources are available for those interested in studying this area. The work by Dr. Van der Kolk is especially significant.[15]

Conclusions from the Research

We can sum up this research in several basic statements, which will help us as we continue to consider the phenomenon of repressed or dissociated memories:

1. Traumatic events seem to be stored in the brain in vivid detail.

2. The brain's chemical response to trauma seems to cover the tracks of certain traumatic events—effectively hiding them from day-to-day memory.
3. This can result in a severing and/or laying down of unusual connections in the brain—a disjointedness of sense memory, emotional memory, and bodily memory—as if pieces of memories are stranded.

What Influences the Accuracy of Memory?

But how do we know these memories are accurate? When repressed memories are played back, can we trust them? Or are these memories somehow compromised in the whole process?

As we examine the accuracy of memory, three separate parts need to be evaluated: the accuracy of the perception, the permanence and possible contamination of the storage process, and the reliability of the retrieval process.

Accuracy of Perception

A car runs a red light on a city street, hitting another car as it moves through the intersection. A third car, tailgating, is unable to stop and slams into the others. Onlookers walking along the busy sidewalks or waiting to cross the street are observers of this crash. Probably all of the witnesses will agree on the central feature, that there was an accident and that three cars were involved. But after that, their stories may differ.

Memory begins in our sense receptors. In order to have an accurate memory, we must *experience the event correctly* through our senses—seeing, hearing, smelling, tasting, and touching. We must also *take in the complete event,* or all the significant aspects, rather than only a portion of it. And finally, we must *comprehend what is occurring,* on at least a minimal level. After considerable research on perception, there is now ample proof of the questionable reliability of eyewitness reports.

Research generally demonstrates that the *central feature* of an event is most clearly and accurately remembered. As facts become more peripheral or less significant to the event, the accuracy of the perception decreases. In the three-car accident, witnesses agree that three cars collided. But who caused it? Who had the light? Where did the third car come from? These peripheral details may not be agreed on, as each witness may have a different view. How do investigators determine what actually happened?

One factor that improves accuracy of perception is the *length of time* spent perceiving the event. So those witnesses who stayed and watched will probably agree on how many people were in each car, and whether they walked away from the accident or were taken by ambulance. The witnesses who left the scene of the accident quickly might forget (or never observe) whether the accident victims were male or female, adults or children, or what colors the cars were. But those who kept watching will have better accuracy.

Our perceptions are also more accurate if we have an interest or *emotional investment* in the situation. For example, if one of the cars looked like the car of a close friend, one of the witnesses may have looked very intently at the passengers, and be able to describe them quite accurately, but be inaccurate about other details of the accident.

The *focus of our attention* also helps determine the accuracy of our perception. Prior to the accident, who was paying attention to the cars or to the stoplight? Most observers won't remember whether the light was red or green, especially if it had just changed—except for those who were waiting to cross. These people would have been watching the stoplight, so they would know best about this detail.

For the same reason, if there is something *unusual or novel,* it is more frequently perceived and remembered. So, if one of the cars was multicolored, like some of the old Volkswagens were painted, or one car is brightly colored and the other two indistinct, the unique color or style would catch the onlookers' attention. If one car was traveling very fast or honking its horn, perceptions would turn in that direction.

Other witnesses might be affected by their *mood or stress level* at the time. An angry man might attribute blame to a driver who didn't really deserve it. A woman walking down the street suffering from emotional pain might notice only whether anyone was hurt in the accident. She might miss all other details.

Accuracy of perception also relies on our *familiarity with the subject.* A traffic cop on the scene might notice many details of the accident that others would miss—because he has been trained to observe such details. An auto mechanic waiting on the corner might remember hearing the scrape of worn brake pads. Others who heard the same sound might not remember it because it meant nothing to them. Young children who are witnesses might not have enough understanding of cars and lights and driving rules to comprehend what has happened except for the loud crash.

Accuracy may also depend on *the number of different facts to take in*. A three-car crash has more details to consider than a two-car crash, or one car crashing into a telephone pole. Remember that short-term memory can hold only five to nine items. Our brains simply cannot hold all the relevant information in the short time we observe such an accident.

Laboratory studies clearly demonstrate what is called the *primacy effect*, which says that the initial event or the first word of a series, or one's first experience, is recalled better than subsequent similar ones. The unique characteristics of that first time seem to stand out, but later memories of similar events may be blurred or combined. Using our accident scenario, we might guess that the first sound or sight of trouble would be remembered better than other details. Also, someone who had never seen an accident before might be expected to remember the major details more clearly than those who had witnessed several accidents previously.

Animal research shows that *severe stress* creates a memory track, and when subsequent severe stress occurs, it will travel the same pathway, activating the previous memories.[16] So, during a time of high stress, we might not only perceive the current situation, but we might flash back to a previous trauma. This has been demonstrated by many researchers, and has been identified by such terms as *screen memories* or *condensed memories* or *combined memories*.

Returning once again to the scene of the accident, let's suppose that Jane, standing on the corner, sees the whole thing. Jane was injured in a serious car accident a year earlier. In fact, she's heading to her lawyer's office because she's being sued for allegedly causing the accident. This is a time of major stress for her anyway, and this new accident will not only bring back those old stressful memories of her own accident—but the details of the two accidents may mesh in her mind. As the police interview her about details of this new accident, she may provide details of her own accident a year earlier—without realizing that they were two separate events. It's also possible that, as she recounts her own accident to her lawyer later that day, she will inject details of the accident she has just witnessed.

Of course, in this book we are not just dealing with a traffic accident. We are dealing with repressed memories from traumatic incidents in the past, most involving abuse of one kind or another. But the same cautions apply. Was the original incident perceived accurately? Even if the central event is accurate, are all the details true, as well? Did the person understand what was going on at the time, and did this affect perception? Were memories of separate events meshed together?

Questions about the accuracy of eyewitness reports and perception in general do not imply that such reports are always inaccurate. Every recovered memory must be carefully evaluated before we determine its truth or falsehood. Remember that the therapist is not immediately concerned with the accuracy of the client's story. We look for the *perception,* and its impact on the client. How was this event experienced? Even if it was not seen clearly or if it was misunderstood, the trauma comes from whatever was perceived or experienced, not from what actually occurred. Facing this is essential to healing.

Permanence and Contamination of Storage

When we have placed information in our brains for storage, does it then stay there permanently in an unchanged form? Not necessarily. The evidence seems to indicate that many memories are modified over time. We often remember the good old days, exaggerating the pleasure and minimizing the pain. Occasionally, we emphasize the negative, such as in the case of a broken relationship, thus minimizing the pain of the loss. Later, we may be unable to remember any bad moments of that championship season or any good moments of that failed romance.

With repeated accounts of a story, we tend to change it a little each time. This change may become the truth that is then stored until the next recall. This very process is a source of healing, for each time a traumatic event is recounted, it is usually with a little less anxiety and pain.

But, as we have been learning, traumatic memories play by different rules. Dr. Terr, well known for her work with children who have experienced trauma, describes it this way: "The memory of trauma is shot with higher intensity light than is ordinary memory. And the film doesn't seem to disintegrate with the usual half-life of ordinary film. Only the best lenses are used, lenses that will pick up every last detail, every line, every wrinkle, and every fleck. There is more detail picked up during traumatic events than one would expect from the naked eye under ordinary circumstances." She believes that trauma leaves an indelible mark on a child's mind at any age. "Traumatic fright is unique. And it is remembered."[17]

How Does the Brain Remember?

As we have seen, details of the place where the trauma occurred—including the sights, sounds, and smells—remain attached to highly emotional events in memory.[18] This is why many therapists encourage clients to picture their childhood homes or other places in their childhood.

It is generally well accepted that meaningful, distinctive events are more deeply processed in memory and somehow leave more lasting and durable memory traces. Consequently, distinctive and meaningful events are easier to remember. Since very few events are more profoundly meaningful than childhood abuse or trauma, "it seems unlikely that childhood sexual abuse experiences can ever be permanently forgotten. While repression and dissociation may suppress retrieval mechanisms of memory, the underlying memory traces are likely to remain relatively intact."[19]

So, these traumatic memories don't fade away, as normal memories do. But it seems that the same emotional heat that etches these memories into our brains can melt the memories, changing or merging them. There are some crucial exceptions we must consider.

The Power of Suggestion

Dr. Loftus refers to the *Misinformation Effect*—changing of our stored memories due to post-event misinformation. She gives many examples where people have been given false information and they have mixed it into their original view of events, confidently passing on their revised and false story. As time passes, memories are increasingly more susceptible to distortions and new information. She also describes *suggestibility* to such a degree that some people come to believe an entire event that never happened.[20]

Details, Details

Dr. Loftus also found that, when people have sharp and clear memories, they tend to resist attempts to change the memory. But, as we have seen, memory is invariably sharper for the main themes of an event—thus less important details are easier to influence and modify. The most durable of all memories, research shows, are those relating to *emotionally charged experiences*. These seem to be less subject to contamination and change, especially in their central features. But even here, less significant details may be lost or modified.[21]

Repetition

If the trauma is a single event, Dr. Terr says, we have almost picture-perfect recall. But if the trauma is repeated, memories about the details of the abuse are more blurred and fragmentary or even blocked. Those who were repeatedly abused as children, for instance, might have difficulty remembering the details of any one particular episode.[22]

The normal stories of our lives can change as we repeat them over and over. Therapists who work with repressed trauma often believe that the recovered memory is *intact* because it has *not* been changed through repetitions of the story, and because of the intense emotions associated with it. Because the traumatic story has *not* been repeated, it remains in a more unchanged state, as it was originally perceived.

The Urge to Merge

In high-stress situations, flashbacks can affect our perception, resulting in combined memories. But it seems that memories can also be combined *in storage,* one folding on top of another.

Dr. Terr studied the case of a busload of children kidnapped from Chowchilla, California, in 1976 and buried alive. She first saw the children and their families five months after the incident and then interviewed them again four years later. Regarding the merger of memories, Dr. Terr gives the example of one of the Chowchilla children who had a big fight with her mother just before leaving for the bus. She later described her kidnapper in terms that clearly fit her mother's description.[23]

Imagining Things?

Dr. Stephen Kosslyn of Harvard has raised serious concerns about the validity of repressed memories. Through the use of PET brain scans he has found that the brain area involved in seeing an image and storing it as a memory is also involved in imagining that image. Thus, he says, an imagined event can seem as real as an actual event.[24]

So as the biological perspective is considered, there's the likelihood that both sides of the repressed memory conflict have validity. "Research in animals suggests that memory storage can be modulated and inhibited, and that once inhibited, memory can nevertheless return. At the same time, we also know that memory can be unreliable and we have an inkling of how fantasy might be mistaken for reality."[25]

Reliability of the Retrieval

The information that we retrieve from our brains seems to be highly dependent on our moods, expectations, current thinking, and the environment in which the retrieval occurs.

Mood

This is never more evident than when we are angry or depressed. At that time, we seem to go through a computer (brain) search for all relevant bad information. Nothing looks positive or hopeful. Everything is wrong, bad, gray, dark, and hopeless. Most of us tend to do the same thing when we are happy. Then the sun is shining, the flowers are blooming, or the rain is refreshing and all is well with the world. Researchers at the University of Oregon found that depressed subjects recalled their parents as being much more rejecting than they did when not depressed.[26]

Expectations

As we search our memories for relevant information, we generally look for information that confirms our bias or beliefs on a subject, or information that confirms our self-concept. We often believe that we are right or innocent. Parents attempting to find out the true story regarding a fight between their children often despair. Each child declares his or her innocence and the other's guilt. In marriage counseling, we often see the same contradictory points of view from the two adults.

We generally see ourselves in a more positive light than is accurate. We like to think of ourselves as good people, whatever that means to us. This makes us likely to deny or excuse behavior that we would judge others for.

Denial

Some people use denial more extensively than others, as described in the following excerpt:

> Anorexics, bulimics and alcoholics tend to be experts at denying painful truths, and the results can be tragic. An anorexic will believe that she is always too fat, even when the mirror and scale offer horrifying evidence of her false judgment. A bulimic may repress the knowledge of her binges and purges despite the all-too-visible danger signs. And alcoholics lie to themselves all the time, claiming that they drink just to loosen up, or that

they always remain in control. Often the families of alcoholics join in a destructive game of deception, avoiding the painful truth.[27]

We find evidence for many different points of view as long as we see what we want to see, and remember what we want to remember. It does not necessarily mean that the information is not true. It does mean that we are not looking at a balanced picture, at both sides. Many psychologists believe that self-concept is formed early in life. After that, we may choose not to see contrary information, we may choose not to retain it, or we may choose to remember only that information that matches our self-concept at any particular time.

Current Information and Attitudes

As our attitudes change, we can retrieve certain memories and reinterpret them. For example, Joe has just had a religious experience. Over the next few weeks, he suddenly remembers all sorts of incidents where God had acted in his life. Previously, he had not seen those events in the same light, but now he makes new sense of them.

Sharon joins a group of Adult Children of Alcoholics. As she learns from others in the group, she begins to evaluate her own childhood memories with terms like the "scapegoat" or "hero" or "lost child," retrieving those events that fit these new concepts.

Suggestion

The manner in which we are questioned often affects our retrieval. Dr. Loftus has demonstrated in her research the ability of an interviewer to change memory. In one experiment, in describing an accident she used the word *smash* rather than *hit*. The word *smash* elicited higher estimates of speed and the addition of nonexistent broken glass at the scene of the accident.[28] Other experiments have indicated that when a question is asked implying something is true, some people will go along with this deception, even creating elaborate details to support it. Yet we must note that the ability to change memory is usually limited to peripheral events; the central theme is seldom altered.

Environment

Finally, the environment affects the retrieval process. The greater the similarity in environment to the circumstances of the original event, the more likely the accurate retrieval. This is the basis for the flashbacks of repressed memories. A similar situation, a picture, smell, taste, sound, or touch occurs and the memories begin flooding back. Dr. Nancy Meyers, a psychologist and memory researcher at the University of Massachusetts at Amherst, states, "Adults could remember much more if they were placed in a physical environment that exactly matched their childhood."[29] (This is often referred to as state-dependent learning.)

Confabulation

Human beings are storytellers. We seem to have a basic sense of what makes a good story. So, if we are missing certain details in a story we're remembering, we often make them up. Scientists call this *confabulation*. Often, it seems, our brains do this confabulation automatically. If a memory is missing a crucial link, we invent something to tie it together. If something in the story doesn't make sense, we adjust the memories slightly to make better sense of it all.

In Cindy's case, she invented the stranger in black because it made no sense for her loving grandfather to abuse her. It is not unusual or surprising for our brains to do this. But it does caution us about believing everything we feel, hear, see, or think we remember.

4

Is There a Case for Repressed Memory?

Between the ages of ten and thirteen, Ross Cheit attended the summer camp of the San Francisco Boys Chorus each year. As an adult, when he learned that his nephew was joining a boys' chorus, he began to have memories of sexual abuse at the camp.

As he pieced it together, Ross, now an ethics professor at Brown University, determined that he had been molested by William Farmer, the camp administrator.

Was this just an invented memory, suggested by the recent activity of his nephew? It seems not. Ross decided to find the perpetrator, and hired a private investigator. He talked with many of the other boys who had attended the camp, who were also abused. He interviewed counselors, a nurse who witnessed the abuse, and Maudi Bacon (the founder of the choir), who said she'd "almost had to fire the man for hobnobbing with one of the boys." Ross eventually located Mr. Farmer, and recorded their phone conversation, during which Farmer admitted molesting him, confirmed that he had lost jobs and fled California because of "it," and admitted that he knew his acts were criminal.[1]

Few victims ever get that kind of satisfaction. Many remain in some uncertainty about their own memories. When the memories return, these people have a gut feeling that they're true, but it's difficult to get corroboration for the details. And there are often skeptics who suggest that they've made the whole thing up.

Yet there are enough stories like Ross's to prove that memories can be blocked and, some time later, recovered with amazing accuracy. In recent years, a substantial body of evidence has been compiled to build a case for the repression and recovery of traumatic memories. This evidence includes: currently accepted psychiatric diagnoses, historical accounts, clinical evidence, and legal evidence.

Psychiatric Diagnoses

In the past few years, many of the popular periodicals have presented both sides of the debate over the existence of recovered memories. A helpful overview follows:

> Sometimes an event, such as being abused as a child, is so frightening or painful that the conscious mind simply can't accept it. When this happens, psychologists theorize, the psyche is protected by one of several defense mechanisms: *repression,* in which an entire experience is sealed off from conscious memory; *splitting,* in which only the good parts of a traumatic event are remembered; and *dissociation,* a process in which the conscious mind literally separates itself from what is happening to the body. . . . Although more common in cases of abuse, the use of defense mechanisms is actually a normal part of life. Everyone has experiences that are psychologically too hot to handle—for example, you may have blocked the time you forgot your lines in the school play and were laughed at, or the day you were hit by a car.[2]

In layman's terms, this nicely explains the commonly accepted psychiatric diagnoses for symptoms such as conscious unawareness, amnesia, blocking, numbing, repression, or dissociation from trauma.

Repression is not listed in the current *Diagnostic and Statistical Manual of Mental Disorders* (DSM-IV). This manual is the bible of mental disorders, put out regularly by the American Psychiatric Association and used by most mental health professionals and insurance companies.

Does this mean repression doesn't exist? Not at all. Several years ago, the editors of this manual decided to describe mental disorders according to observable clinical features, without addressing their origins or causes. Repression is not clinically observable. Its existence is inferred.

Yet repression may be a cause behind post-traumatic stress disorder (PTSD), acute stress disorder, and the dissociative disorders—which are all listed in DSM-IV.

For the purposes of this book, the terms *repression* and *repressed memories* will be used very broadly, to include the above disorders. The term *dissociated traumatic memories* would often be accurate for the memories described.

Post-Traumatic Stress Disorder (PTSD)

Post-traumatic stress disorder is a reaction to trauma or terror, helplessness, or horror. There is often a recurring experience of the event, including repetitive nightmares and dissociative flashback episodes. Or, as a defense against this continuing terror, described as *psychic overload,* it may include emotional shock or numbness, and an inability to recall an important aspect of the trauma—repression. There are also other symptoms, especially those associated with intense anxiety.[3]

PTSD was first diagnosed in soldiers returning from war. Some experts say that as many as five hundred thousand veterans from Vietnam alone suffer from PTSD.[4] It is believed that they had a much higher incidence of PTSD than veterans of other wars because of their mistreatment or lack of support when returning from Vietnam, as opposed to other veterans who were considered war heroes and had ample opportunity to discuss their experiences. At first blush, the ravages of war seem far removed from the experiences of an abused child, but consider the similarities: a trauma of surprising intensity, sudden disillusionment with trusted authority figures, a sense of being trapped, shame, and secrecy.

When natural disasters strike, such as fires, earthquakes, or hurricanes, victims often suffer PTSD, as do civilian victims of war or holocaust. Of course, PTSD also occurs among those who have suffered individual victimization, such as child abuse, rapes, beatings, or other terrifying experiences. Seemingly milder events, such as divorce, or the death of a loved one, or even loss of property, are often followed by PTSD symptoms. Following a minor automobile accident, a three-year-old girl was diagnosed with PTSD on the basis of nightmares, many fears that were specific to the accident, and violent play.[5]

In his thorough book on the subject, *Trauma and Its Wake,* Charles Figley describes many different reactions to trauma.

> Some persons collapse on the spot; others collapse once refuge is attained; some "freeze" and are literally immobilized; still others "click" into a machine-like state and efficiently carry through in their actions; others enter with their emotions raging. If there is a "universal" response, it is the denial or numbing during the trauma, an apparent latency period . . . for days or weeks for acute PTSD . . . or years or decades . . . in chronic or delayed cases.[6]

Acute Stress Disorder

Acute stress disorder is similar to PTSD, except it lasts a maximum of four weeks and occurs within four weeks of the traumatic event. It has three or more of the following dissociative symptoms:

1. Numbing, detachment, or absence of emotional responsiveness
2. Reduction of awareness . . . (being in a daze)
3. Derealization
4. Depersonalization
5. Dissociative amnesia[7]

Dissociative Disorders

The dissociative disorders also involve blocking of traumatic events. In the case of *dissociative identity disorder,* commonly known as multiple personality disorder, there is "the presence of two or more distinct identities . . . [which] recurrently take control," and the "inability to recall." It is a splitting off of a personality or personality state that holds the memory of the trauma. This enables the personality that has forgotten the trauma to go on with life as if nothing has happened. The cause always seems to be severe emotional trauma, usually in childhood, generally of a repetitive nature.

Dissociative amnesia has as its essential feature "inability to recall important personal information, usually of a traumatic or stressful nature, that is too extensive to be explained by ordinary forgetting." *Dissociative fugue* is defined as "sudden, unexpected travel away from home . . . with inability to recall one's past." It may be so extensive that the individual does not even remember his name or any personal information about himself or his life, present or past. *Depersonalization disorder* involves the "persistent or recurrent experiences of feeling detached from, and as if one is an outside observer of, one's mental processes or body."[8] DSM-IV also describes other dissociative disorders.

The previous diagnostic training guide, DSM-III-R, gave a helpful elaboration:

> There are four types of memory disturbance that may be associated: *localized* (circumscribed), in which there is failure to recall the events occurring during a specific period of time; *selective,* in which one recalls only some, not all, of the events occurring during a circumscribed period of time; *generalized,* in which one recalls nothing from his entire life; and *continuous,* in which the patient cannot recall events from a specific time through the present.[9]

Dissociation protects against trauma in two ways. First, it blunts or obliterates the reality of the trauma while it is in progress. And second, it blocks the memory so it prevents repetitive flashbacks.

The psychiatric community of therapists clearly accepts the existence of amnesia, dissociation, or loss of memory due to trauma—involving either partial or complete repression. If a child—or adult—cannot make any sense of a trauma and has no method of coping, they escape the intolerable feelings and unthinkable thoughts, deadening the pain through emotional numbing or denial, or by pretending it never happened (blocking all conscious memory of it or dissociating).[10] As a Christian therapist, I believe this is a God-given method of helping us survive something that would otherwise make us crazy. We truly are fearfully and wonderfully made (Ps. 139:14).

Historical Accounts

Evidence from Concentration Camps

Bruno Bettelheim wrote about repressing his memories of Dachau and Buchenwald concentration camps in Nazi Germany:

> A split was soon forced upon me, the split between the inner self that might be able to retain its integrity, and the rest of the personality that would

> have to submit and adjust for survival. . . . Anything that had to do with the present hardships was so distressing that one wished to repress it, to forget it. Only what was unrelated to present suffering was emotionally neutral and could hence be remembered.[11]

Helga Newmark had a similar experience. When she left the concentration camp, she never spoke of it again to anyone. However, years later, after she was married, she waited at a railroad crossing with her two daughters and, she says, "All of a sudden I flashed back to being crammed into a cattle car on the way to the concentration camp. The memories came flooding in and I was paralyzed." She felt that she would go crazy if she didn't deal with the memories, so she entered therapy. There she remembered even more about the experiences in the camps that she had repressed. "Every memory that I regain is like another layer I'm peeling off, so I can get closer to the person I really am."

Newmark talks about how frightening it has been for her to publicly reveal any of this, because in the concentration camps the only safety was in becoming invisible. She concludes her account by saying that she hopes people will learn from her story that they can "recover from a trauma and go on to a normal, successful, even happy life."[12]

Studies have shown widespread dissociation or depersonalization for women who were survivors of the German concentration camps. They experienced the atrocities as if they were a dream, not real, or as if they were occurring to someone else.[13]

Evidence from War

In World War I, "under conditions of unremitting exposure to the horrors of trench warfare, men began to break down in shocking numbers. They screamed and wept uncontrollably. They froze and could not move. They became mute and unresponsive. They lost their memory and their capacity to feel." This was initially attributed to the effects of exploding shells, thus called "shell shock." In World War II, the episodic amnesia was again seen frequently. "It was recognized for the first time that any man could break down under fire and that psychiatric casualties could be predicted in direct proportion to the severity of combat exposure. . . . With the end of the war, the familiar process of amnesia set in once again."[14]

Other studies also demonstrated that a significant number of veterans had partial or complete amnesia for their combat experiences. Greater dissociations occurred with the more violent and the more stressful experiences.[15] For some veterans, the re-experiencing of their war trauma did not start until as long as fifteen years after the events.[16]

In *The American Daughter Gone to War,* Winnie Smith, a critical-care nurse in Vietnam, writes that she repressed whole segments of her traumatic experiences for sixteen years.[17]

Vietnam veterans who have been diagnosed with PTSD will sometimes demonstrate partial or complete repression for particularly traumatic events. At the same time, they may also have other traumas that repetitively haunt them. The specific events, since they are not secret and are witnessed by others, can often be verified.

Dr. John Briere, a psychiatry professor at USC Medical School, is a recognized authority on trauma. He cites research with soldiers in wartime that validates "a significant amount of combat-specific amnesia, often after especially stressful or violent events."[18]

Other data collected from Vietnam veterans indicates that the severity of the symptoms is influenced by the following:

1. Exposure to life-threatening combat (or contact with death and dying)
2. Taking of life or inflicting serious injury
3. Participation in or witnessing atrocities or other activities that require concealment or lead to moral dilemmas
4. Isolation from peers
5. Absence of permission to discuss the trauma[19]

Through extensive work with Vietnam veterans suffering post-traumatic stress, Dr. Van der Kolk observed how "horrific experiences are stored but 'forgotten.' Some of these memories later return in flashbacks. . . . The body keeps score, but the brain doesn't always remember."[20]

Evidence from Personal Trauma

In 1972, it was observed that some of the symptoms of victims of rape "resembled those previously described in combat veterans." In a study with ninety-two women and thirty-seven children who came to an emergency room, dissociative reactions and other PTSD symptoms were observed. "Only after 1980, when the effects on combat veterans had legitimized the concept of post-traumatic stress disorder, did it become clear that the psychological syndrome seen in survivors of rape, domestic battery, and incest was essentially the same as the syndrome seen in survivors of war."[21]

In 1989, a jogger in Central Park was left for dead after repeated rapes and brutalization. She has no memory of the event. In the jogger's case, the lack of memory could be because her injured brain never had a chance to physically create the memory,[22] or it could be the result of the emotional blocking of the trauma.

A case that received widespread publicity involved a New England priest, James R. Porter. He was accused of sexually abusing Frank Fitzpatrick, thirty-eight, who had repressed the memory of sexual molestation that had occurred at age twelve. The accusations were corroborated by about a hundred other men and women. Porter admitted the sexual abuse, and even confirmed Frank's memory of a rum-laced mincemeat pie. Some of the other victims also had delayed memories. During the trial, church officials "admitted that they had witnessed the priest's assaults or were told of them, but permitted him to continue supervising altar boys and youth activities." When parents had complained, he was quietly transferred to another parish.[23]

For David Clohessy, thirty-six, executive director of SNAP, Survivors Network of those Abused by Priests, memories of sex abuse flooded back after he saw *Nuts,* a film portraying a prostitute's coming to grips with memories of childhood abuse.[24]

Judith Herman, in her book, *Trauma and Recovery,* gives many examples of trauma with amnesia or dissociation. Alice Partnoy, a "disappeared" woman in Argentina, describes her success in dissociating from the trauma of her imprisonment. Elaine Mohamed, a South African political prisoner, writes about her splitting into two parts: "the Elaine part of me was the stronger part, while Rose was the person I despised. She was the weak one who cried and got upset and couldn't handle detention and was going to break down. Elaine couldn't handle it."[25]

Time magazine reported on a woman named Claudia, "who doesn't want her last name revealed." Through flashbacks, she suddenly recalled childhood sexual abuse by her older brother.

> From the time she was four years old to her brother's enlistment in the Army three years later, he had regularly handcuffed her, burned her with cigarettes, and forced her to submit to a variety of sexual acts. Claudia's brother had died in combat in Vietnam more than 15 years before her horrifying memories surfaced. Yet Claudia's parents had left his room and his belongings untouched since then. . . . Claudia searched the room. Inside a closet she found a large pornography collection, handcuffs, and a diary in which her brother had extensively planned and recorded what he called sexual "experiments" with his sister.[26]

Sylvia Fraser, an award-winning journalist from Ontario, Canada, has written *My Father's House: A Memoir of Incest and of Healing.*

> She was a beautiful blonde child, a star student, a quintessential 1950's teen-ager, a model wife. . . . As a girl, she loved Saturday matinees, giggled at pajama parties, ran for student council president, led the cheerleading squad, went steady with the right boy and married him, her proud father at her side. But from the age of seven, Sylvia Fraser shared her body with a twin who lived a separate life from her, with separate memories and experiences. This other self was created to do the things Sylvia was too frightened, too ashamed, too repelled to do—the things her father made her do.

At the age of forty-eight, she "breaks through her amnesia to discover and embrace the tortured self she left behind."[27]

"We tend to think of memory as residing in the mind, but the body has specific memories too," said Fraser, recounting her experience. "My body remembered what my mind forgot, and when the memories came back, they came back as convulsions—the convulsions of a child being orally raped." She now believes the seizures experienced as a child were related to her abuse. For Sylvia Fraser, corroborating came from older relatives and the family doctor.[28]

Clinical Evidence

In the Psychology Literature

One fascinating study focused on 129 girls who were under the age of thirteen when they were brought to a hospital for treatment for sexual abuse in the early 1970s. Seventeen years later they were interviewed and asked about childhood abuse. "38% did not report the sexual abuse . . . that had been documented in hospital records, nor did they report any sexual abuse by the same perpetrator."[29]

Perhaps they were too young to carry such a memory into adulthood. It's true that 55 percent of the subjects who were zero to three years of age at the time of the abuse *did* recall the abuse and, at that age, events are often forgotten. But it is also true that the following did *not* recall: 62 percent of the four- to six-year-olds, 31 percent of the seven- to ten-year-olds, and 26 percent of the eleven- to twelve-year-olds.[30] At these ages, memory for a trauma that was severe enough to require medical attention would certainly be remembered if it had not been repressed.

Did the subjects just neglect to mention the abuse, or not get around to it? Or were they too intimidated to talk about sexual abuse? No, the study involved approximately a three-hour interview with each person, some of whom did tell of other sexual abuse. So the subjects had sufficient time to disclose any information, and apparently felt comfortable to share other similar types of abuse. "Of the women who did not recall the . . . abuse that brought them into the study, 68% told . . . about other sexual assaults."[31]

Or was there a need to keep a secret? Not in these cases. Remember, they went to the hospital after the original incident. The trauma received attention from at least one parent or caretaker who took each child to the hospital, and from at least one medical professional. So the abuse was not kept secret. Yet even under these conditions, there were many who blocked the event. The women who were molested by family members or had genital trauma were more likely to have no recall (43 percent versus 28 percent).[32]

In addition to the 38 percent who did not recall the abuse, 16 percent who reported the event stated that there was a time in the past when they did not remember that the abuse had happened.[33]

It's hard to discount the possibility of repression or dissociation after considering this study by Linda Meyer Williams.

Dr. Loftus is a research psychologist on the board of the False Memory Syndrome Foundation, an organization of parents who claim to be falsely accused. She believes that "repressed or delayed memories may be uncommon." In her recent study (1993) of one hundred women receiving outpatient substance-abuse treatment at a New York City hospital, she and her coworkers found that more than half reported memories of childhood sexual abuse. Of that group, most remembered the abuse their whole lives; "only 18 percent said they had forgotten the abuse for a period of time and later regained the memory."[34] Dr. Loftus says "only 18 percent." But even if this lower percentage is more accurate, it still establishes that traumatic memories can be repressed, and (in her sample) nearly one in five cases of abuse were reportedly repressed.

Dr. Loftus also cites several other studies. Of 590 individuals who were known to have been injured in automobile accidents, 14 percent did not remember the accident a year later. In another study, more than a fourth of 1500 people did not remember a hospitalization that occurred only one year prior to the interview.[35] Both of these studies used documented traumas that were verified, yet repressed.

In one of John Briere's studies, 450 adults reported sexual abuse that had occurred between the ages of five and sixteen. Fifty-nine percent reported that there was a time prior to age eighteen when they had no memory of the abuse. The amnesia was more frequent with violent abuse (which included physical injury), multiple perpetrators, fears of death if the abuse was revealed, an earlier age of onset, abuse that lasted longer, and more current symptoms. They concluded that "amnesia for abuse . . . appears to be a common phenomena."[36]

Professional psychological journals present many cases of repressed memories. Unfortunately, it has been rare for these articles to indicate whether the recovered memories were validated. But we are starting to see some efforts at verification. For example, a 1993 journal describes a case report of a twelve-year-old boy recovering a memory of an attempted strangulation by his mother. She confirmed the event.[37]

A recent survey of the literature of multiple personality disorder found very few publications that present clear corroboration, or that even attempt to validate the truth of recovered traumatic memories. It does cite two corroborated studies, including this one:

> In 1985, Bowman et al. presented a case of multiple personality disorder in an adolescent who reported sexual abuse from age 6 to age 8 1/2. The father was charged with incest, sodomy, and rape . . . [and is] currently serving a life prison sentence. Welfare department records, family interviews, and court transcripts were available. . . . corroboration was explicitly reported.[38]

Dr. Lenore Terr, who has evaluated or treated more than four hundred children exposed to a variety of extreme traumas, presented one study involving twenty children under age five who had documented evidence and details of their trauma, including photographs (such as pornography), police reports, eyewitness reports, confessions, or corroborating injuries. She found that short, single events were better recalled in words. Of the seven children who had suffered repeated traumas, none of them could tell the story in full. For three of these, the repeated events were totally forgotten, at least in words. (These fit the current definition of repression.) She concludes that children who experience repeated and brutal abuse or trauma may forget large chunks of their childhood, not just specific assaults.[39]

According to Dr. Terr, children who experience a single, terrible event—such as witnessing a murder—retain vivid memories of the incident. They devote a lot of time and energy attempting to explain the trauma and how it could have been averted. But repeated trauma produces "amnesia for the events, denial of any past problems, emotional withdrawal, self-hypnosis, dissociation (such as feelings of physical numbness or invisibility), and self-mutilation or other aggressive acts."[40]

Dr. Judith Herman, a Harvard psychiatrist, found that about three-fourths of the women who reported child abuse were able to substantiate it by the admission of the abuser, physical evidence, pornographic pictures, or confirmation by other victims or relatives. Twenty-eight percent of these had repressed the memory of the abuse. Severe memory problems occurred most frequently for those individuals whose abuse began early in childhood and ended before adolescence. Violent or severe abuse was most likely to be associated with "massive repression as a defense."[41] Dr. Herman's recent study interviewed 519 adults suffering from PTSD. At some point in their lives about two-thirds experienced memory loss for early sexual abuse.[42]

Karen Hopenwasser, M.D., clinical assistant professor of psychiatry at Cornell University Medical College in New York City, describes the frequent return of repressed memories: "New phases in life development, from becoming a mother to losing a parent, often release a flood of childhood recollections."[43]

In the Clinic or Clinical Histories

In our clinic, we see many clients with repressed trauma, since that is one of our specialties.

One group of such clients, with partial or full repression, includes *victims of current trauma,* such as rape or other sexual abuse, severe physical assault, or various forms of emotional abuse. In many of these instances, there is extensive evidence of the trauma: police reports, medical evidence, confessions by the perpetrators, and eyewitnesses who saw the traumatic event that our client cannot remember.

Barbara is one of many examples of such repression or amnesia. She was working alone in a small boutique when an armed man came in and brutally raped her, threatening her death if she ever identified him. Fortunately, a passerby saw a man with a gun run out of the shop, recorded his car's license plate number, and called the police. When the police arrived, they found Barbara lying on the floor with multiple injuries. She had no recollection of what had transpired. Physical examination and evidence verified the rape and the identity of the assailant. It also ruled out any form of brain injury causing amnesia. Yet Barbara remained in a state of shock and amnesia. As she began therapy, she clearly expressed her desire to avoid any recollection of the event.

For Barbara, this meant living in a fog with very little feelings and limited capacity to function in her daily life. She had frequent nightmares, slept restlessly, and had high anxiety during the day. She startled easily by anything unexpected, even frequent events such as a door opening, someone speaking, or a phone ringing. She had numerous physical symptoms—nausea, headaches, back pain, diarrhea. She clearly had the symptoms of PTSD. As much as she feared facing the truth, Barbara knew she could not continue with her current symptoms. The therapy process was less traumatic than she had feared. She faced the dreaded truth and the accompanying feelings. She learned ways to protect herself in the future. She found new spiritual strength, coming to believe that, with God's help, she could handle even severe pain.

A second group of clients with partial or full repression or dissociation come to our clinic because of *current symptoms and external information.* With all of the current public information about the long-term effects of abuse, some courageous perpetrators or abusers are contacting their victims to ask forgiveness and to make amends. Many individuals, both victims and perpetrators, have lives changed by this revelation and the subsequent therapy.

> Dan had a history of difficult relationships with women: many ex-girlfriends, one divorce, and current marriage problems. He described his childhood as fairly uneventful. His sexual history, however, was unusual. Like many men these days, Dan was very sexually active in relationships with no emotional commitment. However, whenever he truly cared about a woman, all sexual feelings disappeared. In both marriages, he was unable to respond sexually. He had no memory of sexual or physical abuse or anything that might contribute to this problem.
>
> A few months ago, Dan had a shocking visit from his mother. She requested his forgiveness for sexually abusing him when he was young. She was amazed that he had no memory of this. She carried extreme guilt over this abuse, feeling responsible for his marriage failures. She did not relate the details, but offered to pay for Dan's therapy. The memory of the abuse came quickly for Dan. The specific details were confirmed by his mother. She briefly participated in his therapy, as Dan resolved his feelings and came to a place of forgiveness. Not only did he achieve a rewarding, open relationship with his mother, but his marriage was restored, and the sexual problems became a thing of the past. Dan's mother also sought therapy to deal with her molest as a child and her guilt for repeating the same behavior with her own child.

A third group of clients have *partial memories of an event or the associated feelings,* without the picture of what specifically occurred. Dan, for example, had always had extreme anxiety whenever his wife entered the bathroom. He tried to explain it as modesty, but he felt the same tension even if he was just cleaning the room. At times he had flashes that it was his mother, not his wife. When the memories of the abuse by his mother returned, Dan was not surprised to remember that the bathroom was the primary location of his molest.

Other clients may have a memory of the beginning of an uncomfortable incident, but the memory abruptly stops without a completion or resolution. Some may find strange gaps in their memories. Perhaps there's a person who was very significant in their childhood of whom they have no specific memory. Or maybe there was a recurring event, such as a yearly camping trip, which they cannot recall.

Results of Repressed or Dissociated Memories

When we have partially or totally blocked out a traumatic event we usually suffer difficulties emotionally, socially, physically, mentally, and spiritually.

Emotionally, we are likely to have considerable anxiety or depression, especially when a current event has any similarity to the trauma. We may become overly controlled in order to prevent the feelings from emerging.

Social problems are inevitable because we bring a great deal of pain, anger, and fear from the past into any current relationships. We may be the perpetual victims, or go to the other extreme and become victimizers. Our fear may demand attempts to control circumstances or other people. Childhood trauma inevitably robs us of our God-given personalities.

Physical problems are numerous for victims of trauma. Repetitive nightmares and sleep difficulties are common, resulting in exhaustion. In crisis situations the body pumps adrenaline. But when a trauma is not resolved the adrenaline may keep pumping—the body may stay in a state of arousal until adrenal exhaustion occurs. This then results in numerous symptoms including allergies, immune system disorders, and frequent illness that the impaired immune system cannot fight. Stress-related problems are common, such as headaches, hormonal problems, ulcers, back pain, colitis, TMJ, high or low blood pressure. A seven-year Yale study found many physical problems "as a consequence of pervasive repression, . . . including tension and migraine headaches, Crohn's disease, ulcers, allergies, hypertension, impotence, and vaginal herpes."[44]

Mental distortions in our thinking are predictable results of trauma. When we experience early or repeated victimization, we learn helplessness and hopelessness. We believe we are incapable of self-protection. We accept lies about our worth and what the world expects from us. Some people overcompensate and become very tough, independent, and aggressive, needing no one but themselves. Others remain in the pessimistic, helpless thinking. The Yale study found that repressors had difficulty in "thinking about certain issues in a non-threatened, nondefensive manner . . . with a bias toward seeing their parents and siblings in an excessively positive light."[45]

Spirituality is often filled with conflict for trauma victims. Most people blame themselves and God for the trauma instead of blaming the perpetrator and evil. Trusting God is difficult for many victims because their trust has been shattered. We must come to terms with the question of why God allows evil, especially to children, as well as with the ways in which God is trustworthy.

Legal Evidence

There have been several cases in the last few years which have supported the concept of repressed memory in our legal system.

The Franklin Case

In 1990, George Franklin was found guilty of first-degree murder. He was convicted on the basis of his daughter's recovered memories, which had been repressed for nineteen years. Eileen Franklin-Lipsker's memory of the 1969 sexual abuse and murder of her best friend, Susan Nason, returned in fragmented flashbacks. The events occurred when the girls were both eight years old.

The jury believed Eileen's report of her repressed memory because it matched the details of the murder that were obvious when the body was found in 1969, shortly after the murder. Susan's ring was smashed and there were two blows to her head.

As the memory returned years later, Eileen reported seeing her best friend raped and her head smashed with a rock as Susan had held up her hand to protect herself. Eileen's memory had considerable details, including sights, smells, and sounds. The details matched the physical evidence found on and around Susan Nason's body.

As she grew up, Eileen had displayed behavior that was very suggestive of the specific childhood trauma she described, according to Dr. Terr, who testified for the prosecution. For seven or eight years after the murder, Eileen pulled out the hair on one side of her head, creating a bald spot and bleeding. It was the same spot where Susan had been hit on the head with a rock. She withdrew from all friends. She did not have girlfriends after that—it was too dangerous. When she became a mother, she became the neighborhood vigilante. "Whenever she found a child playing alone, she took that child home. Children alone reminded her unconsciously of Susan Nason, who had been alone when Eileen and George Franklin picked her up."[46]

Eileen's repressed memory surfaced in classic fashion, triggered by a visual cue. The memory flashed into her mind as she watched her daughter playing, turning her head exactly as Susan Nason's had turned a moment before Franklin smashed it with a rock.

This is considered a landmark case, the first time anyone was convicted where the primary evidence was a recovered memory that had been repressed.

Other factors came to light after the trial, as reported by *Newsweek*: "Franklin's probation report, not part of the trial but given to the judge before sentencing, corroborates some of his daughter's testimony. An ex-girlfriend interviewed by police said Franklin asked if he could have sex with her eight-year-old daughter. He also reportedly told the woman he belonged to a society whose motto was 'Sex before 8 or it's too late.'"[47]

When George Franklin was arrested, his apartment was filled with "child-size dildos, child pornography, and books on incest."[48] When the inspectors advised him that they had reopened the murder case of Susan Nason, he immediately asked if they had been talking to his daughter.

Two of Eileen's sisters also revealed their sexual abuse by their father; two of her other sisters called them liars and publicity seekers; and their mother said she had no awareness of any sexual abuse within the family. There were also reports implicating George Franklin in the sexual assaults and deaths of other children.[49]

The Crawford Case

Recently, the police arrested a murder suspect, Franklin Crawford, after a year's investigation of John Reed's recovered memory—a memory that had been repressed since 1971. Reed was a terrified teenager when he reportedly heard a scream, followed the sound into a park, and saw Pearl Altman on the ground with her attacker standing over her. John ran, looking back to see if he was being followed, and he saw Crawford throw Pearl down a river embankment onto the rocks and into the water. "He observed a woman at the checkout counter [of a supermarket]. As she turned toward him, she reminded him of the [victim]. It triggered his memory. Investigators believe the man repressed the memory because he was afraid of the town bully."[50]

The Lawrence Case

As an adult, Lana Lawrence suddenly remembered being sexually abused by her father when she was nine. She had similar flashbacks of episodes going back to the age of three. On the basis of these memories, her father was prosecuted and convicted in Michigan, pleading no contest to this crime. In a newspaper interview, he reportedly admitted the abuse.[51]

The Mudd Case

A man was found guilty in a murder case that hinged on a flashback memory of the night of the crime by the victim's son fifteen years after it had taken place. In what became known as the "Total Recall" trial, John Mudd, Jr. suddenly remembered details of the night in 1975 when his father, John Mudd, Sr., was killed in their home. John was five years old at the time of his father's murder. His testimony was the key element that led a jury to find Steven Slutzker guilty of first degree murder.

John Mudd, Sr. was shot six times when he went to his basement in Wilkinsburg, Pennsylvania, to find out why the lights had gone out. The police found later that someone had removed a fuse. John testified that he suddenly remembered that he had heard seven shots and then saw his father's body at the bottom of a flight of stairs in their basement. He then saw Slutzker emerge from his family's kitchen.

As a surprise witness during the trial, Amy Slutzker, twenty-two, testified against her father. As a six-year-old, she saw her father take a gun out of his dresser drawer and leave their home minutes before Mudd was shot.

Slutzker admitted he was having an affair with Mudd's wife, Arlene, but denied committing the murder.[52]

An appeals court upheld the murder conviction, after Steven Slutzker asked Pennsylvania Superior Court to invalidate his 1992 conviction. He said John Mudd, Jr. shouldn't have been allowed to testify against him.

A psychiatrist said that John had suppressed the memory of the slaying because it was traumatic for him.

The younger Mudd's testimony was "markedly consistent with the testimony of others about events that night and with the physical evidence," said the trial judge, Jeffrey Manning of Allegheny County Common Pleas Court. Superior Court agreed with Manning. Slutzker was sentenced to life in prison. In 1976, he was charged with killing Mudd, but prosecutors lacked evidence and had dropped the case.[53]

The Bruen Case

The Nevada Supreme Court, on May 10, 1990, allowed a delayed discovery lawsuit against Ned Bruen by Tor Peterson (case #19878). Bruen was a "big brother" to Peterson under the Big Brother program. He violated this trust by sexually abusing Peterson from 1975 to 1983, beginning when Peterson was about seven years old. Bruen committed various acts of sexual battery, taking photographs of Peterson before, during, and after sexual involvement. As a result of Peterson's disclosures and a subsequent investigation, Bruen was eventually convicted of sexual assault, attempted sexual assault, lewdness with a minor under the age of fourteen, use of a minor in producing pornography, and possession of child pornography. Peterson blocked out the eight years of sexual molestation by Bruen until vividly recalling it during his therapy. The courts agreed that there was sufficient objective evidence for Bruen's conviction.[54]

New Statutes

Because our courts accept the existence of "repressed trauma," in recent years at least twenty-one states have passed "delayed discovery" statutes allowing a plaintiff to sue for damages caused by long-forgotten abuse, within a designated time period from when he or she recalled the abuse.[55] Those statutes emerged in response to suits brought by attorneys representing incest survivors and clergy-abuse victims.[56]

The California legislature has recognized by statute the concept of delayed memory. A victim of childhood sexual abuse, who is now an adult, may in some circumstances sue the offender. The statute also provides safeguards to prevent such lawsuits from being filed without any basis in fact (Section 340.1 Code of Civil Procedure).[57]

Summary

There are still some who say repression of a traumatic event *cannot* occur. Such people are simply uneducated on this topic. Publications, such as the *Journal of Traumatic Stress,* numerous books on the topic, and even television programs present documented cases. Well-trained professionals have seen many clients with repression in which the trauma has been documented or verified.

Even many of the supporters of "false memory syndrome" agree that repression does occur, though they are quick to point out that there are many claims of repressed memories that are not true. This is a valid point, and this book will deal with it.

One cannot throw out the baby with the bathwater. Yes, some recovered memories may be false or partially false. This does not mean, however, that repression or dissociation does not exist at all. The psychological community is far past the question of whether repression *can* occur. Instead, the more appropriate question is whether it *has* occurred in a particular case and whether the memory has been accurately recovered. We need to focus on ways of determining the accuracy of recovered memories, and, above all, effective methods of treatment.

Some research psychologists claim that because they cannot prove repression in the laboratory it does not exist. But the very nature of the cause of repression—extreme trauma—means they will never be able to produce it in the laboratory with human subjects. Instead, we must examine it after the fact, after the trauma has occurred. This is currently being done in numerous studies.

Many therapists report numerous specific cases of repressed memory. As Dr. Briere puts it, "It is widely held among trauma-specialized clinicians that survivors of severe abuse usually come to psychotherapy with incomplete memory of their maltreatment."[58] From my own clinical experience, I concur.

The evidence for the existence of repressed memory is just too great to be ignored. We all must move on to the new issues that arise when we accept the truth that traumatic memories *can be* repressed and, in many cases, *are* repressed.

5

Can Memories Be Distorted by Outside Influences?

Jack was a successful businessman in his mid thirties. He came into my office reporting that he was "falling apart." His wife had unexpectedly left him three months earlier to move in with another man. She took their two preschool girls with her. About a month later, he was contacted by Child Protective Services and informed that all visitation with his children had been suspended due to charges of sexual molestation.

Jack was sure there was some error, but all attempts to call his wife were unsuccessful. As his fear rose, he began calling more frequently. His wife, Carol, then got a restraining order to prevent any further calls to her or the girls. A week or two later, Jack's parents called him and tearfully relayed that they had also been charged with sexually abusing the two children. They added that both girls had reportedly given many details of both abuse and threats by Jack and the grandparents.

Jack described the terror he experienced at these false accusations. He hired an attorney who advised him to seek counseling and a psychological evaluation. Extensive testing revealed no sexual attraction to children, no acting out behavior, no evidence of lying, denial, or distortions of reality. It did, however, suggest a somewhat overcontrolled, perfectionistic, work-oriented man who had been unaware of and insensitive to his wife's emotional needs.

No testing can rule out sexual abuse, but there were no factors supporting it, either. Psychological and medical examinations of both children were court-ordered, as well as a psychological examination of Carol. At that point, Carol began calling Jack, offering to drop all charges if he would admit his guilt. She explained that the quickest healing for children comes when they are believed and the abuser confesses his wrong actions. (This is correct *if the accused abuser is guilty.*) Under these conditions, she would allow supervised visitation with the girls for his parents and for him. Jack was excited. At least he could see his girls. He would do anything to get his family back.

The more Jack thought about his girls, the more he thought that perhaps he really had abused them. Certainly his wife and girls wouldn't lie. Yes, he concluded, he had abused his daughters. What a horrible, despicable person he was. He tearfully begged his wife and girls to forgive him. Carol agreed and began to permit supervised visitation. As the counseling continued, Carol and the girls agreed to participate. Eventually, through further investigation and honesty on Carol's part, the full story emerged: neither Jack nor his parents had ever abused his daughters. It was merely Carol's ploy to gain full custody.

Anytime an allegation of sexual abuse occurs during a divorce and custody battle, it is suspect. Occasionally such allegations are true, but so much of what we hear from divorcing parents about each other is an exaggeration of the negative. We must evaluate these charges carefully. The allegation of abuse is the easiest way to gain custody of children and to hurt an ex-mate. If the accusation occurs before a separation, and in fact caused the separation, it is much more likely to be accurate. If it occurs after a divorce is in process, the likelihood of deception is high.

Consider the Source of the Memories

The sources of our memories are a very important consideration in evaluating their truth. Other people may have influenced us to believe exaggerations, misconceptions, or lies. Most of these people have done so unwittingly. But a few people may knowingly scheme to trick us. We must not allow anyone to convince us of our own reality, unless we are certain that he or she is an accurate eyewitness.

Family and Friends

It's sad that we can't trust everyone. Nor can we trust anyone, even trustworthy people, in every area all of the time. We all are human and sometimes we blow it. Even those we've trusted in the past are capable of deceiving us, especially if they are angry at us.

There's an old saying: You always hurt the one you love. Relationships can sour quickly, as we fail to meet high expectations. Friends who used to be close and affirming may now be saying many critical things to us and about us to others. That hurts! But it happens. Because they have been unwilling or unable to resolve things with us, they hang on to their anger. To preserve their self-worth and to protect their feelings of guilt, they do whatever is necessary to make us the bad one or wrong party, even using lies or exaggerations. More often, they really convince themselves of our badness and their goodness.

Few people are more vindictive than those with whom we have had the greatest intimacy, followed by a break in the relationship. Ex-mates or ex-friends often tell negative stories. Custody battles give rise to false accusations with the intent of gaining control of the children. Many parents trick themselves into believing that a lie is in the best interest of their children. Some will do anything, including things that are illegal, immoral, or dishonest, if they feel the children's best interests are at stake. And in a divorce, each parent tends to feel that he or she is the better parent. Custody evaluations usually reveal false or exaggerated stories that each parent tells about the other in order to buttress their own case. In fact, it's become so common to involve the children in these negative beliefs about the other parent that the term *parental alienation syndrome* has been coined.

Are your memories a result of accusations by an ex-friend or ex-mate? If so, question them. Don't assume that the accusations are true, even if the friend or spouse has previously been trustworthy. That's what Jack did, and it nearly wrecked his life.

We remember what we have perceived. And our perception is colored by our attitudes toward people, things, or events. Love is blind, they say. What does that mean? When we are in love, we ascribe to the person we love all positive, wonderful qualities. The object of our affections can do no wrong. We idealize the person. But what happens when the honeymoon is over? Exactly the opposite. All sorts of irritating habits we had overlooked are now obvious to us. When a couple is fighting, separating, or divorcing, it's hard for them to see any good in each other. The same experience may be perceived—and remembered—in completely different ways.

Consider how the same quality can be viewed in a positive or a negative light:

Qualities of the One We Love		Qualities of the One We Hate
Responsible		Rigid
Hard working		Workaholic
Stable		Nonfeeling or boring
Intensely feeling	*changes to*	Irrational or hysterical
Neat and orderly		Neurotically compulsive
Spontaneous		Irresponsible
Funloving		Childish
Patient and kind		Passive

If you have been very close to someone, they probably know enough about you to say the very things that will cause you to question your own reality and memories. This is especially true about your shared experiences with this particular person. But they may also influence the memories of your childhood. Most people do begin to believe anything they have been told frequently enough.

The *New Yorker* gives a long, detailed account of a father who was accused by his daughters of sexually abusing them. Initially he reported no memory of any abuse, but as time went by, he remembered all of the incidents they recounted. As a test, he was also told of an incident the daughters did not describe. He soon remembered that as well.[1] We don't know what really happened in this family. Only God knows the full truth. But this test does show how easy it is to rewrite our own histories. Even our memories can be heavily influenced by lies, distortions, and exaggerations.

Family members and trusted friends have an enormous influence on what we believe—even when it comes to remembering our own past. Dr. Loftus has demonstrated that some people can be convinced of events that never happened.

"Do you remember when you were five years old and you got lost in the shopping mall?" That was the scenario Dr. Loftus set up, choosing subjects of different ages and getting trusted family members to relate the story. Later some of the subjects remembered the event, elaborating on the details, and some even described it with strong emotion.[2] The problem was—it never happened! A few of the subjects were talked into this memory.

But perhaps this is too generic and common a fear; we must have all been frightened about losing our parents at some point in childhood, and so we could easily imagine that scenario. In fact, because this is such a common fear, many children have heard the Sesame Street book *Ernie Gets Lost,* a story about Ernie getting lost in a shopping mall.

Dr. Loftus clarifies that 75 percent of those studied did not manufacture false memories in this experimental situation, despite the implicit pressure to produce one. About 10 percent of the adults did create a specific false memory in response to the suggestion or story from a family member whom they apparently trusted. About 15 percent said they felt a vague sense that the event had occurred.[3]

Support Groups

We have already met Greg, the man who wept in my office as he dealt with memories of childhood beatings. We will soon get to know his wife, Melissa. But now let's meet Lynn, Melissa's daughter from a previous marriage.

The church Lynn attended had a support group for adults who were molested as children. Lynn found some of these people to be open, loving, and supportive. More than that, they expressed feelings.

Lynn had no memories of her father from the first six years of life, and her mother always seemed busy with work and school. After Melissa married Greg, the home was stable, but people didn't communicate. Remember Greg's nonconfrontational patterns; he avoided hearing or sharing feelings. So Lynn often felt lonely as she grew up. She yearned for a feeling of family.

When one of the support group members suggested that it was obvious that her home was a place of hidden secrets, probably incest, Lynn accepted the idea and joined the group. At the suggestion of others, she became convinced of her abuse, soon creating rather elaborate stories of abuse by her biological father. She decided to verify this abuse through hypnosis (which we'll discuss more completely in a later chapter).

Recovery groups are wonderful ways to receive support and encouragement. Many therapists recommend them as an addition to individual therapy. A group is a place where we can tell others about those painful areas in our lives. Our healing is facilitated by talking about our pain to those who understand and accept it.

However, recovery groups also have the potential to influence us to believe inaccurate memories. As we hear the stories of abuse from others, it is easy to empathize deeply with them and cross the line into feeling the pain ourselves. We may begin to believe that we must have experienced similar abuse, particularly if we have similar symptoms. We see the attention, caring, and affirmation received by those who share certain experiences and we want to receive those things, too. We may sense an underlying competition to tell the worst story in order to get the most care from the leader. Or we may identify with an individual in the group who shares a story of abuse and assume that story as our own.

This may sound cold and calculated, but in many cases people do not even realize what's going on. We want so badly to be part of this caring group that our brains invent ways to make that happen.

Women seem to be more susceptible to group influence. We live in a time of isolation for many women. We no longer experience the life of years ago, when women gathered together to cook, sew, knit, shop, garden, can fruits and vegetables. We no longer have the extended family to teach a young woman about childcare, to gather around her during childbirth and family illnesses or crises, and to listen with empathy, support, and direction when needed. Women seem to be craving this kind of interaction with other women—thus the power of a group where intimate and personal issues are discussed, where people care.

When a support group lacks a leader, or doesn't have an agreed upon structure to resolve issues, it is more likely to foster false memories. Without someone who is knowledgeable guiding the group, it may follow a spiral of stories that escalate in their severity of abuse. But if these groups are structured to focus on the positive or on the successes of the group members, rather than focusing predominantly on retrieving more memories, the support and friendships can provide valuable assistance.

The power of suggestion has been confirmed in numerous experiments. In one, people at work were told by several different people that they were not looking well. Most people who received this observation went home sick before the day was over, even though they had felt fine when they arrived. The impact of suggestion, particularly the negative, is immensely powerful.

We know this from our own experience. As children and teenagers, we desperately sought to fit in with the group. We borrowed ideas about fashion, morality, and even about ourselves from our friends. That's why parents are so concerned about the friends their children choose. We instinctively know that friends influence friends.

Even as adults, we often yield to the influence of the groups we find ourselves in. If you're at a concert and the crowd starts applauding, what do you do? You probably applaud whether you liked the song or not. Or if you're in a conversation where several others begin agreeing about some moral or political issue, but you disagree—what do you do? It's easier to go with the flow, especially if the group is made up of friends you like whom you want to like you.

This is the principle behind the success of many cult groups. When surrounded by a loving group of people who all agree on some basic truths, some people will tend to go along with the crowd, accepting those truths into their own belief system, no matter how preposterous they may be. Perhaps the most shocking example of this in our time was the Jonestown Massacre, in which 913 followers of Jim Jones committed suicide in Guyana. This American cult leader commanded his followers to drink a cyanide-laced punch. Apparently they passively obeyed, even killing their 276 children. We were stunned to hear the incomprehensible obedience to an unknown self-declared leader. The same kind of influence may occur with memories about our own lives.

I have seen many clients who sought therapy because a friend or family member told them that it was obvious they were victims. Some of these well-meaning friends continued playing amateur doctor, giving the diagnosis about how the victimization had occurred. *You can always tell by the symptoms,* they said. Well, this is simply not true. Even if one person exhibits certain symptoms and is a victim of abuse, it does not follow that everyone who shows those symptoms has also been abused.

People sometimes will join a support group for incest survivors because they have vague suspicions of abuse in their past, or because they have certain telltale symptoms. But this may be premature. You should first try to establish your own history with a certain degree of confidence (a therapist can help with this). And if you feel you do need the emotional support of such a group, at least be aware of the possibility that you might be influenced to believe that the stories that happened to other group members also happened to you, when in fact they did not.

Guard your past and your memories of it. It is not the same as anyone else's past. You are special and unique.

The Media

TV, movies, newspapers, and magazines have been filled recently with stories of childhood abuse. Unfortunately, these media presentations can sometimes spark false memories in people who suspect they've been abused.

This is the power of suggestion at work again. We can have so much empathy for the characters on the screen or on the page that we put ourselves in their situation. It's hard to separate fact from fiction, or someone else's story from our own. Especially if people have a memory gap to begin with, they may be susceptible to stories seen or read. There's a short jump from *It seems like it could have happened to me,* to *Maybe it did happen to me,* to *It must have happened to me.*

Certainly some genuine recollections can occur by hearing, reading, or seeing something very similar to our own experiences. Sometimes true memories can be sparked in this way, but the potential for distortion or fabrication is also present.

One great problem in this area is the profusion of experts who write books that essentially try to convince the readers that sexual abuse has occurred to them, whether they know it or not. Readers are urged to imagine the abuse happening, in an effort to free up those blocked memories. But many of us have vivid imaginations. We can imagine most anything.

And, once we imagine something, we might have the corresponding feelings. But this does not mean that the imagined event really happened.

Be careful about these books, and use your imagination wisely. Unless you know that abuse occurred, do not assume it did. Do not set out on a course to prove sexual abuse unless you're fairly sure that it happened.

Books are viewed by some of us as authoritative sources of truth. It's hard to question a published author who seems to be an expert. But we must question what we read, especially in this area of repressed memories. We need to assess our susceptibility to what we read or see on television. We need to question and prayerfully think through assumptions and opinions of others, no matter how confident and informed they may seem. We can find support for almost any truth and be misled.

In the case of memories, there is conflicting information presented from people who are highly educated, knowledgeable, and respected. Different views of memory are well presented and well documented. Most of these authors are presenting the truth as they understand it. But sometimes we don't even know we are presenting only one side of the picture. We can be so devoted to one theme that we can be completely off base in another area and not even realize it. Consider Dr. Benjamin Spock, who wrote a book on child rearing that many parents considered the absolute truth on the subject. In his later years, however, he is reported as saying that he was wrong about some of his very permissive attitudes.

Books can be wrong. And we must never suspend common sense as we read any book, even this one. Although I have spent considerable time in research, there may be information that I've missed. If there is, it could change the conclusions I've reached. I am doing my best to provide you with the most accurate information available. But this work should not be viewed as authoritative or definitive. Question it. Do your own research. Tell me if I'm wrong. I sincerely seek the truth, and remain open to all options concerning the truth of memories.

Psychology sections in bookstores are filled with many self-help books for survivors. One of the most controversial (and best-selling) is *The Courage to Heal* by Ellen Bass and Laura Davis, a book often referred to as the bible of the recovered memory movement. It has some excellent, helpful information and exercises, but it also includes inaccurate statements such as, "If you think you were abused and your life shows the symptoms, then you were," and potentially dangerous advice such as, "If you don't remember your abuse, you are not alone. Many women don't have memories . . . this doesn't mean they weren't abused."[4] Like many of the authors of these self-help books, neither Davis nor Bass has any academic training in psychology, learning theory, or memory. Many of these books contain lists of symptoms of repressed memory that are so general and all-inclusive that almost everyone fits the description.

A San Luis Obispo, California, woman, Kimberly Mark, has filed a suit against Davis. An article on the case states

> She was emotionally damaged because the book induced her to believe she'd been molested when she hadn't. . . . She came to believe she had 400 personalities and had suffered satanic ritual abuse. . . . It (the book) tells her you have to work at recovering your memories. So she works more and more. It tells her you must believe. So she believes. . . . It tells her (she) must not have anyone around her that is not a believer—so she doesn't go seek orthodox treatment. . . . Last fall, a *Time* article made her doubt that she'd ever been abused. . . . By then, her emotional health had been destroyed and she couldn't work.[5]

A survey was conducted of several hundred families who have been accused of abuse but claim they are innocent. These families had something interesting in common. "In almost all cases," the study reports, their children had read the book *The Courage to Heal*.[6] The primary complaint about this book is that it suggests that you do not need any memories or any evidence to believe that you were abused, just symptoms. This approach can obviously lead to many false memories. This book also encourages revenge, anger, lawsuits, deathbed confrontations, and suggests that there should never be forgiveness.

On October 1, 1993, the Supreme Court of Minnesota overturned the previous conviction of Robert Huss for criminal sexual assault of his three-year-old daughter. They found that the book *Sometimes It's OK to Tell Secrets* "is a highly suggestive book and . . . its repeated use by the child's mother and therapist, combined with the mother's belief that abuse had occurred, may have improperly influenced the child's report of events." The book comes with a tape in which the words of the book are set to music. It refers to acts of abuse as "yucky secrets." The child repeatedly sang this song at home.[7]

A friend gave Melissa a book about sexual abuse shortly after she learned of Greg's affair. Melissa devoured the book, looking for the reasons for her failure as a wife, as well as reasons for Greg's affair. She concluded that they both had been sexually abused. Probably, she figured, all of her children had been abused too, since they had all spent time with their grandparents, the suspected perpetrators. She could see symptoms in every one of them.

Fortunately, Melissa was in therapy at the time, and did not pursue some of the suggestions in the book, such as imagining what might have happened. Since almost everyone has some of the symptoms in the book's list, it creates many false leads. In the case of Melissa and her family, sexual abuse occurred for only one of the six family members, and the perpetrator was not the person she initially suspected, as we'll discover later.

Suggestibility through books and teachings often plays temporary havoc with medical students and nurses. As they study each disease, some begin to worry that they themselves display the symptoms. A kind of hypochondria sets in. Fortunately, there are often concrete tests that can confirm or rule out the diagnoses.

Psychology students experience similar confusion and suggestibility through their studies, particularly in their first class of abnormal psychology. It is very easy to see themselves in many of the disorders. The same sort of temporary hypochondria occurs with some of these students who imagine that they suffer from some new emotional disorder with each new chapter of the textbook. Psychological testing courses in graduate programs have relieved the anxiety of many future psychologists.

That's something we can laugh at later as we realize that it's just our sensitivity to what we've been learning. But it's no laughing matter when people continue to believe that they are emotionally disturbed when they are not. The false suggestion of sexual abuse in an otherwise healthy family can be very destructive.

Over the past twenty-five years, I have watched the waves of popular illness, both physical and emotional. Television talk shows popularize certain abnormalities. Repressed memories, incest, and ritualistically abused victims have been featured prominently on *Geraldo, Oprah, Don-*

ahue, *Sally Jessy Raphael*, and other daytime TV talk shows. These may be true or false accusations of the reported abuse. We don't know.

The sad part is that the people who truly are the victims get lost in the masses and may not receive the treatment needed. We must not climb on the bandwagon of sexual abuse, the current popular choice, unless we know that sexual abuse has occurred. Symptoms alone are not convincing—all of the symptoms could have other causes. Treating the wrong cause will not bring about healing or freedom.

Statistics can also scare us into assuming that we've been victimized. The occurrence of sexual abuse, for example, has varying numbers. Dr. Briere presents several studies that concluded that sexual victimization of girls is between 20–30 percent, and 10–15 percent for boys.[8] Whatever the frequency, it is far too common. But this does not automatically mean that you too have been abused. Do not let yourself be drawn into believing something without the facts. Know that we are all subject to being influenced in positive ways and in negative ways.

There are books that currently are receiving wide acceptance from the therapeutic community, but have some inaccurate information with both positive and destructive suggestions. They have become popular because therapists and clients are looking for answers. Before accepting or believing anything, there are four steps we need to take.

First, we must evaluate the *qualifications* of the writer or speaker in the specific area in which we are considering their information.

Second, we need to consider whether this is a presentation of *facts or opinions.*

Third, we should look to find any facts that might support the *opposite point of view,* in order to see the entire picture. In the area of memories, some highly qualified professionals are presenting only the ideas and research that support their points of view, rather than providing a balanced picture.

Fourth, we need to ask ourselves, do their answers seem *too simplistic or all-encompassing?* For example, if a book states or implies that your abuse is the cause of all your problems, past and present, that is an irresponsible conclusion. It seems to be feeding your need to shift responsibility to others rather than helping you to take responsibility for your growth.

An excellent book is *The Suggestibility of Children's Recollections*, published by the American Psychological Association. The foreword of this book explains that it does not "hide the differences of opinion among these scholars, but . . . afford[s] opportunities for disagreement." The twenty-three contributors to this book include "psychology's leading authorities on the suggestibility of children's recollections."[9] It is a very informative presentation of varying perspectives and research, and is essential for any therapist who works with children or childhood memories.

It is of critical importance that our beliefs are accurate and based upon truth because when we have come to believe something, we act accordingly. "As [a man] thinks in his heart, so is he" (Prov. 23:7 NKJV). We look for evidence to support our beliefs. We close our minds to evidence that is contrary to our beliefs. It is essential to remember that we all are suggestible in varying ways. Remain open to the truth! It is a warning sign when we are dogmatic about any memory, convinced that it absolutely did occur just as we remember it. Allow yourself to consider the opposite point of view, that it might not be true or that it might be partially true.

Therapists

The False Memory Foundation newsletter often suggests that it is the therapists who are implanting false memories. At times this may be true, especially if they are inadequately trained or biased. We might include in this category lay helpers or other authority figures who offer counseling.

There is information given by nonprofessionals and "professionals" in books, magazines, and on TV and radio that is perceived as truth when it isn't. We must be diligent in questioning the validity of the information we receive. Why should we accept the information or perspective that someone is presenting? Does the person have the proper training or experience to teach us this? Too many of us are gullible and ready to believe what anyone tells us.

It's more understandable that we would accept the opinions of a trained, licensed, and experienced therapist. But many people who offer therapy are lay people, interns, new therapists, or counselors who have little training in memory or repressed trauma. These people may help in certain ways, but do not trust them to work with your repressed memories, if indeed you have any.

Perhaps we need to learn to be more discriminating consumers of health care. Many of us grew up not questioning the doctor, and that attitude seems to carry over into counseling. But now, even in medicine, second and third opinions seem essential. And the same should be true in psychological therapy, especially for something as important as a belief that would cut off relationships with family or dear friends (not to mention the major change in self-perception). You might go to the retired nurse next door with a sprained thumb, but if you need heart surgery, you'll consult an expert. You should consider the recovery of repressed memories as serious as surgery.

Unfortunately, even well-trained therapists can have uninformed biases regarding repressed memory of abuse. The psychiatric community has been strongly influenced in the area of child abuse by untested theories from nonacademic sources. Anyone who writes a book becomes an instant expert. It is such a new field that not only clients, but also therapists are looking for answers. And our society often believes that if something is written, it must be true—unfortunately this holds true for professional therapists, too. Thus some of these dubious answers have been accepted by some therapists, opening the floodgates for false memories.

Dr. Michael Yapko, an author and psychologist in San Diego, devised two questionnaires. The Memory Attitude Questionnaire (MAQ) was "created to assess the range and depth of therapists' understanding of the workings of human memory, especially in relation to clinical issues and treatment." Dr. Yapko discovered that many therapists have inaccurate knowledge of memory. About a third believed that the mind functions like a computer, with accurate recording. About 10 percent thought that memory was not influenced by suggestion. About 25 percent believed that feelings of certainty about a memory made it more likely to be accurate. More than 25 percent trusted that, if the client said something happened, then it did actually occur. Forty-one percent believed that "early memories, even from the first year of life, are accurately stored and retrievable." Fifty-seven percent did not do anything to distinguish truth from fiction.[10]

I have never met a therapist or lay helper who purposely set out to deceive or trick a client into believing a falsehood. The current attacks on therapists, suggesting such sinister motives, have been very painful, frightening, false accusations for many. In the past, very few therapists ever considered that clients' allegations could be false. Nor were they aware of their ability to lead clients into false assumptions. The training in the area of treating child abuse never included either. In fact, the opposite was stressed. We were taught that it was irresponsible and therapeutically destructive to question or not believe a child who was reporting abuse.

For example, an article printed in 1979 suggests that "authorities now strongly encourage that reports [referring to incest] be considered reality unless very clearly demonstrated to be fantasy. . . . An error in this direction is far less serious for victims than problems which ensue when they encounter disbelief in the face of reality."[11] This is the pervasive teaching that counselors receive.

Our training in this area has been inadequate. Many have had little or no course work in memory or learning theory. Until recent years there was no training for therapy concerning sexual abuse. Some counselors have begun working with repressed trauma after only attending a seminar or reading a book.

Yet a very positive climate is now emerging, which should allow each person to question memories, both conscious and repressed. But some therapists still see abuse in every client. In some cases, the therapist will offer conclusions about the client's childhood. And if the client disagrees, a few counselors may even go to the extreme of saying the client is in denial. This is totally unacceptable, yet I do not believe it is done maliciously.

There are several ways that distortions can enter therapy.

1. The client could have misperceived what occurred.
2. The client could relay what happened in a confusing or false manner.
3. The therapist could hear the client improperly or incompletely.
4. The therapist could fill in missing details with inaccurate information.
5. The therapist could inaccurately communicate his or her interpretations or conclusions.
6. The client could misunderstand the interpretations or comments of the therapist.
7. The therapist could come to the wrong conclusion.

It's obvious that there are considerable opportunities for errors to occur.

Most therapists have a strong theoretical perspective on the cause of the presenting problem, and of the necessary steps for healing. It is time that we all take another look at our biases and consider other alternatives to those we have previously accepted.

In "Guilt by Memory," a TV documentary on CNN, a private investigator was seen going undercover to a therapist. She presented complaints of depression and problems with her husband. The therapist told her, in the first session, that she was a classic case of an incest survivor. During the second session, when the "patient" said she had no memory of anything like incest, the therapist told her that her denial was typical and that she had repressed the memory because it was too painful.[12]

ABC's *Prime Time Live* presented a similar experience by an attorney, Greg Zimmerman. He consulted a therapist concerning his depression after his father's suicide. He felt he was unable to talk about this pain, but was pushed to find something else, with the therapist informing him, "I don't know how to tell you this, but you display the same kind of characteristics as some of my patients who are victims of Satanic ritualistic abuse."[13]

How frequently do therapy sessions like this occur? We don't know. There should be a dramatic change following a recent court decision in Napa, California, May 13, 1994. In a civil suit, despite the unwavering beliefs of the daughter and her mother that the abuse was true, the jury supported the father. Gary Ramona was awarded $500,000, instead of the $8 million he was asking. The jury did not rule that the therapists had acted maliciously, but that they had been careless and had failed to consider alternatives in the treatment of bulimia. They did not rule on the truth of the memories.[14] With the threat of lawsuits looming, and the publicity concerning suggestibility, many therapists have realized the destructiveness of their tendency to diagnose sexual abuse when the client has no awareness of it.

Our clinic is seeing more and more clients who are seeking to assess the truth of their memories. They report the inability to find therapists who take a middle ground. There currently seems to be a polarization, with some counselors denying the existence of repressed memories, therefore concluding that all recovered memories are false. Others apparently believe that all memories are accurate, and questioning is a denial of reality. We do encourage questioning. I do not believe people will be healthy until they allow their doubts to be heard and considered.

If you have been coached into recovering memories, it's important to take time to evaluate them. Think back to the times before your memories emerged. Were you told by a therapist that you had all the symptoms of abuse? Did the therapist encourage you to imagine or create a story of abuse, and then accept this story as factual? Did your therapist consider other possible causes of your problems besides child abuse? Have you had doubts about the accuracy of these memories, and have you expressed these doubts? If so, how has your therapist responded?

A strange thing happens in a counseling situation. Most people want the approval or at least the attention of their therapist. You want to be a good client. As a result, the therapist has a subtle power over what you say. If a therapist brightens up and asks more questions when you talk about your parents—then you will try to talk about your parents more. This therapist-pleasing is a natural, documented phenomenon.

Many therapists have a theoretical bias of what causes emotional problems. Through the therapists' subtle clues, clients learn to give them what they want—the information that fits into their theories. In the case of repressed memory, the clues may or may not be subtle. As we have said, some therapists see child abuse as the cause of everything, and they may coach you into remembering something that didn't occur.

This is not to suggest that your therapist is deceitful or manipulative, but it is essential for you to examine what's going on in your therapy sessions. Question. Seek the truth. If your recovered memories are accurate, they will bear up under scrutiny. If they are not, your therapist should join you in discarding them. Questioning is not denial—it is merely intellectual honesty.

The *New York Times* describes the experience of Jan Downing, a special education teacher from Newbury, Massachusetts, who said she sought counseling for her son's behavior problems. She had a good relationship with her parents, but within the first few sessions her counselor told her that she was an "adult child of an alcoholic and compared my childhood to growing up in a concentration camp," she says. "If I resisted he would rephrase my realities for me."

Jan became depressed and increasingly more dependent upon her counselor. Then he said she had all the symptoms of sexual abuse by her father. Jan had no memory of this, but she followed her counselor's advice, cutting all contact with her family, except for "horrible" letters. Her parents were devastated.

After six years of therapy, Jan says, she was so depressed she underwent a series of hospitalizations that lasted weeks at a time. Her therapist kept telling her that unless she retrieved memories of sexual abuse, she would never get better. Finally, she began to have memories of sexual abuse that included her father. But when her mother died in the early 1990s, Jan began to question the validity of her memories and the methods of her therapist. She eventually decided that her therapy was a sham. Jan Downing, forty-three, has filed a lawsuit against her therapist and is trying to rebuild her life, with the loving support of her father and brothers. Her greatest pain, she says, was not being able to resolve the issue before her mother died.[15]

Barry is a middle-aged man with a history of marital problems. He had been in therapy for a year before seeking intensive therapy. He knew he had been sexually abused because a leader, whom he respected and trusted, told Barry that he fit the symptoms of sexual abuse. Barry felt like such a failure because of his poor memory. He believed that if only he could remember the abuse, then he would complete his therapy, and everything would be fine.

In his intensive work at our center, however, sexual abuse was not the issue. Instead, Barry faced his feeling of extreme worthlessness, resulting from abandonment by his mother at age four. He recalled his vow never to allow anyone to hurt him like that again. He kept his vow, displaying many behaviors that brought distance with women. But at the same time, his need for a mother continued to draw him into relationships with women. To use a familiar phrase, he couldn't live with them and he couldn't live without them. Resolving his anger, hurt, and fears of abandonment finally permitted intimacy and a successful marriage relationship.

I am often surprised at our influence as therapists. I recall Jimmy, a nine-year-old boy who came into our clinic for an assessment of learning disabilities. He was doing poorly in school and believed he was "dumb."

Jimmy did not have any learning disabilities. In fact, he was very intelligent. The results of an intelligence test changed his life from that day on. His school performance immediately improved and today Jim is in medical school.

Jenny, Greg and Melissa's youngest child, was described as having only average intelligence. However, with the family history of high intelligence on both sides, no evidence of learning disabilities or neurological impairment, no reported difficulties during Melissa's pregnancy with her or in the labor or delivery, no high fevers or accidents during childhood, the conclusion seemed questionable. Testing, as with Jim, revealed that Jenny was very bright in verbal and social areas, but that she rarely persisted or put much effort into completing tasks. Furthermore, she wasn't about to compete against "all the brains of the family." So Jenny had laid claim to a different area of success—socializing—where she was the shining star. As her school became aware that Jenny qualified for the gifted program, their attitudes and expectations of her changed. Despite some reluctance, Jenny entered the higher-level classes. Within a few months, she was doing very well academically, with plenty of time left to socialize.

Many adults with normal to high intelligence grew up believing they were "dumb." Therefore, they do nothing with their talent. It's amazing to observe the dramatic change caused by a two-hour intelligence test, or tests assessing abilities. People have made career changes, have gone to college, or have completed college as they revised the truth about their intelligence. Since they believe that the perceptions of the therapist and the test are accurate, they store that information, and then they retrieve it whenever needed and they act accordingly. If they fail a test after that, they may respond by thinking, "What happened? I'm really smart. This isn't like me." So they examine the test, discover their errors, and do better the next time.

But individuals who believe they are stupid may fail the same test and react by saying, "See, I knew I was dumb. I can't ever pass a test." Such people will not learn from their errors. They will continue to act dumb, and probably do as poorly, if not worse, the next time.

Therapists often have tremendous influence over clients, especially when they are hurting and vulnerable. We must take that responsibility very seriously, and guard diligently to insure that we never influence anyone to believe a lie.

Abusers

Clearly, the perpetrator of abuse wants to remain undetected. So he will do whatever is necessary to deceive his victim about his identity.

Some children have reported the forced use of drugs prior to the abuse that resulted in a confused memory of the event. In many cases, young children have believed that their mothers or fathers were present during the abuse, though they never really saw them there. Upon investigation in most of these cases it turned out that the abusers merely told the children that the parents were there and wanted them to be good and do what was asked. Abusers often make children believe that the parents are in on the abuse so the children won't tell their parents about it. Anything that alienates the children from their parents can help to ensure secrecy.

In other cases, clients report wildly impossible scenarios of abuse. These might merely be fantasy, but it's also possible that these were staged by the abusers to make the victims' stories more outlandish.

Thus, abuse occurred, but the victims' memories of many of the circumstances and details may be inaccurate.

Factors Distinguishing True from False Accusations

Dr. Richard Gardner, Clinical Professor of Child Psychiatry at Columbia University, has written *True and False Accusations of Child Sex Abuse.* He suggests thirty factors in distinguishing true from false accusations. I will list some here that are consistent with my experience.

Children who have been genuinely abused are often more hesitant to reveal the abuse, feeling guilt or shame over their participation, not wanting to reveal their "special secret."

They may fear retaliation, and may show fear of the perpetrator, sometimes generalizing to others who are the same sex as the perpetrator.

Abused children can usually give specific details, because they can refer to their internal visual image. In the case of actual abuse, these details do not significantly change over time, except with younger children and/or a prolonged delay before the abuse is told.

The emotions are usually appropriate to the content of the abuse, as it is experienced by the child. They often have sexual knowledge and activities beyond their ages, and feelings of sexual damage or deformity.

Their play is often symbolic of the abuse. They are often depressed and withdrawn, showing pathological compliance. They are more likely to have psychosomatic disorders, such as nausea, vomiting, and stomachaches, as well as regressive behaviors (bed-wetting, uncontrolled bowel movements, thumbsucking, baby talk, and separation anxiety) and sleep disturbances. Many have the symptoms of PTSD as described earlier.[16]

In general, the more of the above behaviors or feelings in evidence, the greater the likelihood of the truth of the accusation. Dr. Gardner concludes that, in his experience, "children between three and four are the best subjects for programming a false sex-abuse accusation. Two-year-olds do not make reliable informants and five-year-olds are less readily brainwashed, although they are certainly not immune."[17]

Dr. Gardner also presents indicators of a falsely accusing parent (usually the mother). She often has a history of attempts to destroy, humiliate, and hurt the accused mate. She will go to any lengths to exclude him from their children, and has often made it difficult in the past for the accused to have any time with the children for numerous reasons. Often these mothers have grown up in homes where their own mothers hated men and severed all relationship with the fathers. They tend to exaggerate and show deceitfulness in other ways. They are often impulsive, angry perhaps to the point of paranoia, and may be excessively moralistic. They often go to great lengths to validate the abuse, even if it might be harmful to the children, finding counselors and attorneys who strongly support them. They resist taking lie detector tests or cooperating with any impartial examiner. They rarely consult the accused first, but immediately contact police or child protective services, and may include extended family or friends in the accusations.[18]

These are indicators only, and certainly do not determine whether an accusation is true or false. But they are helpful to consider.

Let me repeat what I have said throughout this book: *I definitely believe that some people repress traumatic memories.* I have seen lives changed through the recovery of memories, the resolution of the feelings, and the correcting of conclusions that resulted from the repressed trauma. I have seen marriages restored, families reunited, and people healed spiritually and physically. However, this does not occur when the memories are false. In the physical realm, you must identify and treat the right disease—the wrong treatment can make people worse. The same is true here. We must take the time and effort to evaluate the truth of our memories.

If you have recovered memories, they may be true. Or you may have been influenced by friends or family, a support group, a book or TV show, or perhaps your own therapist. These may be good, well-meaning people—but they don't know what happened to *you.* Don't let anyone else find a memory for you. Diligently seek the truth and be open to it. The Bible says, "Test me, O LORD, and try me, examine my heart and my mind; for your love is ever before me and I walk continually in your truth" (Ps. 26:2–3 NIV).

6

Would *I* Ever Create False Memories?

Penny gave the appearance of being an independent and successful career woman, but under that facade was a very frightened young person. She was referred to the McDonald Therapy Center after four years of therapy. According to her therapist, "she had recovered many memories" through group and individual therapy, but was feeling worse. Her finances were drained, so therapy had continued without charge for the previous year.

It became apparent that Penny had developed a very close and caring relationship with her therapist, group, and friends in recovery. None of them had directly influenced her to believe that abuse might be in her background, but as she remembered incidents of abuse from her childhood, she became a part of the group and experienced great empathy and caring.

Penny's parents had both been successful in their careers—and very busy. As a child she felt the pain of emotional neglect from them. Now, as a troubled adult, she had found a group of people who gave her the kind of care she had never received. Her ticket into this group, as she saw it, was her story of abuse.

When she was asked what might happen in her life if the memory were not true, if the abuse had never really happened, she reacted with panic. She believed she would lose her entire support system. In the past, because of her distrust and distant attitude, she had been unable to make any close friendships. Without this supportive group, she believed that would be the case again.

Penny was not trying to deceive anyone. But in the process of discovering whether or not her memories were true, the deck was stacked. She had a major incentive for wanting them to be true—the group that loved and supported her.

There was simply too much riding on the accuracy or inaccuracy of her recovered memories. We decided to shift the focus of her therapy. Her therapist was advised to set a time limit for the free therapy, while they worked on specific ways in which Penny could develop intimacy. Both the therapist and the group agreed to validate Penny's needs for attention and her pain based on the neglect she had experienced, not on any abuse she may have suffered. They directly stated that she did not need to remember additional abuse—or even any abuse—to qualify for their care or inclusion in the group. She no longer needed that ticket. Under these conditions, Penny began to experience freedom to evaluate the truth of her memories.

In the previous chapter we considered external factors that might influence our memories—the people and forces around us that might talk us into remembering childhood abuse. Now we will look at internal factors that can also affect these memories. Why would a basically honest person create a false memory? Is that something that you or I would ever do?

We will look at the following areas as they relate to false memories: gratifying unmet needs, justifying behavior, expressing feelings, pleasing others, and confusing imagination with fact.

Gratifying Unmet Needs

We might create false memories to gratify unmet needs. Every person has unmet needs. None of us had the perfect parent or the perfect childhood. As a result, we are in a continuous search for that person or situation which will satisfy these unmet needs. Sometimes we like to think of ourselves as selfless, giving, and without needs. This, unfortunately, puts our needs into the unconscious realm rather than in our conscious awareness.

So without realizing it we may develop an addictive attachment to a therapist, a recovery group, or a Christian leader or friend. Without understanding the needs involved, we may be drawn to those people or groups that meet those needs. This was clearly Penny's situation. She had deep emotional needs which were met by the support group. She wasn't consciously aware of those needs—she just enjoyed the group and couldn't imagine leaving it.

In some counseling relationships and support groups there is a subtle incentive to fabricate memories. Penny's case is classic. One of the most dangerous scenarios occurs when a therapist sees a client without the usual fee, as long as the client is recovering memories. Such a client has every reason to continue to produce more and more memories, and every reason to avoid questioning their accuracy. And if the therapist becomes more interested as the memories become more horrible, then the client's stories may become more and more bizarre.

> Melissa's unmet need was the inability to have intimacy with a man. This was a major obstacle in her relationship with Greg. From a book she had read, Melissa had concluded that sexual abuse was the reason for her lack of intimacy. But apart from this unsubstantiated hunch, there were already several other obvious causes—the lack of intimacy and trust with her father, his control and criticism as she was attempting to establish her autonomy, and the example of distant, parallel marriages she saw in her parents and extended family.
>
> If Melissa had focused on only the possibility of sexual molest, she would not have resolved this unmet need. If marriage counseling had not occurred Melissa would never have found intimacy with Greg, even if her childhood pain was resolved. She still did not have the tools to develop intimacy, nor did she trust Greg, because of the history of their relationship.

When people create false memories as a way of gratifying unmet needs, there's a double danger. Not only is there the general havoc caused by the false memories themselves, but those memories can serve as a smoke screen, blinding people to the true causes of their unmet needs.

Justifying Behavior

We might create false memories to justify behavior which has caused guilt and shame.

Penny had become a Christian when she was eighteen, six years before she came in for counseling. Prior to that time, she had been promiscuous. As hard as she tried to control her sexual behavior, she could not. As a Christian, she began to feel guilty about her past. That is what initially caused her to seek therapy.

In her group, Penny heard that early sexual abuse can cause either avoidance or acting-out of sexual behaviors. She felt great relief as sexual abuse memories began. Suddenly there was a reason for her teenage promiscuity. Not that it was okay, but there was a reason for it. When she realized this, it drastically reduced her guilt and shame.

However, again, the issues that Penny needed to address were the overwhelming loneliness and need to be touched that had gone unmet in her neglectful childhood. Her sexual behavior was her desperate cry to be wanted, held, and touched by someone. She didn't need to concoct a memory of abuse to find a reason for her promiscuity. The reasons were already there.

Melissa had similar feelings of guilt around her sexual behavior, which had resulted in her pregnancy with Lynn. In counseling, she expressed the desire to discover sexual abuse as a reason for this behavior. Somehow, she figured, her actions would be more understandable, perhaps even excusable, if she could blame them on her own abuse by someone else.

It was difficult for her, as it is for all of us, to take responsibility for the choices she made. Until she faced her own shame—"badness," as she described it—she remained the helpless victim. Fortunately, Melissa was willing to look at all of the issues that made these choices more likely, including her part in it.

The opposite need existed in a thirty-two-year-old woman named Samantha. She had grown up in a very close, caring family, and now was married, with four children of her own. Until two years earlier, she had talked with her mom on the phone two or three times a week and had seen her parents several times a week. Whenever they needed something, they called Samantha, and vice versa. Her parents had been her best friends. Samantha's husband, Jim, resented the time it took from their relationship and frequently told her that she had never cut the apron strings.

As they began marriage counseling, it was recommended that Samantha look to Jim to meet some of these needs. As she started to call less frequently and was occasionally unavailable, both parents expressed disappointment and hurt. Samantha felt extremely guilty. Although she felt the need to "grow up," as she expressed it, her guilt and need to please her parents was so overwhelming that she felt unable to pursue her desire for independence. She knew her parents loved her; that made it all the harder. Soon she began having dreams about a couple physically and verbally abusing a child. The child was Samantha at age seven and the couple were "obviously my parents."

This changed everything. Samantha immediately confronted her parents and refused to see them again, despite their denial of the incident. She finally had the independence from her parents that she needed and her husband demanded. It was without guilt, since they had so betrayed her and now were lying about it.

Five months later, Samantha came to our center, severely depressed. She had no idea what had caused it, except for the realization of the betrayal by her parents. She was making no progress in working through any of the depression. In fact, it kept getting worse, and was now to the point of suicidal and hopeless feelings. Her therapist recommended medication, which she tried, but the improvement was minimal. Nothing seemed to be working. Jim wanted her to do some intensive therapy in order to get through this depression.

The truth of Samantha's memories will be evaluated in later chapters. But she certainly had motivation to create a false memory. It enabled her to achieve independence without guilt.

Expressing Feelings

We might create false memories because we need a framework to express and accept specific feelings.

Dennis was very depressed. In an unhappy marriage and an unsatisfying job, he felt it was his lot in life just to put up with it and say nothing. He stated that he never felt anger, but had been depressed for as long as he could remember. He knew little of his childhood except what older family members described. They relayed that his father was an alcoholic and physically abusive at times. They described his mother as critical and controlling, rarely satisfied with any of the children's accomplishments. Dennis did not remember any of this.

One day Dennis came in with a memory of his father beating him. Dennis was furious for the first time in his life. After doing anger work and rage reduction, the depression lifted. Dennis was amazed at the energy he felt, but in the following weeks he became concerned—it seemed to have opened a Pandora's box. He was starting to feel angry at work and at home as well. This became the focus of therapy, with Dennis releasing anger in a safe place and learning to identify the unmet needs below the anger.

Soon Dennis began the process of directly asking for what he wanted and needed. Marriage counseling began to address the many unmet needs for both partners. Vocational counseling set Dennis on the path of a different career. As he considered and explored the truth of his memory, he discovered it was not possible as he pictured it. It occurred during wartime, and his father was not home at all during a two-year period. Dennis's terror over anger (his own or anyone else's) was the important issue. As that was resolved, Dennis could learn to trust himself and others, including God, whom he had previously viewed as angry and out to get him. It was not long before he began to recall Dad's verbal abuse and Mom's criticism.

Memories may be symbolic rather than factual. Although Dennis was not beaten by his father, he was certainly emotionally beaten on numerous occasions. The picture of a physical beating may better communicate the intensity of fear and anger that Dennis, as a little child, experienced during the verbal abuse. As an adult, he minimized the impact of "just words," but could understand the terror of physical abuse. His adult mind supplied the pictures he needed for his childhood terror.

Each of us has a broad range of feelings of varying intensity. We grow up believing various messages about these feelings and their acceptability. We may feel anxious about particular feelings or behaviors, such as anger or crying, but have no idea why. We may at some point recall an incident where we faced frightening consequences for the expression of specific feelings. How many boys learn not to cry because tears get jeers from their buddies or because their dads tell them that men don't cry? How many children learn not to express anger, because it only brings an angry response from a stronger, more violent parent?

So, as adults, we continue to do all we can to avoid tears or angry words. But as we stuff more and more feelings inside us, we become like a balloon that is ready to pop with the slightest touch. Finally, we might remember or experience an incident that is so intense that we can't avoid these feelings any longer. These memories may have great therapeutic value in that respect, but may not be factually true, or may be only partially true. Because the feelings inside us are so intense, it is not unlikely that we might create a memory that will fit the strength of these feelings.

As we saw with Dennis, the created memories had therapeutic effect. He was suddenly able to express his feelings, and that changed his life. But, as he discovered, the memories were not wholly accurate. Fortunately, he was able to accept those memories for what they were—symbolic expressions of the feelings he had bottled up for so long.

Lynn, Melissa's daughter, rarely let anyone see her feelings, a pattern she learned from her mother and her mother's family. But as part of the support group she joined, Lynn was able to experience many emotions. As she pictured the hurt little girl who had been abused in her memories, she felt free to feel pain, sorrow, and anger—and was encouraged by the group to do so. She subsequently allowed herself to feel empathy for other group members. This was an emotional outlet she needed, and her memories made it happen.

We have seen many cases where memories of abuse exposed the problems of families that were distant, uncaring, unemotional, or violent. But pictures of sexual abuse can also be symbolic of an intimacy with parents that felt *too close.*

In this day of single-parent homes or homes with an emotionally absent parent, a child can have the responsibility, attention, affection, or dependency that is usually reserved for a spouse, without there being sexual overtones or abuse. But this can confuse a child. It feels great to be special, loved, wanted, and enjoyed. Yet often it demands too much and feels too intrusive.

As an adult, such a person might look back and see a nearly ideal childhood, with a loving, supportive parent. But those confusing feelings of overintimacy are still bottled up inside. In some cases, memories of physical sexuality are created as a symbol of the overwhelming emotional intimacy. It's as if the child's brain is trying to express its anger, hurt, and confusion in ways the adult brain will understand. No, it wasn't actually sexual abuse, but sometimes it felt like emotional incest.

Pleasing Others

We might create false memories to please others.

> Dennis was the fourth of six children. He especially admired his two older brothers, who were in therapy to resolve their anger and episodic alcoholism. Dennis did not have either of those problems, but he felt that he could identify with them when they talked of the beatings from their father. As he created his own memory of the beatings, he wanted to identify with and be like his older brothers. It was a mark of masculinity—the girls in the family were not beaten, only the boys. As Dennis understood his need for acceptance and validation of his masculinity from his brothers, he was able to seek it directly and accept the truth that it did not depend upon beatings from his father.

Often clients will seek to please their therapist by offering information the counselor seems to be looking for. I have not seen any therapist who desires a client's victimization, but that may be the message received when a therapist is convinced that the cause of current problems is a repressed memory. We therapists must learn to not communicate that message. Maybe a repressed memory does contribute to the client's problem, but rarely is there only one cause for any particular difficulty.

There are untrained lay people who claim to know the source of individuals' problems, even without taking the time to know the individuals. Some have written books or led groups. Some have claimed to have a gift from God of discernment, freely telling a stranger that God has revealed things about him or her, such as childhood trauma.

Norma had such an encounter. A woman at church claimed to have had a revelation from God that Norma's dad had sexually abused Norma repeatedly during her childhood. Norma was instructed to "pray for this truth." When she replied that she had no awareness of anything like this, she was scolded for being unwilling to know the truth. She wanted the acceptance of this woman, so over the following few months, Norma was able to "come up with the memories," as she puts it. She then sought therapy at our center. There was no evidence of her dad's abuse. Norma was very suggestible and always tried to be a "good girl." So, unfortunately, it now meant discrediting a Christian leader whom she admired, and one who was irresponsible and destructive in her claims to know the truth about someone else's reality. Only God knows that!

The Lord wants us to know those truths that will bring us to wholeness and healing. This refers to all aspects of our thinking and behavior, not just the truth about the past. It refers to truths about God, about ourselves, and about others.

Confusing Imagination with Fact

We might create false memories as we confuse facts with fantasy or imagination.

Suggestibility

In her group Lynn was told to imagine what could have happened to her that would account for her lack of memory about her biological father. Obviously she had blocked out traumatic events, the others said. So Lynn began to picture his sexual abuse, gradually adding more and more details.

In repetitive fantasy, some people come to believe the fantasy is true. They can create conversations, react emotionally, experience bodily sensations, and live in "virtual reality."

Larry Squire, a neuroscientist from the University of California, San Diego, has written a book, *Memory and Brain,* in which he evaluates the relevant research. Chemical activity in the brain during active memory search suggests that different areas of the brain store parts of the same memory, with visual, hearing, language, and spatial memories in different areas. The part that records visual memories also records dreams and visual fantasy. Squire believes that it could be confusing or difficult to distinguish between these forms of visual input. It isn't until we add the other parts of the memory that we have a whole memory. This is probably why dreams or imagined events sometimes seem as real to us as if they had actually occurred.[1]

Discover magazine cites similar evidence from the work of Stephen Kosslyn at Harvard. Using brain imaging techniques—PET scans—he demonstrates that the "brain area involved in perceiving an image and storing it as a memory is also involved in imagining that image. . . . Thus an imagined event might be mistaken for a perceived event."[2]

When people are instructed to imagine or picture specific types of abuse, they become especially vulnerable to memory contamination and the confusion of fact and fantasy. Many of us can imagine unlimited scenarios of events that have not occurred for us. We can even imagine the associated feelings. This does not make them true. Tears come to many people's eyes as they imagine the death of a loved one. Most of our anxiety is created by situations that we imagine or fear might occur. People react in anger at imagined conversations or conclusions about another person's motivations—without any factual information.

Children are often more suggestible than adults. Although the research results differ on this topic, most of it does indicate that there are significant age differences in suggestibility, with preschool children more suggestible than school-aged children or adults. "Some children can be led to make false or inaccurate reports about very crucial, personally experienced, central events."[3]

There was a recent meeting at Harvard to discuss children's susceptibility to suggestion. Dr. Stephen Ceci, a psychologist from Cornell University, is one of the recognized authorities on the suggestibility of children's recollections. He reported one study of four- to six-year-olds who were asked about two events that had occurred (according to their parents) and eight events that had not occurred. They were asked the same question each week for ten weeks, such as, "Did you ever get your finger caught in a mouse trap?" At first they answered "No" to the events that had not occurred. But within a few weeks some of them began answering "Yes," even creating detailed stories about how it happened. Fifty-six percent of the children had made up stories for at least one suggested event, and a quarter of them made up false stories for most of the phony events that were repeatedly suggested. Even after they were told it was not true, and the experiment was explained, one child continued to believe the story he had created. In fact, "the false memories were so elaborate and detailed that psychologists who specialize in interviewing children about abuse were unable to determine which memories were true."[4]

Another study by Dr. Ceci introduced a man named Sam Stone. A preschool class was told before he came to their class that he wasn't nice, he sometimes took things and broke toys. When Sam did come into the classroom for a few minutes, he touched nothing and said nothing but hello and good-bye. For the next ten weeks the children were placed in simulated therapy sessions lasting just two minutes each. They were intentionally asked suggestive questions, such as, "Do you remember when Sam Stone spilled chocolate on that white teddy bear? Did he do it on purpose or was it accidental?" At the end of ten weeks, 72 percent of the three- and four-year-olds reported Sam's misdeeds. When pressed, 44 percent said they had seen him do it. About one-fifth of the children even added additional events that had not been suggested, filled with details and appropriate emotions.[5]

Commenting on Dr. Ceci's findings, Dr. Marsel Mesulam, head of the neurology department at Beth Israel Hospital at Harvard Medical School, said, "Young children may be led into concocting memories so easily because their frontal lobes are immature. Until age 7 or 8, children respond to neurological tests like adults with frontal lobe damage."[6]

Most of the studies indicate that children do not just make up abusive events. However, some children can be led by an interviewer's suggestions, especially when "they are younger, when they are interrogated after a long delay, when they feel intimidated by the interviewer, when the interviewer's suggestions are strongly stated and frequently repeated, and when more than one interviewer makes the same strong suggestion." But if children can tell their experiences shortly after they occur, in a supportive environment, with a warm, skillful, nonleading interviewer, their "accounts of the extent, duration, and sequence of the experience core are highly reliable."[7] (These studies do not, however, examine the memories of repeated events of situations involving familiar people.)

Certainly the research by Dr. Ceci and others is an important warning about leading questions and suggestibility. However, the research by Gail Goodman presents a somewhat different picture. Dr. Goodman is a professor of psychology at the University of California, Davis. Her research is internationally known and has been cited in several United States Supreme Court decisions.

Dr. Goodman points out that "the vast majority of scientific studies of children's testimony do not concern genital touch but rather focus on children who are bystanders to brief events of little importance to their lives. Is a child's memory, suggestibility, and willingness to disclose the same for personally significant events involving intimate body parts as for brief, neutral events watched from afar?"[8]

Children who had experienced genital examinations were studied by Dr. Goodman. She found that open-ended questions, like "What happened when you went to the doctor?" resulted in very few reports from the children who had been examined. The use of an anatomically correct doll and the leading question, "Did the doctor touch you there (pointing to the genital area)," resulted in the majority of the children correctly reporting their examinations, but also 8 percent who had not been examined said they had been touched there.[9]

Studies by Dr. Goodman of three- to six-year-olds in stress—receiving medical inoculations—revealed that the younger children were less accurate in answering questions and correctly identifying the culprit who caused the pain than were the older children. Younger children made more false identifications. All age groups were even more inaccurate in peripheral details, such as details about the room where the shots occurred. With a delay of seven to nine days the accuracy of identifications for the younger group decreased. Concerning suggestibility, five- and six-year-olds were resistant to 75 percent of the leading questions.[10]

Dr. Goodman has summarized some of this research indicating factors that affect child witnesses. Increased errors occur when the questions are not age-appropriate, or when the interviewer is accusing or intimidating. The presence of the perpetrator can substantially reduce a child's willingness to tell what happened. Those who expressed strong fears of the defendant had a more difficult time answering the prosecutor's questions, whereas children who had their parents or a loved one present were better able to respond.[11]

Misunderstanding Child Development

In evaluating the truth of memories it is essential to understand the intellectual, verbal, imaginative, and emotional development that is normal for a child at the age when the alleged trauma is believed to have occurred.

Very early childhood memories are usually suspect, especially in the accuracy of peripheral details. Most research demonstrates that our earliest verbal memories begin at age three or four, although one study did report memories at age two. Memories prior to this age are generally believed to be the result of imagination, often of hearing the story told. For twenty-five years I have asked people their earliest memory. It is generally of an incident around age three or four, very rarely is it earlier.

Child psychiatrist Lenore Terr agrees that preverbal children lack the verbal memory of a trauma, but she states "even infants have behavioral memories of traumatic experiences that are reenacted in play behavior and fears." She reports on twenty preschool children with medical charts or pictures (such as pornography) that clearly document specific traumas that these children have endured. Many have partial or no verbal recall of the trauma, but they did show behavioral memory for the trauma, acting out the central elements. In her experience, this is an almost universal event.

She gives examples from her clinical experience, including that of Sarah, who was sexually abused in day care when she was fifteen to eighteen months old. Dr. Terr saw her at age five, when pornographic pictures involving Sarah surfaced, and her father was contacted by the police. Sarah was able to confirm some of the details of the abuse by physical complaints and emotions. No one had ever told her about it. This did not mean she could give a narrative description of the trauma.

If the trauma occurred earlier than twenty-eight to thirty-six months, the children could not remember most of the trauma in words. Some had a vague sense about it. No memories from before twenty-eight months were complete. Dr. Terr states, "The cutoff age for verbal retention of what happened, twenty-eight to thirty-six months at the time of the trauma, fits in well with some new, convincing research on the physiology of young children's brains. A tremendous spurt in left brain development (verbal skills reside in the left brains of right-handed people) occurs at around age three. Complete verbal memories can be established once the verbal centers are well-developed."

Eighteen of the twenty children in the study by Dr. Terr acted out the trauma in their behavior, including a child who was sexually abused between birth and six months. She concludes that, "These behaviors turned out to be the truest, most accurate indicators of what traces of memory still existed in the mind of a child exposed very early in life to a traumatic event or a series of events."[12]

The form a memory takes depends on your age at the time of the event, not at the time the memory is recovered, explains Dr. Terr. If you were too young to have highly developed cognitive and verbal skills when the original event took place, the memory may come back only as a vague emotion, image, or bodily sensation instead of a detailed recollection that can be described in words. But "behavioral memory (fears, play, reenactment, dreams) is almost universal."[13]

Today, many psychologists think that the lack of early memories is simply the result of immature brain development. Studies have shown that, although babies can recognize people and places they've seen before, their memories aren't permanent—when something is out of sight, they have no memory that it exists. For example, it's not until about nine months that a baby will look under a blanket to find a toy she's seen someone hide.[14]

It is important as we seek to determine the truth of our memories to understand the evidence for a "dual memory system."[15] The first is present at birth, continuing throughout life, including images, behaviors, and emotions. As Dr. Terr has demonstrated, children do have primitive behavioral and feeling memories, even when they cannot put them into a story yet. But if we do have a memory from the first year or two of life that is clearly told in story form with details, it is unlikely to be accurate in all its details, and possibly not true at all. We may have created a story that fits with the early images, fragments, behavioral and feeling memories. In this case, the story is in the ball park, but still questionable in its details. Or we may have created a story that is totally imaginary.

The second memory system emerges during preschool years, and allows narrative memories or the ability to describe a past event verbally. This starts around age three, but is rather limited to answering objective questions, rather than free recall, which gradually increases over the next couple of years. By three, memories of specific events that are unique or unusual appear with some frequency. This is also the age of most adults' earliest memories. Research does indicate that even three-year-olds are pretty accurate in answering specific questions, but their reports are loose and disorganized, with random associations, unless the adult provides the organization. When their recall was behavioral (reenacting the event), it was very accurate and organized, even for toddlers.

In addition to the belief that language development is essential for the recall of memories, other research presents biological reasons, specifically that the part of the brain that is essential for adult episodic memory, the hippocampus, is not fully developed at birth, maturing perhaps around age two or three.

Dr. Terr also found differences in memory for those who had experienced a one-time event and for those having repetitive traumas. Only one child in the latter group recalled all of the events, and the accuracy was much less, whereas all of the children three or older remembered the single traumatic event, and could verbalize it quite accurately. Why the difference?

> It appears that sudden, fast events completely overcome any defenses that a small child can muster. Long-standing events, on the other hand, stimulate defensive operations—denial, splitting, self-anesthesia, and dissociation. These defenses interfere with memory formation, storage, and retrieval. When the defenses are completely overrun by one sudden, unanticipated terror, brilliant, overly clear verbal memories are the result. On the other hand, when the defenses are set up in advance in order to deal with terrors the child knows to be coming, blurry, partial, or absent, verbal memories are retained. The child may even develop blanket amnesia for certain years in the past.[16]

In clinical practice over the past twenty-five years we've seen many children who have been abused. I cannot recall any of them who did not show behaviors similar to the reported abuse. Our experience in play therapy, projective techniques, sand tray, and so forth, all correspond to Dr. Terr's observations. Rarely have the children been questioned directly about specific kinds of abuse. Instead, they demonstrate, without questions, what has occurred. Then, open-ended questions about their play or drawings elicit other known details.

Adults who were abused as children also demonstrate corresponding behaviors, if they feel it is acceptable to act in that manner. Those who have validated their repressed memories have all expressed the desire to do things such as hiding in the corner and covering their heads to avoid beatings, or keeping their mouths tightly closed to avoid oral rape.

This is important to understand as we evaluate the truth of our own memories. The most powerful validation of early memories will probably be our unusual behavior following the trauma, behavior that sometimes continues into our adulthood. If you have a clear verbal memory from the first couple years of your life, it is probably something you imagined or a story you've been told, or perhaps a re-creation of something that may have happened with the addition of details from your fantasies. There may be brief snapshots in your mind from that period, but your brain has certainly added words and interpretations at a later stage.

Most experts agree that the absence of early verbal memories, especially prior to age three, isn't necessarily evidence of hidden trauma.

Preschool children are generally trusting of whatever they hear. Especially when a trusted authority figure, such as a parent or teacher, tells a story or describes another individual, young children usually accept the truth uncritically, in a very concrete interpretation of what they hear. When they hear that someone is "tied up" at the moment, they picture the ropes and the method of constraint, not that the person is too busy. If an angry adult yells, "I'm going to kill you," a young child anticipates murder. During the divorce process and custody battles, one parent can relate stories about the other which are totally believed by most preschool children.

Children may also trust an adult's line of questioning. That is, they figure out what information the adult wants and they provide it.[17] They usually want to comply with authority figures, and they perceive adults as credible and accurate sources of information. So when they are asked the same question more than once, children may assume that their previous answer was unsatisfactory, and change the answer to whatever they think the adult wants to hear. It appears that some children fill in memory gaps in order to please the interviewer. A neutral, nonsuggestive interviewer elicits the most accurate information on the first interview.

Discrimination between imagination and fact can be difficult for preschoolers. Many parents of young children are appalled at their child's lying, until they discover that the child has difficulty distinguishing between fact and fantasy. Something in a book or on television is as true as the objects they can touch. Their thoughts and fears are as believable as the event that actually occurred. Many four-year-olds, for example, assume that they have their eyes open when they dream, since they cannot see with their eyes closed. Thus it is not unusual for them to believe that a dream is a factual event. Research shows that younger children have a harder time than older children distinguishing between things they've actually witnessed and things they have imagined. Drs. Ceci and Bruck summarized the research prior to 1993.

> These data reflect the fragile boundaries of children's fantasy-reality distinctions. When situations become intense, children appear to easily give up these distinctions . . . 4-year olds had more fragile boundaries than did the 6-year olds. . . . Apparently, the cues involved in differentiating between certain types of actual and imagined events may not be well developed before late childhood.[18]

If someone recovers a memory of something that supposedly occurred at age three, it may be an accurate recovery of something that was inaccurately perceived to begin with. That is, it may have been a dream or story that the child assumed to be true, but wasn't. It is important to evaluate the source of this memory, if possible. But we may never know the source. All we know is that something (probably) happened that elicited the thoughts or fears or imagination of the event.

If children see something frightening on television, they may place themselves in the story and be traumatized by it, especially if it is a story of other young children or of animals. Some parents, thinking their children are asleep, will watch pornographic movies. Or a baby-sitter might be watching pornography or might secretly have a boyfriend over and be sexually involved, not knowing the child is watching. All of these can produce memories of abuse that did not directly occur to the child.

A clinical case from 1955 describes a twenty-seven-year-old man who suffered from "twisting sensations, wry neck, feelings of choking and of his upper torso being separated from the lower parts of his body." During therapy, he recovered memories of his mother's attempted suicide by hanging when he was three years old. His father verified that this had occurred, and that his son had witnessed it. Symptom relief occurred for the son, following the recovery of the memory and his father's confirmation.[19] Although this man was never hung by his neck as a child, the occurrence of seeing this traumatic event was remembered in his body, as if he were the victim of the hanging.

The reasoning of young children differs from that of adults or older children. They think in a concrete manner, reasoning from specific to specific, and sometimes connecting events with no objective association. They combine categories that do not belong together, and often this gives them a distorted picture of reality. For example, if a child takes a nap every afternoon and one afternoon he does not take a nap, he may conclude that it is not afternoon. Or if he falls and cuts his knee while playing with a friend, he may believe that his friend cut his knee. If another child was hurt by his daddy, this child may believe that all fathers hurt little kids in the same manner. Adults who describe multiple abusers might be combining actual events and fears, especially the incidents of abuse that occurred in the preschool years. Melissa, for instance, remembers thinking that her family lived in Grandma's house, because Grandma was her primary caretaker in the early years. Even though Grandma did not live with them, she was there often and had the primary authority over Melissa.

The memories of even very young children can be accurate, especially those of a personally meaningful event in which they are involved and which they understand. Free recall brings the most accurate stories. Highly misleading questions result in the most inaccuracies, especially under repeated questioning by any authority figure. Children can be most easily influenced by suggestions about peripheral details, and situations they did not clearly see or understand. Suggestibility seems to decrease with age, but even adults can be misled under certain conditions. There are even occasions when younger children are *more* accurate—in an area where they have superior knowledge (e.g., cartoons) or when something is very bizarre to them or very different from their usual experience.

Harvard-educated psychiatrist Dr. Jean Goodwin teaches at the University of Texas Medical Branch in Galveston, and is the author of *Sexual Abuse: Incest Victims and Their Families.* She states, "Perhaps five percent of all articulated accusations involving children involved intentional lies or psychotic misperceptions. . . . Data show that most child abuse is never reported to anyone. . . . My experience is that individuals who came from traumatic environments are often quite confused about what happened to them. I don't call that false accusation; I call it massive confusion."[20]

Children may knowingly lie under certain conditions. Summaries of the research indicate some of those conditions:

1. To avoid punishment
2. To sustain a game
3. To keep a promise (even more readily if it protects a loved one)
4. For personal gain (like gum balls)
5. To avoid embarrassment[21]

Many parents have experienced the deception of children, probably under each of the conditions just mentioned. We are more likely to lie in childhood, but many adults also admit they readily lie if it seems warranted to them.

There are many other developmental issues that are relevant but beyond the scope of this book. The content of the reported trauma must be understood in the context of the level of development normal for a child at the age the trauma occurred. Healing will require attention to the task which needs to be completed at that age, in order to proceed with normal development. Trauma usually interrupts the development process in some way.

Often people assume that recovered memories are true because they can't imagine why they (or someone else) would make something like that up. We have shown several reasons for the fabrication of false memories.

Not all claims of recovered memories are false, but we cannot *assume* that they're true, as many seem to do. We need to investigate the facts before we take any rash action. We must always give ourselves time to evaluate any memories, prayerfully asking the Lord for truth. Do not confront or cut off relationships until you have considered all the material in this book.

How Can I Know the Truth of My Memories?

Are you confused right now?

If you have been recovering memories of your own, of course you are eager to find out what they mean. Are they filling in some missing piece of your past? Can these memories be trusted?

Be patient. Take the time to sort through these memories. Understand that this is a process that will take some time. There are all sorts of evaluations that a good therapist can help you with, but the most important step to start with is your willingness to be open and to consider all possibilities.

Beware of those writers, speakers, and counselors who say, "All recovered memories are accurate." But also beware of those who say, "There's no such thing as a recovered memory." The overwhelming scientific and clinical testimony indicates that the truth is somewhere in between. Some memories are repressed and later recovered accurately. Sometimes, however, there are things that seem to be memories from long ago, but they are actually fabricated, suggested, or distorted, and thus partially or totally inaccurate.

But we're dealing with *your* memories now, not *all* memories. You want to know if your memories are true—or perhaps you know someone who is working through this. However, before we do anything else, we need to calibrate the scale, to wipe out all preconceptions and biases.

Be Open to All Options Regarding the Truth of a Memory

If we are to deal properly with the issues raised by our recovered memories, we must look honestly at the incidents involved, our original reactions to them, and their continued impact on our lives.

The existence of a memory does not obligate us in any way to believe it is true. Nor does the fact that a memory was repressed mean it is *un*true. Every memory is unique. We will find no general rule that applies to validating every memory. But the first step must be our openness to each memory being fully accurate, completely false, or a combination of true and false. We will never be emotionally healthy if we hang onto a false memory or refuse to believe the truth of an accurate memory.

If you have been recovering memories, you may have already made some preliminary decisions about their truth or falsehood. It's hard to change your view. None of us likes to admit that we're wrong about something this important. Especially if you've already talked with others about these memories, it's very difficult to go back to square one to decide fairly about their accuracy.

Sometimes we must first explore the reasons we are unwilling to be open to all options. As we saw in the last chapter, Penny was terrified of losing all her support and intimacy, and never having close friends again if she discovered the memories were not true. With her history of neglect and promiscuity, as well as all of the attention and love she received from her therapist and the group, she had strong needs to prove the truth of her memories. The threat was reduced by the recovery group's acceptance and inclusion of her whether or not she had been sexually abused. She also benefited by her growing confidence that she was capable of developing other friendships as well. At that point, Penny was willing to begin considering all options concerning the truth of her memories.

Why Might I Not Want to Believe a True Memory?

Some people express the fear of believing a repressed or negative memory because *they assume it will require confrontation with the supposed abuser or the end of the relationship with that person.* Neither is necessary, as we will discuss later.

If a person has done something very wrong or bad, that does not mean he has never done anything right or good. Whatever negative interaction has occurred with, say, a father or grandfather does not eliminate the positive interactions with that same person. We are usually reluctant to believe a memory about someone we have idealized. Yet, by allowing them to be human, and still loving them even if they are imperfect, we can come to accept ourselves and other imperfect relationships. Until we see the reality of those we have idealized, we will not fully understand the badness that everyone has, and the need of every person for forgiveness from God and others.

Some people think that only emotionally disturbed people would repress memories. This assumption makes people shy about admitting their own repressed memories. In fact, the opposite is true. Repression is a gift from God to enable a child, or adult, to cope with something that is overwhelming. It's the only method the child can imagine to continue receiving good things, such as love, attention, touching, gifts, feeling special, and so forth. Repression is actually a healthy alternative to psychosis, or withdrawal into a world of unreality. It enables a child to stay in reality, except for the specific event repressed. Even many adults need temporary amnesia or repression when the trauma is so overwhelming that they can cope with only a portion of it at a time.

With most repressed memories of abuse, there has been a time when *the abuser threatened the victim with greater danger if the event were ever revealed.* The threats might include harm to the child or the family or its possessions. In cases when a parent or stepparent is the perpetrator, the child is threatened by abandonment, destruction of the family or home, or "no one will believe you if you tell." Repression—essentially deciding the event didn't happen—is a way to stay safe and functional, a sign of good internal strength. But fears of those old threats die hard. Many people, even as adults, still fear revealing such secrets. Initially, they may not even know the reason for the fear, but it's deeply ingrained from their days of victimization. Even when the memory comes seeping out, they may instinctively deny it.

We may want to avoid the pain, anger, and other feelings that will occur if a memory is proven true. We assume that if we say it didn't happen, we can feel as if it didn't happen. It doesn't work that way. Once the memory has emerged, it's too late to simply dismiss it and hope the feelings will go away.

We may not want to accuse an innocent person. This is a good desire, which should motivate us to seek the truth sincerely and prayerfully.

Every person should be innocent until proven guilty. Every caution must be used to avoid believing a lie. That is why no accusation or confrontation should occur before moving through all of the steps in this book—if ever.

Sometimes we do not want to believe repressed memories because we do not want to believe that traumatic things like this happen to anyone. We all hate to hear of abuse to anyone, but especially to children. It goes against all of our protective instincts. It's difficult to comprehend that it might occur from trusted caretakers. We do not want these things to be true. We do not want to believe that some people might even knowingly choose evil, and repeatedly abuse children in horrible ways. It makes us feel very unsafe when we think of living in a world where helpless children might be tortured. We would all like to believe that people are good, that they love and protect children.

The story of the murder of O. J. Simpson's ex-wife and the possibility of his involvement have been difficult for many. He's been a hero, a good person. We want him to stay like that. We don't want to hear that he physically abused his wife on previous occasions. It shakes our trust in our own perceptions and judgment of people.

Why Would I Want to Believe a False Memory?

Some people fear they have gone too far down the road with a false memory to change it now. Even if we have acted as if the memory were true, and cut off relationships, it is not too late to reverse our thinking about any particular memory. I have not seen any family that was unwilling to welcome back their child. The biblical story of the prodigal son is an excellent example of the joy and celebration over the return of a son who rejected his entire family and their lifestyle and values. Few parents would act differently.

It's embarrassing to concede to someone that we were wrong about them. Pride can keep us from admitting that a memory is false. The more people we have told about it, the more difficult it becomes to consider that it could be false.

Lynn told her support group and her father's family, including grandparents and some of his extended family, about the alleged abuse. She also wrote a paper about her abuse for a school project.

She had not talked with her parents because she was angry at them, and she saw them as too involved in their own problems. After all this, she admitted she would be very embarrassed if none of it were true.

It's very difficult to admit an error like this without placing the blame on someone else, such as one's therapist or friends or a group. They may share the blame, but we must take responsibility for a major part of such a false judgment. It takes great courage to say, "*I* was wrong."

We might be afraid of our reactions toward others who have encouraged a false memory.

Lynn was encouraged to explore all of these feelings. Her reaction, after considering the embarrassment, was anger at the hypnotist. Could he have let her believe something that might not be true? As she expressed these feelings, she had to admit to herself that she went into hypnosis already convinced it was true—she was just looking for the details. Then she became angry at the group, specifically those members who told her that she had all the symptoms of sexual abuse. It had to be their fault! Soon she began to question why she had allowed them to influence her, if they had.

Many people have expressed the fear that they are crazy if they have made up a memory that turns out to be false, thus they are entrenched into proving its truth. All of us have had dreams that were so real that we were unsure if they actually occurred or not. We all have believed misperceptions, only to discover that we did not have all the information or that we had inaccurate information. Everyone has blamed the wrong person for something that happened. All of us have had fears and fantasies that feel totally real, though we know they are not true. All of this is human nature; it does not mean we're crazy.

As discussed previously, there is believed to be a neurological basis for false memories. A recent conference on this topic was held at Harvard Medical School.

> Part of the fragility of memory is due to the way the mind encodes a memory, distributing aspects of the experience over far-flung parts of the brain, various researchers said at the meeting. The brain stores the memory of

> each sense in different parts of the neocortex—sound in the auditory cortex, sight in the visual cortex, and so on. . . . Another part of the brain, the limbic system, has the job of binding these dispersed parts of the memory together as a single experience.
>
> One of the more frail parts of a memory is its source—the time, place, or way the memory originated. . . . Source amnesia is the inability to recall the origin of the memory of a given event. Once the source of a memory is forgotten, scientists say, people can confuse an event that was only imagined or suggested with a true one. The result is a memory that, though false, carries the feeling of authenticity.[1]

Source amnesia is common for all of us. It occurs when we recognize a face but have no idea where we saw the person before. We retain the memory for the face, but not the memory for the time and place the face was first seen. We recall a particular story, but we're unsure if we read it or if someone told it to us.

> Lynn did feel that she had to be crazy if she could possibly make up an entire story of abuse. But, she decided, it would be even crazier to continue believing something that wasn't true. Her group had reassured her at the time of the initial memory that people don't make up stories like this. Two group members who had doubts had checked out their memories and found them to be true. The other group members believed their memories based on the experience of the two who had checked out the details, assuming that all memories must be accurate.

We may be afraid to doubt a memory for fear that we could no longer trust our perceptions in any area. But believing untruths about another person or event is what eventually robs us of confidence in our instincts and in the accuracy of our perceptions. It opens the door to unreality. You may have known people who exaggerate or lie so frequently that they no longer seem to know when they are doing it. They've lost their conscience or critical judgment. They also lose intimate relationships because people come to mistrust their word. It is important for all of us to know that we cannot trust our perception 100 percent of the time. It is healthy and wise to question openly what we think we perceive and remember.

But if I made this story up," Lynn wondered, "how can I ever know what's true?" She was encouraged to always practice a little doubt in life, being open to the possibility of her inaccurate perceptions and conclusions. She felt relieved to grasp this concept, acknowledging that she did not want to be a "rigid know-it-all," as she put it.

We are sometimes afraid of alienating people by changing our beliefs about memories. This might include a therapist or recovery group or anyone who has given a tremendous amount of support and caring. If the memory is false, it feels as if we have used these people, or we fear they may feel used. We might anticipate that we will no longer fit into this group of people with whom we have identified, thus losing important relationships. Most people who have risked openly discussing this have found they did not lose their close friends, unless they had nothing in common except the similar abuse.

Lynn was very concerned about the loss of her support group. She described the group as a place where she was herself for the first time. Even as she said that, she laughed, commenting that maybe she feared that she could be herself only as long as she agreed with them. We discussed possible reactions. The reactions did occur. One of the young women who had checked out her memories and had them confirmed felt insulted that her experience wasn't sufficient evidence for Lynn. One question brought immediate insight for this woman. The question was, "Would someone else's experience have been enough for you?" She acknowledged that it would not have been.

Believing false perceptions robs us of relationships because we begin to develop a paranoia or suspicion. Instead of checking out our thoughts or feelings, we allow ourselves to build a negative fantasy world. We gradually move into more and more distrust, withdrawal, and inability to interact with certain types of people or situations.

This definitely occurred for Lynn. She became more distrustful of all men, discontinuing any dating or even friendships with the young men at school.

Some people fear that, if their memories are false, others will feel that their own memories are invalid also. This is frequently true if we share a memory of abuse from the same person. For example, two sisters may remember abuse from their dad. It is very possible for one of their memories to be true and one to be false. It probably will be difficult for the sister whose memory is true. She is likely to be disappointed and feel abandoned when the support is no longer there. Giving emotional support and love, even though the memories are different, can bridge this difficult time.

During the therapy process, we are trying to make sense out of our feelings and behavior, and anything that gives some answers is appealing. Since we are exploring dreams, feelings, vague memories, and so forth, we are working with input that can have several different interpretations. If we do attempt to validate memories, we can minimize the possibility of belief in a false conclusion.

When Lynn began to question her memories, it was difficult for those group members who had not made any attempt to validate their own memories. Several felt very fearful. One member was angry that Lynn was questioning and not believing. We had anticipated all of these reactions. Lynn handled them well, assuring the members that this was only about her—she was not questioning them. She asked if they would accept her even if she might come to the conclusion that her remembered abuse had not actually happened. Lynn stated her commitment to remain caring and supportive of them, whatever their point of view. The group honestly struggled with these issues for several weeks. One member expressed anger that this was taking them off track from their recovery. Lynn also expected this reaction, and gave her opinion that the denial, as they described it, was a part of her that needed to be addressed as well. Eventually, two of the other group members also came to our clinic to evaluate the truth of their memories, and three others searched out validation on their own.

People may believe a false memory because they can't make any other sense of why the memory came to them. This is probably the most common reason. But when people understand the symbolic nature of some memories, it helps them to work through the feelings and the conflicts without being glued to the necessity that the memory be factual. When they understand displacement, they realize that the remembered event might have occurred, but not with the person they remember. Generalization causes us to fear that other people will do what one person has done to us. Our repressed memories can be symbolic of this fear, which can be just as real to a young child as something that actually happened.

Lynn knew that she was angry at her father for abandoning them, and for not supporting them financially. She felt that he had robbed her of a carefree, happy childhood. Instead, Mom worked long hours to support them, and she felt very alone. Whatever else had happened, her memory helped her to understand some of her anger.

We may be very suggestible. The imagination is a wonderful thing. It provides deep empathy for others, because we are able to imagine ourselves in the same situation. It can also create false memories that are as powerful as the real event. Very creative, imaginative people should question and pursue validation of significant memories. We should recall if there was a similar story on TV, in a book, or in a group we attended.

If we are highly suggestible, we are susceptible to believing false memories. Once a memory has occurred, we may not have any awareness of its truth or falseness. Outside validation becomes essential.

Lynn appeared to be strong and independent, needing very little from anyone. Exactly the opposite was true. She learned at a very young age to take care of her mommy when she came home from work exhausted. She didn't want Mommy to be unhappy with her. So these needs were huge for Lynn. As a result, if someone was nice to her and cared about her needs, she would do anything for that person. This had occurred with a couple of teachers and with the mother of a friend. Whatever they said, she accepted.

Even as she struggled to question the truth of her memories, Lynn was discovering these things about herself. She recognized her suggestibility, her fears of rejection, her caretaking of others—but not of herself—and her tendency to blame.

Can My Memory Be Partly True and Partly False?

Recovered memories are often partly false or are exaggerated truth. If we have not allowed ourselves to change our initial stories, we may be trapped in partially false memories. Many children change some aspect of their stories some time after the emotion subsides. Even as adults we often initially exaggerate a highly emotional event.

Screen memories may occur, where similar events are combined and perceived as one. This means there is an element of truth, but many of the details do not fit together. Some of the details belong to another story.

Some memories are partial imagination. If an event begins in a similar manner to a previous trauma, some children fill in the blanks, completing the second event in the same way that the first event turned out. Often children were so frightened by the first event that they are unable to perceive that the second event is different. This makes it possible to imagine the wrong perpetrator. It is like looking through abuse-colored glasses. We may see abuse when it is not there. As soon as the memory trigger for the abuse occurs, we lose the reality of the present event.

People who have high susceptibility or who are very imaginative are more likely to have partially false memories. People who spend a lot of time daydreaming become quite adept at believing fantasies.

If we frequently use dissociation or repression, our later memories may be contaminated with our thoughts or fears or fantasies of childhood.[2] People who have learned these defenses have initially done so out of a need for survival. After a while, though, they may become habitual. With any hint of danger, the dissociation and repression recur. This prevents accurate attention to the details of what is currently happening.

Accept That You Might Never Know If a Memory Is True or False

You could proceed through all of the suggested steps, and still be uncertain about the truth of your memory. In that case, it is safer to assume it might be false if you are accusing another person. If the person is no longer in your life because of death, divorce, or a move, then the present consequences are not as significant. People must be considered innocent until proven guilty. False accusations destroy people's lives.

Whether you are the person with the memory, the therapist, the accused party, or an involved observer such as another family member, you need to understand all of the possible options regarding this memory. In summary, here are the possibilities:

The abuse did not occur and the memory is false	The abuse did occur and the memory is true	The abuse is partly true and partly false
1. The accuser is lying deliberately	1. The accused is lying deliberately	1. The abuse is symbolic of the relationship with the accused
2. The accuser believes the accusation (due to factors considered in chs. 5–6)	2. The accused falsely believes he is innocent (due to factors to be considered in ch. 14)	2. The abuse occurred, but with a different perpetrator
		3. Several memories are combined, confusing the facts
		4. Child development issues have distorted some of the facts

Continue to Pray for the Truth

God's desire for us is that we know and live by the truth: the truth about him, the truth about ourselves and others, and the truths about living life. Seeking truth and wisdom is often mentioned in the Bible. Jesus told his disciples, "When the Holy Spirit comes, He will guide you into all truth" (John 16:13 LB); and "I am the way and the truth and the life" (John 14:6 NIV).

"Test me, O LORD," the psalmist prayed, "and try me, examine my heart and my mind; for your love is ever before me and I walk continually in your truth" (Ps. 26:2–3 NIV).

David, once called "a man after God's own heart," stated, "I have chosen the way of truth; I have set my heart on your laws" (Ps. 119:30 NIV); and in Psalm 51:6, "Surely you desire truth in the inner parts; you teach me wisdom in the inmost place."

Paul advises us in Ephesians 6:14 (NIV) to "Stand firm, with the belt of truth buckled around your waist." And the Book of Proverbs urges, "Buy the truth and do not sell it; get wisdom, discipline, and understanding" (Prov. 23:23 NIV).

God also promises to reveal to us the truth we need. In Daniel, it says that God "reveals profound mysteries beyond man's understanding. He knows all hidden things, for He is light and darkness is no obstacle to Him" (Dan. 2:22 LB). And Jesus promises in John 8:32 (NIV), "You will know the truth and the truth will set you free."

Is there any better expression of what we want our memory evaluation to achieve? We want to know the truth and, knowing it, be set free to find healing.

8

Am I Ready for My Memories?

Melissa's first marriage ended shortly after the birth of her daughter Lynn. Initially critical and controlling, her husband became distant and unavailable as the marriage went on. He was unwilling to work on the marriage. Melissa was relieved when he left.

After considerable caution and five years of occasional casual dating, Melissa met a "wonderful man," Greg, who loved both her and her daughter. They married four months later. But within a couple of months, Greg opened his own business, a very time-consuming project. As Melissa tried to be supportive of Greg and his new venture, she could feel her loneliness, depression, and helplessness. Many of the feelings subsided with the birth of three children in the next four years. "I was so busy," Melissa said later, "I didn't have time to feel."

The feelings emerged again when their youngest child, Jenny, began school. It was at this time that Melissa first sought counseling to resolve her conflict between parenting and career possibilities. She felt satisfied at the resolution, deciding how she could do both. Her feelings of depression and loneliness lifted as she became busy and successful again. She continued to seek support and acknowledgment outside her marriage, while she and Greg carried on peaceful but parallel lives—this was just like her parents' marriage.

But Melissa saw a major problem in this second marriage: there was little intimacy or sexuality. Throughout her life, she had been very successful academically and professionally. She had close women friends and many acquaintances. She enjoyed her home and children and was described as an excellent mother. And, during the previous few years, Melissa had developed a strong and positive sense of her own identity, a task she hadn't completed in adolescence.

But after fifteen years of marriage, Melissa was devastated by Greg's request for a divorce. He was "in love with someone else" and planned to marry her. The relationship had been going on for several years.

Melissa went into a major depression, with intermittent anxiety attacks. Initially, Greg agreed to counseling in order to "help Melissa," and to end the marriage peaceably. Because of his Christian commitment, the children, pressure from his extended family, and Melissa's inability to cope, Greg reluctantly agreed to end the affair a few months later. He would stay and work on the marriage, to see if their problems were resolvable, even though he did not have much hope.

Meanwhile, individual therapy helped Melissa to begin looking at her anger. She faced up to her feelings of neglect from her distant dad and the fear of abandonment that had occurred with her mother and grandmother. In the depth of her pain, she sought to find God, and became a Christian. She was deeply moved by the awareness of God's love and acceptance and healing.

This encouraged Greg to end his secret identity, not just his affair, but his whole style of privacy. They both expressed their desire to attempt to develop intimacy with each other, limit their busyness, and commit to more open communication. With the help of marriage counseling, individual counseling, and a lot of hard work, they were able to return to their early love and commitment. They terminated therapy on a happy and hopeful note.

But seven months later, they returned to therapy. Although their relationship was growing and going well, Melissa was unable to enjoy a sexual relationship. She was no longer depressed, but she did have intermittent anxiety attacks, frequent, repetitive nightmares, and a generalized fear of men. Counseling continued, but little progress was made. Melissa and the counselor wondered about repressed trauma, and she was sent to McDonald Therapy Center for an evaluation.

Even though we suspected that there might be some incident in Melissa's early years that she was repressing, we did not leap into the discovery process. There were many issues to consider first. It would be different if Melissa's trauma were recent. If she had recently been attacked, for instance, she would need immediate treatment. But when someone has lived with a trauma for years, and it is not in their conscious awareness, it is advisable to set up the best circumstances possible for the easiest and quickest recovery—or else a person may feel re-abused by the therapy process.

Some people say it's best to leave repressed memories alone. They say that repression is God's way of protecting you from the hurt that is too painful for you to endure. On the other side of the question, some say you must face the truth or you will never be whole, never be what God created you to be. God intended repression, they say, as a temporary measure; if you hide from the truth, you're showing a lack of faith in God's ability to heal and restore.

I take the middle ground. Some memories are best left buried. But when such memories affect our daily life, keeping us from living fully and freely, it's important to face them, and go through the recovery process, in order to leave them behind. But before beginning that process, several preliminary steps are in order.

Deal with Any Known Childhood or Adult Traumas, Conflicts, or Difficulties

Melissa had been in psychotherapy twice previously. She had resolved her conflicts over career and parenting. There were no major problems at work. Family counseling and the restoration of the marriage assisted the children with their feelings, and family counseling was continuing. Melissa had spent time understanding, feeling, and resolving the known pain with each of her primary caregivers, Mom, Dad, and Grandma. She had established a satisfactory relationship with both her mother and father, with the hopes and plans that she and her father would grow closer. Major time and attention had been given to her feelings about Greg's affair and proposed abandonment. Other marriage issues, such as the need to spend time together in both fun and communication, were being addressed and improved. In individual therapy, Greg had made significant changes in both his behavior and feelings. The marriage was generally at a secure and fulfilling place for both of them.

This family had worked through a lot of difficulties! But if any of these areas had not been resolved, that would be the focus. One should not consider working with repressed trauma at any crisis points, such as when Greg asked for a divorce. Melissa was already overwhelmed and could handle no more.

Repressed trauma work is usually similar to elective surgery. Before surgery occurs, one needs to be in optimum health. There are exceptions, such as when one is having flashbacks that are so debilitating that functioning is difficult. Even then, there are often ways to put the memories aside temporarily in order to deal with other issues, if that seems to be indicated. As in a physical injury, if the trauma has just occurred, it needs immediate treatment, even if it is not the ideal time.

If a person has not worked on known areas, false memories are more likely, in an attempt to explain all the present and past difficulties. We all prefer the easy answer and solution. We'd love to hear that one treatment will cure all ills, that one trauma has caused all of our problems. Since we are very complex, and our symptoms are generally diverse, we would have to make up or exaggerate a trauma in order for it to cover every difficulty we are experiencing.

Evaluate Current Strength and Health

How are you doing today? That's a key question to ask before jumping into repressed memories. How are you handling your life, your impulses, your feelings, your conflicts? Do you have a healthy control over your actions even though your emotions or impulses may be different? Can you accept your imperfections, failures, and badness, without beating yourself up emotionally or hurting yourself physically? Do you feel a healthy guilt for wrong behavior, a guilt which leads to change instead of never-ending shame? Can you forgive yourself and accept God's forgiveness? This is the ideal, although many people require assistance to arrive at this point.

Melissa was fairly strong emotionally, although her earlier intermittent depressions, anxiety, and helplessness over her husband's business did indicate some problem. It is normal to be upset if a mate asks for a divorce, and even more painful if there is already someone else in your mate's life. When this was resolved and the childhood issues of abandonment were faced, Melissa's depression lifted. The helplessness and the depression did not return with the sexual problems. Her ability to cope in previous therapy and her successful resolution of difficult problems, such as the marriage conflicts, both indicate how strong she is. Her success in her job, parenting, and friendships are all evidence of her competence.

Anxiety and nightmares, however, may be symptoms of repressed trauma, especially when they emerge at a positive and successful time of life. This suggested that she might be ready to take the next step in her possible recovery of repressed memories. When these symptoms had occurred in the midst of other chaos, her ability to cope was breaking down. So in evaluating Melissa's history and psychological testing, we concluded that she did have the emotional strength to deal with repressed trauma, if it had occurred.

Identify Any Addictions or Escape Behaviors

Most of us have established some method of dealing with uncomfortable feelings or impulses. People who have repressed a trauma have already unconsciously decided that some feelings and events are beyond their coping ability. Many have developed a way to keep these from their current awareness, often through some form of addictive or escapist behavior. These might include alcohol, drugs, food, exercise, sex, work, television, sleep, fantasy, involvement in others' lives, addictive relationships, or other ways.

Escapist behaviors can occasionally be helpful and useful as a temporary break from the pain. However, we must be willing to give them up and face the pain if we are to deal with repressed trauma successfully. With serious drug or alcohol addictions, the addiction must be treated before proceeding with the uncovering of blocked memories. Both the past and present look very distorted through drugs and alcohol, and memories may be very inaccurate or false.

Melissa's addiction was busyness, or workaholism. She was well aware of how driven she had been since childhood and her grandma's death. In order to continue this pace, she consumed large amounts of caffeine daily. She was willing to discontinue both addictions and to face any pain that might be buried. To avoid the headaches she had experienced in the past with rapid withdrawal from caffeine, she began a program of gradually decreasing her intake over a month's time. Her primary addiction to excessive work had decreased as she was able to grieve her grandmother's death. But it still remained a habit; with four children, a husband, and a career, there was always more to do. To decrease Melissa's responsibilities involved planning by the entire family.

Melissa began by taking fifteen minutes a day to play or relax. Her goal was to have some time daily and most of Sunday for fun and relaxation. She was taught to begin listening to her body to hear the pain and exhaustion, to her mind to hear her thoughts, and to her emotions to experience the feelings. She began to journal about all three areas. She was also in a class at her church where she was learning about listening to God, and writing what she believed God's response would be to the content of her journaling in the other three areas. All four would involve growing and learning and were not expected to be very accurate in the beginning. But the journaling would begin to reveal distortions in thinking, feelings, and perceptions of God, as well as an awareness of the degree of pain that was converted into psychosomatic symptoms. Within a couple of months, Melissa (being the hard worker she was) was doing an excellent job in breaking her addictions and beginning to be more in touch with the physical, emotional, mental, and spiritual aspects of herself.

Establish a Supportive Environment

It is very dangerous to proceed with work to uncover repressed trauma until clients have a relatively supportive environment, especially if the nonsupport or opposition is occurring on a frequent basis or from someone within their circle of closest relationships. Some of the primary causes of repression are the aloneness one feels when the trauma occurs, the belief that no one is there to help, and the fear of not being believed. A therapist cannot and should not be the only, or even primary, support person. A mate, friends, parents, or a recovery group need to be in place to meet this need. If people have been very damaged in childhood, they might not be able to trust enough for intimacy, but they must have people who have the time and desire and personality to care and nurture.

> Melissa had a good support system. Her husband was willing to do anything to help, even taking off work if necessary. Her mother was similarly available. In fact, she suggested that Melissa get away and do the intensive therapy while she stayed in their home as long as necessary. Melissa's church and pastor were well versed in the pain of childhood trauma. They had recovery groups within the church and a well-established method of helping individuals in needs of all kinds. Melissa also had several very close friends from whom she felt she could receive support.

So, with the supportive environment in place, we moved to the next consideration.

Assess the Cost

The cost of moving into treatment of the possible repressed trauma must be assessed in terms of time, money, emotions, and health. For most people, this is "elective surgery" and therefore can be scheduled. Often the seriousness of the symptoms is the offsetting factor. The more debilitating the symptoms become, the more people are willing to pay the cost. I have never seen a client who was just curious about his or her past and therefore entered therapy. Why bother?

The Cost of Not Seeking Treatment

Although repression or dissociation provides an immediate coping advantage, it has serious long-term consequences when it continues.

Among these are such symptoms as severe depression, anxiety attacks, addictive behaviors, and the numerous symptoms of PTSD and the dissociative disorders, as discussed in earlier chapters. Because it walls off the traumatic experience, it prevents us from coming to terms with the trauma at a later date.

There are also many more medical complaints among people who have suffered trauma. Chronic pain, headaches, gastrointestinal disorders, pelvic pain, exhaustion, and immune deficiency disorders are all more frequent. Higher rates of surgery and diagnostic testing have also been noted.[1]

Many physical complaints occur for victims, but especially the victims of repetitive trauma. "In studies of survivors of the Nazi Holocaust, psychosomatic reactions were found to be practically universal. Similar observations are reported in refugees from the concentration camps of Southeast Asia."[2]

Children who have blocked out prolonged abuse display some of the following telltale signs and symptoms, according to Dr. Lenore Terr. They typically show an indifference to pain, a lack of empathy, an inability to define or acknowledge feelings, and an abhorrence of emotional intimacy. She also describes four responses common to almost everyone exposed to extreme terror as a youngster: (1) trauma-specific fears, such as avoidance of any sexual posture similar to that assumed during sexual abuse; (2) repeatedly visualizing or reexperiencing the feelings associated with the trauma, often in response to reminders of the event; (3) reenacting traumas in childhood play or through repeated behaviors; (4) a change in attitudes about people, various aspects of life, and the future. This includes a sense of having a severely limited future, often accompanied by distrust of others.[3]

When we have blocked a trauma, we consume enormous energy keeping the memories and feelings from our awareness, paying a price physically, mentally, and emotionally. There is considerable research that demonstrates the many physiological reactions to trauma.[4]

The St. Louis Project was a fifteen-year study of high-risk children, specifically the children of schizophrenics and manic-depressives. They generally had horrible lives, with a great deal of chaos and trauma. Many reacted with severe problems, but about 10 percent were described as superadjusted or "invulnerables." These children seemed to steel or harden themselves, becoming capable of mastering most any obstacle. However, they did pay a psychological price. Because they used defenses of distancing, isolation, suppressing, externalizing, rationalizing, and intellectualizing, it was hard for them to allow closeness or intimacy in any relationships. They had a lot of success and superachievements, but they weren't very satisfied with life.[5]

> Melissa had a history of medical problems—headaches, high blood pressure, asthma, severe allergies, insomnia, and tiredness. The emotional symptoms were mostly anxiety related, once the depression was gone. The primary social difficulty was in the sexual area and trust of men. She had never developed intimacy with any man, and used many of the above-mentioned defenses, especially intellectualization, rationalization, and suppression.
>
> Spiritually, Melissa was doing quite well, although she felt distant from God most of the time. All of these difficulties combined to provide a powerful motivation for Melissa to pursue therapy to resolve the problems.

Time

The anticipated time of both therapy and recovery needs to be assessed, although the estimate might not be completely accurate. As in an exploratory surgery, the results could be nothing wrong, or a minor difficulty, or one or more serious problems. However, the symptoms do not usually mislead. Generally, our time estimates have been quite accurate because of all the years of experience our staff has had in treating trauma. Many who are able to devote a period of time to the intensive program can complete much of their work in two to three weeks, with weekly follow-up. In a safe, secure environment, on an outpatient basis, many clients are able to break through their defense mechanisms, enabling memory retrieval and the release of feelings, and to begin to identify their self-destructive thinking. Getting away from work and home enables them to be free from the distractions of daily responsibilities and to accelerate this aspect of their therapy.

In order to proceed, it should be a good time physically, mentally, emotionally, and spiritually.

Health

Physically, optimal health is preferred. But since research indicates that repression is often related to physical problems, these and psychosomatic illness might not be eliminated until the cause is resolved. The therapy should not occur during a pregnancy, or recovery from surgery or illness. A body that is as strong and healthy as possible shortens the healing process.

Mentally, one should not be overwhelmed. Since we see many therapists, doctors, ministers, and other busy professionals at our clinic, we urge timing that is not concurrent with excessive school demands, licensing stress, or unusual job pressures. The freer one's mind is to focus on the trauma, the quicker the results. A time of change, such as a move, a new marriage, or the birth of a child, is generally not the best time to focus on the past.

Melissa was the healthiest she had been for many years, although there clearly were medical problems. After a physical examination and discussion with her physician, steps were taken to deal with the high blood pressure and other potential problems that could arise. Emotionally, spiritually, and socially, Melissa was also at her best.

Money

Financial considerations must also be addressed. How often I've wished for a way to eliminate this as an obstacle to anyone's healing. Yet, on the other hand, I have seen times when this was the very tool God used to lead people to the right time for healing. As clients have prayerfully sought God's will in this area, many miracles have occurred, bringing money for therapy in some unexpected ways. Some churches have established funds to assist their members in therapy. Many people have insurance coverage that also pays a portion of the costs.

As with other medical bills, each person has to determine the worth of mental health, the seriousness of the disability, and the time and the treatment indicated. Whenever we face a critical need, we usually find a way to pay for it. When my son broke his arm, I did not pause to consider treatment, even though I did not know what the cost might be. On the other hand, allergy tests waited until a time it fit into our finances.

Emotions

The emotional cost is another consideration. There will be some fear, sadness, anger, confusion, and other feelings connected with the trauma. Are we ready to deal with them?

However, if we do not choose to deal with the root causes, we usually continue to experience the emotions in some form. They may be attached to the wrong people and the wrong circumstances. They may be converted into physical problems. Addictions may cover the feelings, and have consequences considerably worse than the initial problem.

Melissa counted all of the costs I've mentioned. She could take as much time off work as necessary, as soon as she finished a current project. She could take time away from home, with help from her mother and husband. She did not want to do it during vacation times from school, preferring to be more available for her children at that time. Money was obtainable through insurance and savings, so it was not a major obstacle. Melissa decided the emotional cost was worth it. After attempting sex therapy, she believed she could not resolve the sexual problems without pursuing this option. She decided she wanted to experience everything God had for her in her marriage. She had the love and support of the Lord and of her friends and family during her previous therapy, and she knew she could handle the pain. She had experienced the wonderful healing power of tears and anger and honest confrontation of the problems. So Melissa declared herself ready.

But where and how should she best proceed?

Find the Best Facility and Therapist for This Type of Therapy

The traditional office building is often a disastrous setting for intensive therapy. It may not be conducive to privacy, comfort, and recovery. At its worst, it prevents the expression of feelings and leaves us feeling unsafe and vulnerable to unknown eyes and ears in the waiting room. It also places us at risk by requiring us to drive home while we are still feeling all the emotional trauma. To drive safely, we must erect mental defenses to stop the feelings, which can undo a lot of the valuable therapy that has occurred, or stop the emotional release before it even starts.

I have worked in several different offices. In some, there were complaints from other tenants or even our own clients if there was loud crying or anger. That's obviously very inhibiting (even for traditional therapy). After such frustrations, I had the dream of doing this type of therapy in an inpatient setting, where it would be private and safe and free from other distractions. I was hired to develop and direct such a program. But I soon discovered that a hospital setting often feels intrusive, controlling, and frightening. Since psychiatric hospitals are designed to provide safety for suicidal or severely disturbed patients, or for those with chemical dependency, the state has many requirements that are not the best milieu for other clients, especially abuse victims who need both safety and freedom from feeling trapped, but do not need the security of a hospital.

With considerable thought about our previous unsatisfactory experiences, we designed the McDonald Therapy Center as the kind of place we would like to go for therapy. In order for maximum speed and minimum interference in recovery, we designed privacy, safety, and contact with God's handiwork, the outdoors. Soundproofing, sound screens, and a separate building ensure privacy and avoid the embarrassment of entering a therapy office for the "emotionally disturbed," as some fear they might be labeled. The theme of safety comes through in the setting, locale, private neighborhood, view, and limited access by others. Our clients often tell us how safe and private the center feels to them, even when they're outside where they can sit, walk, lie down, or climb into a tree house.

But perhaps the greatest safety and privacy comes in the individual therapy room. We try to set it up so that an individual in the intensive therapy program can remain in the room after the sessions, whenever that is needed. One client described it as her "hospital room." Clients cannot be expected or required to leave immediately after their sessions. They must have the time and space for recovery. There also must be a place to release anger, a room that will not get damaged, and methods available for successful expression of these feelings. Due to the unique environmental needs and scheduling intensity, many therapists send their clients to our center for one to three weeks to do the initial work with trauma and/or the expression of feelings. The client then returns to the referring therapist for the next steps in healing.

The therapist is the final, and perhaps most important, consideration. Therapy with repressed trauma requires specific training. It should never be undertaken by an untrained counselor or a lay person. A lay counselor could be skilled in listening, but for such a person to work with repressed trauma would be like someone performing surgery because he was pretty good with a penknife. There are many inherent dangers that must be understood and addressed in the training.

Not only must the therapist be well trained and experienced in repressed trauma, but they must be comfortable with this type of intensity. Most of our staff have chosen this specialty primarily because they too have recovered from blocked memories and have experienced their healing in an intensive program. I see them as uniquely gifted and called to "bring good news to the suffering and afflicted . . . to comfort the broken-hearted, to announce liberty to captives" (Isa. 61:1–3 LB).

The therapist's emotional, physical, and spiritual health are also considerations, just as they would be for a surgeon. Unless we therapists take time in personal therapy and resolution of our own anger and pain, we are likely to project our own agenda onto our clients' experiences. Work with repressed trauma is especially draining for new therapists, who are shocked to hear the horrors that an individual has endured. If our own pain has not been healed, we are overwhelmed. A team approach brings the greatest support, with the team including other therapists, family, friends, and pastors.

The therapist must also be open to memories being true, partially true, or false. The therapist should know how to help a client in determining this. Without this understanding and balance, clients may be trapped in a world of unreality that is worse than their real world.

Above all else, clients must feel that the therapist they choose is someone with whom they can work, the person God has selected for this aspect of their healing.

Melissa and her husband came to discuss all the issues mentioned in this chapter. With prayerful consideration, we all came to the consensus to plan for Melissa to spend two weeks in the intensive therapy program. The time was scheduled in nine weeks, to allow for completion of her project at work, to break the addictive behaviors, and to develop better listening skills.

If we suspect we may have blocked traumatic memories, we need to evaluate our readiness to cope with them, including recommended prerequisite steps. Optimal physical, emotional, and spiritual health are advisable, unless it is a very recent trauma, which should receive treatment immediately. The cost of this type of therapy should be assessed in terms of time, health, money, and emotions. The cost of continuing without this type of therapy should also be evaluated. It is helpful to view this as a specialized surgery, requiring therapists with specific training and experience, unique facilities, and intensive care options.

9

How Reliable Are the Different Methods of Recovering Memories?

There are several different methods used for the recovery of memories. Each will be considered in terms of reliability, risks, side-effects, and expected outcomes.

As discussed previously, one school of thought suggests that the human mind functions like a video camera, automatically recording each experience, and storing it for instant replay. Because of the limited room in this video recorder, some of the older, less important pictures are put in a less accessible space. Nevertheless, they are not lost, and can be recalled if needed or desired. The methods of obtaining this replay of memory vary.

A second school of thought rejects the exact recording model. It believes that the mind does perceive information and does store it. New information, however, may modify the original input. Therefore, retrieval of memories or information results in more of a composite of old and new and does not necessarily represent an accurate or completely reliable picture of a specific past event. This point of view is generally accepted by the scientific community.

The view which is often held by the clinical community is the third, that memories may be changed by subsequent experiences, information, or feelings, and thus reconstructed, as the second theory purports. However, traumatic or intensely emotional events are viewed differently. Because of their intensity, they are somehow seared into the mind and thus not as subject to modification. Repressed memories are traumatic events that are stored differently, and also preserved from the changes that occur through repetitive telling of the story.

Naturally, the way people view the reliability of repressed memories will depend on which of these general views of memory they accept. Acknowledging the uncertainty over which is the correct view, and with the awareness that further research may resolve this conflict, let's examine the various methods being used to retrieve memories.

Dreams

Since dreams are a normal and healthy part of our daily (or nightly) routine, there are no added risks when therapists attempt to understand our past through our dreams. We all dream, whether or not we recall the dreams. Dreams are generally assumed to be the road into our unconscious, and our attempt to resolve those conflicts, fears, or feelings that we have not completed on a conscious level. Our dreams are often outside of the possibilities of reality. They might include flying, breathing under water, men giving birth to babies, running faster than a train, and so forth.

Groups that have studied dreams extensively generally believe that dreams are valuable in therapy in working out powerful dynamics that drive our thoughts, feelings, and actions. They view dreams as symbolic. Some therapists (Jungian) interpret every character in a dream as an internal part of the dreamer, and the interactions in the dream as the conflicts or dynamics among our own mixed thoughts, fears, desires, and feelings. Most groups who analyze dreams do not take the contents as factual or literal.

Many of us have awakened on occasion with a dream so real that we felt compelled to verify it. Our feelings and thoughts at the moment lead us to believe the facts of the dream, until it is disproved. On very rare occasions, we hear of someone dreaming of a disaster that was occurring at approximately the same time as the dream. But these same people indicate that most of their dreams are not literally true. Very few people assume that dreams are an accurate or reliable representation of repressed events.

Repetitive dreams or nightmares are of greater significance. Since we assume that dreams resolve internal conflicts, if a dream recurs, its purpose has not been accomplished. Dr. Terr discusses the relationships between childhood trauma and dreams. She observes four kinds of recurring dreams in traumatized children: exact repetitions, modified repetitions, deeply disguised dreams, and terror dreams that couldn't be remembered after awakening. All types leave the dreamer feeling anxious and uncomfortable. In the repetition of these dreams that are related to trauma, the central theme stays the same, even though other details may change. The dreams don't ever seem to dissipate the anxiety. They generally continue sporadically throughout one's life, especially when any current event triggers the same feelings as the trauma, such as helplessness or loss or an emotional overload, or threatened emotional harm.[1]

Dr. John Briere specializes in psychological trauma. Most adolescent and adult survivors of abuse report that they experience abuse-related nightmares of two types: (1) graphically realistic pictures of the original trauma appearing soon after the abuse and decreasing in frequency over time, or (2) symbolic pictures of "victimization, involving themes of intrusion, violation, violence, and/or danger."[2]

Barbara, the victim of rape in her boutique, had terrifying nightmares of torture, threats, physical assaults, and sexual abuse. Her dreams accurately represented the central theme of her repressed trauma, but not the correct location or perpetrator.

It is important to note that Dr. Terr found two themes common for *all* children, not just abused children: dreams of falling and dreams of being chased by huge animals. She suggests that these might reflect every child's deepest fears, an instinctive fear of falling and of looming objects.[3]

Dr. Terr also noted the frequency of unremembered terror dreams for abused children, probably due to their desire and need to keep the abuse secret. These children are often afraid of the dark and of sleeping alone.[4]

If our recovered memories are from our dreams, the likelihood of accuracy is small. We should never construct reality on the basis of a dream alone, even if it is recurring. That does not mean these dreams are worthless. It is valuable to sort through their symbolic meanings. They may indicate feelings that are unacceptable to us consciously, and thus provide a road map to locate the source of these unacceptable feelings or the reason for the unacceptability. Dreams may indicate internal conflicts that are keeping us trapped in unresolved difficulties and destructive behavior. They may indicate external trauma, especially if they are recurring.

Melissa had frequent nightmares prior to her intensive therapy. The content was often similar, that of various people terrifying children in different ways. The young children ran away in panic until they reached a safe place. The safe place soon disappeared, and Melissa woke up in terror, unable to return to sleep. At these times, she reported accomplishing huge amounts of work, sometimes staying up all night. Melissa had similar dreams as a child, but was told that most kids have nightmares about someone chasing them. She did not tell anyone that they continued for many years on a recurring basis. Nor did she tell anyone the content. Prior to her intensive therapy, Melissa had two dreams of her dad trapping and molesting her.

The recurring dream could be understood as representing Melissa's message to herself concerning how dangerous her world was, and the best she could hope for was a life of running to escape to a temporarily safe place that would soon disappear. Considering the content of the dream, these messages could be coming from a nurturing part in her that wished to protect herself. The messages could also be coming from a very angry, forceful part that frightened her vulnerable "child," wishing to destroy the naive, gullible, trusting aspects of her personality. The internal conflict may be that of Melissa trying to find safety from her own anger and feelings of inadequacy, as they return time and time again. With the recurring nature of the dream, it *might* also indicate an external event of a traumatic nature. The central theme was this: the terror of children who found no permanent safety from frightening adults.

None of us can successfully escape awareness of our own anger. Eventually, we must face it and deal with it. Melissa has expressed fear of her own anger, but seemed to have faced some of that in her previous therapy. The self-destructive behavior and depression did not recur, but the repetitive nightmares continued.

The question then arises as to other possible causes of such a perception. She felt abandonment from her parents and grandmother, but not fear. Melissa had described her father as controlling, when he was not absent. But Melissa presents no pictures of anyone frightening to her, except for her kindergarten teacher. Since she was quickly removed from her class with no further contact, ongoing fear that would last into adulthood is unlikely to be related to the known events with this teacher.

When Melissa dreamed of her father molesting her, she immediately believed it was factual. She didn't like him anyway. But she was encouraged to seek the truth, without jumping to any conclusions.

These dreams have not recurred since her intensive therapy of several years ago. During this therapy, Melissa faced the truth and feelings about her dad and others, as will be discussed in later chapters.

Many other clients have had dreams of abuse which were symbolic. Most of the dreams were not taken literally. They were very helpful in pointing the direction to the internal conflicts or to an external trauma. Our clinic sees many children and adults who have just experienced a trauma. Rarely is every detail of even a recurring dream the actual replay of the trauma. All of these clients with recent traumas have had recurring nightmares, with the central theme an accurate depiction of their trauma.

Hypnosis

Last year at the San Diego County Fair, a hypnotist had twenty or more volunteers acting in humorous presentations of the likes of Miss Piggy and Kermit the Frog. They were given posthypnotic suggestions, or directions to act in a specific manner when they heard a prearranged word. When they became aware of what they were doing, most of these subjects showed shock and embarrassment.

Hypnosis as entertainment is often demonstrated at county fairs, lounge shows, or parties. But increasingly, hypnosis is being used for memory retrieval. This is not a recent development. Freud used it for age regression, taking a patient to an earlier time in life when a traumatic event occurred. He initially believed that these recovered memories were an accurate description of the past event. He later concluded that they represented an emotional reality, not a historical event, and that they combined fears, fantasies, and desires with actual events. The American Medical Association's Council on Scientific Affairs came to the consensus "that hypnotic age regression is the subjective reliving of earlier experiences as though they were real—which does not necessarily replicate earlier events."[5]

Lynn, Melissa's daughter, sought a hypnotist to verify the truth of her memories of sexual abuse by her father. Lynn was able to visualize specific details of her father and his behavior. She apparently did not regress to the age in question, nor did she experience much emotional reaction, except anger. But she felt confident of the truth of this memory, and she did see many vivid details. Did this hypnosis help Lynn get to the truth of her memories, or did it draw on her preconceptions, merely confirming what she wanted to believe? We need to investigate the process of hypnosis and its reliability.

Hypnosis is an altered state of consciousness that depends upon suggestibility, in which we are receptive and responsive to the hypnotist's directives. At the beginning stages of induction, neither the subject nor the hypnotist can tell if the subject is hypnotized. Gradually, suggestions are given that demand increasing distortions of reality, such as, "Your eyelids will become heavier and heavier and soon you will find you are unable to open your eyes." Or the hypnotist's suggestion can be entirely unintended. Subjects can pick up subtle cues about the hypnotist's wishes from the hypnotist's body language, tone of voice, and approving or disapproving expressions.

The AMA has defined hypnosis as a "temporary condition of altered attention in the subject which may be induced by another person and in which a variety of phenomena may appear spontaneously or in response to verbal or other stimuli. These phenomena include alterations in consciousness and memory, increased susceptibility to suggestion, and the production in the subject of responses and ideas unfamiliar to him in his usual state of mind."[6]

A dramatic example of the power of hypnosis is in its use as an analgesic for the numbing of pain. It is believed that this works through selective attention, since nothing happens to actually remove the physical discomfort. A number of findings indicate that the body still registers the pain, as evidenced by physical reactions such as heart rate, even though the conscious mind may not feel it.[7]

Some hypnotists have used a "hidden observer" technique. After analgesia has been successfully established, the hypnotist attempts to communicate with a "hidden part" of the person that may know about the pain. Many times the hidden part will give pain reports comparable to those who have not been hypnotized.

It is possible to change a person's beliefs, actions, and perception of reality through hypnosis. During graduate school, a friend complained of weight gain primarily because of the irresistible doughnuts served at her sorority every morning. She asked if I could do anything about it, so we tried hypnosis. I gave her a posthypnotic suggestion that the next doughnut she ate would taste like cardboard, but that she would not remember this suggestion. At the time, neither of us thought the hypnosis worked.

A couple of weeks later, I inquired about her eating habits. She said, "I wish I could have been hypnotized, but I guess I don't really need it anymore. The sorority must have started ordering doughnuts from a new company. They're so dry, they taste like cardboard!"

In fact, my friend must have generalized the suggestion to include not only doughnuts, but the deliciously moist chocolate cake we were both eating. After only one bite, she commented that it must have dried out in the freezer.

Hypnosis can require the construction of a whole new reality in order to justify or explain the suggested behavior. Because of this, hypnosis has been quite successful, especially in weight control, the elimination of smoking, or other behavioral changes. It has also been used successfully to resolve conflicts with others, without the necessity of their presence. Many hypnotized subjects can picture another person in the room with them, and then say whatever needs to be communicated. This has been helpful in bringing emotional resolution with someone who has died or whose whereabouts is unknown, or when a direct confrontation is not advisable. Clinicians who use hypnosis report that it seems to bring as much closure as if the person had really been there.

Hypnosis is often the treatment of choice for dissociative disorders. It is generally a much quicker method to get to the causal events of the splitting. As clients and therapists are faced with insurance and financial limitations, hypnosis has become more popular.

Although I was trained in the use of hypnosis with repressed trauma, I do not use it for three reasons. First, it may access memories that clients are not ready to handle, overwhelming them and the therapeutic process. When the client is ready, the memories come without hypnosis. Second, the accuracy is questionable, even when great attention is given to avoid leading the client in any way. Third, some clients do not remember the session afterward, and so it becomes a waste of time. I have found other methods to be more effective, without the risks. Other well-respected clinicians, however, view it differently.

Dr. Yapko, author of a widely used textbook on the use of hypnosis in therapy, believes that many of the therapists who use hypnosis do not understand its limitations or dangers. He developed a questionnaire to assess therapists' attitudes toward hypnosis.

Eighty-three percent agreed to the statement, "Hypnosis seems to counteract the defense mechanisms of repression, lifting repressed material into conscious awareness."

Forty-seven percent agreed that "Therapists can have greater faith in details of a traumatic event when obtained hypnotically than otherwise."

Forty-three percent believed that "Hypnotically obtained memories are more accurate than simply just remembering."

In his book, *Suggestions of Abuse,* Yapko disagrees with these statements and other widely held views of hypnosis by clinicians.[8]

Contrary to what many therapists believe, research using hypnosis often demonstrates that it does result in more details, but with greater inaccuracy. Courts in most states do not accept testimony that has been obtained by hypnosis because they do not trust the accuracy or reliability. It is widely accepted that, by suggestion, a hypnotist can change a person's sense of reality. During the state of hypnosis, which is by definition a state of heightened suggestibility, new memories can be introduced or old memories altered in the laboratory. Research has demonstrated that hypnotized subjects may borrow from fantasy to fill in the gaps of what they actually recall. Leading questions are very powerful in determining the content of this fantasy.

Dr. David Spiegel, a psychiatrist at Stanford University, has commented: "Psychotherapy patients who undergo methods like hypnosis, which heighten suggestibility, can easily become 'honest liars,' convincing themselves of the truth of a false memory." He described a study in which twenty-seven people were told while hypnotized that, as they slept the night before, they were awakened by the sound of a car backfiring. They were questioned a week later and almost half of them (thirteen) reported hearing the backfiring of the car. Six of these thirteen were so convinced they persisted in the false belief even after experimenters explained how the memory had originated. "Under hypnosis people can experience themselves as retrieving a memory when in fact they are creating it, and also develop an inflated conviction that the fabricated recollection is accurate," Dr. Spiegel said.[9]

Research has demonstrated that our prehypnotic belief system is a powerful factor in the content of our imagery. With hypnotic age regression, those who believe in past lives have pictured experiences in another lifetime, and those who accept UFOs have recalled being abducted by aliens.[10] Hypnosis intensifies the subject's powers of imagination.[11] The vividness of hypnotic imagery makes it difficult for hypnotized subjects to distinguish imagined events from things they have seen and experienced.

During hypnosis, there is also a loss of critical judgment.[12] Ideas that would be discarded under normal conditions may be acceptable under hypnosis. So the information obtained under hypnosis could be accurate, could be partially accurate, or could be totally false. Upon emerging from the hypnotic state, a subject is often very confident of the truth of this new memory, often more confident than without hypnosis, even when the memory is totally false. Furthermore, many cannot distinguish between what they knew prior to hypnosis and what details they added during the hypnotic process. They no longer possess their own memories of the past; instead their memories are a blend of fact, fill-in fantasy, and suggestion by the hypnotist. Some courts will allow testimony if the hypnosis is taped and safeguards are taken to prevent any suggestion. Other courts will not accept any testimony if a subject has been hypnotized.

The limitations of hypnosis in court came about primarily from a 1980 article in the University of California *Law Review,* in which Dr. Bernard Diamond presented the unfavorable research on the impact of hypnosis on memory. He concluded that using hypnosis to refresh memory was "tantamount to the destruction or fabrication of evidence . . . and testimony by previously hypnotized witnesses should never be admitted into evidence." The majority of courts followed his lead.[13]

The AMA Council concluded, "The current literature does not support the use of hypnosis for casual or moderately involved witnesses. . . . hypnosis can increase the number of meaningful items remembered but it also increases overall productivity; thus, hypnosis increases the number of both correct and incorrect statements."

Data received through hypnosis, the Council said,

> may include accurate information as well as confabulations and pseudomemories. These pseudomemories may be the result of hypnosis transferring the subjects' prior beliefs into thoughts or fantasies that they come to accept as memories. Furthermore, since hypnotized subjects tend to be more suggestible, subjects become more vulnerable to incorporating any cues given during hypnosis into their recollections . . . in order to minimize a potential miscarriage of justice, it must be communicated clearly to the authorities that neither the subject nor the hypnotist can differentiate between accurate recollections and pseudomemories obtained through hypnosis without subsequent independent verification.

Those clinicians who are proponents of hypnosis point out that research in the laboratory is very different than in clinical practice. It is well accepted that eyewitness testimony is of questionable reliability. Yet it is admissible in court. It is believed that powerful emotions create much greater stability of memories, and thus these clinicians believe that the retrieval of memories by hypnosis *does* elicit accurate memories. The AMA Council concluded: "With respect to cases where there is a preexisting psychopathology and/or extreme emotional trauma, the current experimental literature is not definitive." As a result, they urge courts not to disqualify witnesses that are otherwise qualified.[14]

Case studies provide evidence that hypnosis does not distort the central features of a memory, even though some of the peripheral or less significant details may be inaccurate. Since most therapists accept the third theory of memory, which states that traumatic memories have much greater permanence than other memories, then traumatic memories should not be subject to the same distortions. Since most of childhood trauma is from someone known to the child, and the event is generally very clearly seen close up, without distractions, the memory should be durable and not easily changed. People usually have fairly sharp, clear, and accurate memories of the personal traumas they have suffered, making it difficult for them to mistake imagined traumatic events for real-life occurrences. In order to make this mistake, the imagined event must be sufficiently lifelike to create a subjective sense of remembering. Only an extravagant imagination can accomplish this feat. The sensory vividness needed to transform an imagined experience into a memory is beyond the imaginative powers of most people. Only those who are highly hypnotizable have imaginative powers that are rich enough to experience their fantasies as real.[15]

Most clinicians agree that hypnosis minimizes the defenses of the patient, especially the defense of repression. While under hypnosis, self-reactions of embarrassment, guilt, and anxiety are reduced. The subjects turn their focus inward, and it is believed there is accessibility to deep, emotional material of which the individual is not normally aware. It becomes a safe way to see and experience events that are frightening under normal conditions.

Proponents of hypnosis often believe that it enables an individual to regress, or return, temporarily to a time, place, and event in his or her childhood, thus accurately regaining blocked memories. A review of the literature for the past sixty years on hypnotic age regression concluded that there is no evidence that "hypnosis enables subjects to accurately reexperience the events of childhood or to return to developmentally previous modes of functioning."

Although they may demonstrate dramatic changes in behavior and in the way they experience the event, "their performance is not accurately child-like. In fact, equally dramatic and subjectively compelling portrayals are given by hypnotized subjects who are told to progress to an age of 70 or 80 years . . . pre-natal life or even past incarnations."[16]

Some clinicians view hypnotic age regression very differently, as they see their clients reexperiencing a trauma that they believe could not be just acting, and in fact the client would not even know many of the reactions without experiencing the specific trauma. Whether age regression stimulates an actual return to an earlier state and the literal reliving of past events, nevertheless, remains a subject of lively debate.

Even though hypnosis may not improve the memory of normal subjects, if trauma has interfered with memory retrieval due to splitting or amnesia, then anything that can cause relaxation, break down defenses, or re-create a similar feeling to the time of the occurrence of the trauma might facilitate the recovery of the memory. As a result, hypnosis may work in clinical situations in ways that hypnosis laboratory researchers have been unable to observe.

Clinicians are faced with an extremely difficult task—demonstrating that hypnosis is capable of recovering memory accurately. Except in rare cases in which the perpetrator confesses or other members of the family have knowledge of the event, the therapist must rely on his or her own clinical judgment to evaluate the accuracy of a memory.

Opponents of hypnosis mention the ability to implant false memories in subjects; however, research demonstrates that this is true of only the most suggestible of hypnotizable subjects—10–15 percent. Attempts to implant false memories through hypnosis failed with those in the lower range of hypnotizability. So if we can figure out who is most vulnerable to suggestion, then we can determine when it's most likely that a memory being recovered through hypnosis is actually being made up. Tests like the Stanford Hypnotic Susceptibility Scale are helpful in assessing this vulnerability to the implantation of false memories.

But there's a further complication. What causes high suggestibility? It is believed that there are two causes: one is the continuation of the childhood capacity to imagine or fantasize; the second is childhood trauma, and the dissociation which often results. So it is possible that the very person who has a legitimate legal case because of abuse would be disqualified as unreliable because of his or her high susceptibility to suggestion. Research has demonstrated that the correlation between hypnotizability and childhood trauma is particularly high for individuals diagnosed with a dissociative disorder. A common reaction to childhood trauma is emotional escape into fantasy, which is very similar to hypnotic suggestibility.

The difference of opinion between experimental research and clinical experience has not yet been resolved. Obviously, experimenters cannot cause severe trauma to their subjects in order to study them. It will require research that can validate or invalidate the truth of traumatic memories that have been repressed that are recovered by hypnosis. Until this occurs, memories obtained under hypnosis will continue to be suspect. Such memories may be true, may be false, or may be a combination of true and false. As with all memories, verification should be sought.

Truth Serums

Truth serums are barbiturates, with the generic name of amobarbital. This includes the commonly known Pentothal and Amytal as well as Seconal and Nembutal. The benzodiazepines (Ativan and Valium) are also sometimes used. During the '30s and '40s they were used quite frequently for psychotherapy and for examination of the unconscious. These substances produce a twilight state, in which the interviewer questions the subject, who has received the drug intravenously. It's a relaxed, warm situation, and the subject generally feels close to the interviewer. It was believed that people did not lie while under the influence of this drug, thus the term *truth serum*. It was believed to "be able to draw forth the concealed contents of a person's mind and compel him or her to reveal those contents . . . and that the procedure uncovers accurate, true-to-life memories that have been stored in the brain."[17]

According to Dr. August Piper, a psychiatrist who summarizes the research for about sixty years, under truth serums people can lie deliberately, can choose to withhold information, and they can report exaggerated symptoms of psychological disorders. Details of their past may be untrustworthy. Patients often have a distorted sense of time, show memory disturbances, and have difficulty evaluating and selecting thoughts. They are more susceptible to suggestions by the interviewer. And they may not be able to reliably distinguish between fact and fantasy.

The courts in most states do not accept information obtained under Amytal interviews as accurate or reliable.

As with hypnosis, memories obtained under Amytal may be a combination of fact and fantasy, with neither the subject nor the interviewer able to determine which is which. Dr. Piper states, "By definition, . . . during an Amytal interview, a patient is in a hypnotic state."[18] Dr. Piper concludes:

> The degree of agreement in the literature . . . is striking . . . not a single investigator who had actually conducted Amytal interviews endorsed this procedure as a means of recovering accurate memories of past events . . . [they] may be worse than useless, because they encourage patients' beliefs in completely mythical events.[19]

For more details of the research, consult Dr. Piper's review of the literature.

"In summary, any memory surfacing under Amytal should be considered of questionable reliability until independently corroborated. Memories retrieved in an Amytal-induced trance are likely to contain both fact and fantasy in a mixture that cannot be accurately determined without external verification."[20]

Body Memories

It has been postulated by some psychologists that our bodies hold some memories, particularly those involving physical trauma. Therapists have reported numerous cases that seem to be relevant.

Many cases of asthma have been tied to memories of an oral rape or a choking incident. The asthma stopped after the recovery of the associated memory.

Other clients report vaginal pain that they believe is indicative of an early rape.

Of the many theorized cases of body memories, a few have been validated and the repressed event verified, according to clinicians' reports. Dr. Lenore Terr describes eighteen very young children who remember aspects of their physical trauma, without verbal memories or visual pictures of the details. All have documented external evidence.[21]

However, there are others that have no substantiated connection with the suspected trauma. There could be several causes for the same physical feelings, coming from fact or fantasy, from a time in the past or from the present. Body memories alone are not sufficient to assume a past history of abuse. And yet there are some cases where the physical sensations are proven accurate.

One woman had suffered from various physical ailments since childhood. As an adult, she began to get memories of being victimized in a terrible gang rape and left for dead. As she put the pieces of her memories together, and researched their accuracy, she realized that many of her physical difficulties were caused by the trauma of that awful event. Her body had been remembering all along what her conscious mind had blocked out.

Yet we should not rush to believe body memories with no corroboration. This can lead to inaccurate conclusions about ourselves and our past. It can also delay or prevent treatment of a medical condition that needs attention, when it is believed that the physical problem is rooted in a memory and will disappear as the trauma is resolved. If body memories become the primary focus, we can easily move into the pathology of hypochondria.

Guided Visualization

Guided visualization is generally used as a way of fostering healing and changing the childhood perceptions that are destructive distortions and lies. Spiritual input can be very powerful with this method.

Since guided visualization does include suggestions, it can also produce false memories, especially if it includes specific people or events.

For example, "Picture your father in your bedroom," might elicit pictures of sexual abuse that did not occur. More general guiding, such as, "Picture yourself as a child. Tell me what you see," opens the door to many options, including positive, negative, and neutral images. If a memory is partially recalled, specific directions that go back to the situation but suggest nothing more, can be helpful.

There is no available research that evaluates the accuracy of memories occurring with guided imagery. But the work of Loftus, Ceci, and others, as discussed in previous chapters, certainly indicates that false memories can be implanted for some suggestible clients.

Visual Imagery

Visualization may be the safest method of retrieving memories. The client at all times retains full consciousness and control. There are no drugged effects, and there is less increased suggestibility. Unless there is a severe degree of dissociation, the whole process is fully remembered, including questions or any possible leading. The client is later free to question the visualization and to sort out the facts from the fears and fantasies. He is able to visualize with all of his critical skills in place.

Is the information obtained fully accurate? The answer is *probably not*. It is a beginning place for checking out the missing pieces, after other therapy has not resolved the internal conflicts and anxiety. The information is likely to be partially true—and it will at least reveal our fears or fantasies. It is not strong enough evidence, however, to stand alone to convict the accused.

In Melissa's intensive therapy, she was very surprised by two memories that she visualized. One occurred when she was five. She was outside playing, and a neighbor man invited her into his home for milk and cookies. Her mom had told her not to go next door. But she really wanted the cookies, so she went anyway. Once she was inside the house, the neighbor molested her, and told her she could never tell anyone, or he would come over and hurt her family. He said he was right next door, so he could hear her if she ever told.

The second memory involved Melissa's dad and herself when she was seven. It was a picture of Dad becoming very angry at her, throwing a vase, and yelling. Melissa was terrified of him. Both memories will be discussed more in later chapters. But let me repeat that these images must be accepted *for what they are*. They may or may not reflect actual events, but at least they tell us something about Melissa, something that may help her deal with the many issues of her present-day life.

Visual imagery can be a helpful method, providing a safe opportunity for someone to bring up memories, as long as no one assumes that those memories are automatically true. As with guided visualization, there needs to be more research to indicate the accuracy of the recovered memories. But clinical evidence has provided support for the accuracy of *some* visualization. Dan was an example of this, with his mother verifying the details of the molest. Many clients with recent trauma, like Barbara's rape in the boutique, accurately recall a documented trauma through visualization. With some other clients, it is quite clear that the visualization is their fear or fantasy. Sometimes it is impossible for the client or the therapist to evaluate. As with every other method, external corroboration is required to accuse or convict anyone of the alleged abuse.

Prayer

There are some professionals and lay people who are involved in healing prayer. There are two aspects: the first is praying for the truth, for wisdom, or for specific needs; the second is listening for God's answers. However, since no one hears God perfectly, it is important to understand that we are likely to hear our own thoughts in some combination with God's wisdom. When the ideas we hear are from God, they will never go against biblical truth—God does not contradict himself. And such prayer is a process, not a one-time event.

Some excellent books are available on learning to listen to God. It may be helpful to study these before assuming we are correctly hearing, and it's a good idea to check out our perceptions with others whom we trust concerning spiritual matters. Any memories recovered this way should be subject to the same scrutiny we are recommending for other recovered memories.

Several classic books on prayer were written by the Reverend Andrew Murray in the late nineteenth and early twentieth centuries. One, *Waiting on God,* is structured around thirty different Bible references, all with the message that we are to be still before God and wait to hear and understand his voice.[22] How foreign this is to our society with its fast foods, instant potatoes, and television trauma resolved in one sitting! So much of the damage we cause comes from our impulsiveness and unwillingness to even attempt to hear God, let alone wait to make sure we are hearing him clearly.

Another excellent book, with specific exercises, is *Lord, I'm Listening* by Donna Leonard. She presents the following "Steps for Listening":

1. Sit silently before the Lord (Psalm 62:1)
2. Begin praising and thanking God
3. Ask the Lord to penetrate and guide your thoughts as you read His Word, and to make His presence felt to you as you read
4. Write your feelings in a letter to God
5. Pray for items on your prayer list
6. Learn by memory a verse of Scripture[23]

Prayer is powerful not only in bringing us a settled peace about the truth, even if the initial memory recovered is not accurate, but also in directing us to the next step of our recovery. (See Ps. 40:1, 3; Isa. 40:31.)

For those who have a strong, trusting relationship with God the healing process is dramatically shortened. Each person's road to recovery is unique.

A dangerous practice is to pray for someone else's truth, and then to inform them about your insights into their childhood, perhaps even giving your ideas authority as if God were speaking through you. We have seen people at our clinic who have experienced this type of so-called prayer and have found it very destructive. For some, the information was false, yet very traumatizing while they imagined it to be true. For others, the information may be accurate, but they were incapable of coping with it at that particular time in their lives.

Barry, you remember, was a victim of someone's revelation of truth. The Christian leader who told Barry he showed symptoms of abuse also told him that he had prayed about Barry's problems, and that God had revealed to him that the issue was sexual abuse. This demoralized Barry because he couldn't remember any abuse, and it sent him down a false path, delaying the healing for the real problems he needed to resolve.

If you think you have an insight like this about someone else, it is usually advisable to wait. God is capable of dealing with each of us in his own time and in the manner best for us. And any truth will survive investigation—not demand blind acceptance.

Eye Movement Desensitization and Reprocessing

The newest method for treating trauma, Eye Movement Desensitization and Reprocessing (EMDR), often rapidly and effectively releases the anxiety, emotional impact, and negative thinking associated with trauma. It was developed by Dr. Francine Shapiro in 1988. The treatment of traumatic events with the EMDR method is based upon the theory that there is a physiological aspect to each trauma. It is theorized that trauma causes an overexcitation of a specific place in the brain and a physical brain abnormality occurs. This abnormality may be said to "freeze" the information in its original anxiety-producing form.[24]

The training in EMDR includes a focus on potential dangers, such as unexpected flashbacks or overload. Thus it should only be used by well-trained therapists. It is a powerful tool that successfully identifies connections between current anxiety and childhood trauma. (The treatment aspects will be discussed more in a later chapter.) But does it elicit accurate childhood memories? The method is so new that its accuracy is unknown. To date, there has not been sufficient research to validate the truth of the memories. Dr. Shapiro does not claim the memories are accurate. The perception of the incident, rather than the factual information, is what causes the trauma. Thus the information produced cannot be more accurate than the perceptions. If an adult suffers anxiety, it could just as easily stem from childhood fears as from actual incidents. So the memories will probably be some combination of fears and events, and are not to be taken as literal or accurate without further validating research. There has been no evidence that EMDR implants false memories. In fact, there is no therapeutic method that is less suggestive, since all of the initial information and the ongoing connections come from the client.

Dr. Shapiro recently reported an initial legal test for EMDR in the state of Washington.[25] There was the attempt to liken EMDR to hypnosis, an altered state of consciousness, thus making it inadmissible in court. However, on the basis of EEG research that demonstrated normal brain waves during EMDR, unlike the EEGs of hypnotized subjects, it was determined to be unlike hypnosis and admissible in court.

In reviewing each of the methods of obtaining childhood memories, especially repressed ones, the same conclusion occurs. We currently know of no method that will always produce accurate memories or will always produce false memories. Instead, we are likely to find memories that are true, some that are false, and many that are a combination of facts, fears, and fantasies. That does not trivialize the importance of each person's memory. Sometimes our fears have a more profound effect upon us than events that actually occurred. With a real event, we may have discovered the means of surviving that trauma. But with a fear, our reaction and ability to cope remain in the realm of the unknown. Resolving these fears and anxieties, whatever their sources, is the work of therapy, and not to be ignored or minimized.

10

How Can I Re-create My Past?

History can be very intriguing, especially when it's your own. So much of what we perceive, feel, and decide is based on our past experiences—and what we have learned from the experiences of our parents and ancestors. Many clients are amazed to discover the threads that have continued down through their family history, through their own upbringing, and into their present lives.

When we try to recover our repressed memories, we are doing the work of a historian. We may have bits of "testimony" from the pieces of memory we summon up. But how accurate are these memories? Have those events been perceived accurately, stored properly, and called back clearly, or is there some distortion? Just as a historian would study the context of an ancient inscription seeking verification from outside sources, so we must put together the context of our own early lives.

Compiling your most complete and accurate personal history usually involves getting as many sources of information as you can find. Most relatives and friends enjoy talking about the past, reliving both the happy and painful times in their lives. As you begin to construct your personal history, a tape recorder or video camera is an excellent companion, allowing you to ask questions, listen attentively, and later retrieve the details. (Additionally, this recorded history could be a wonderful gift for children and grandchildren.) Some people may be initially uncomfortable with the idea of putting their thoughts and memories on tape, but they may be swayed by the idea that this will be of help to you, and that the general information they provide will be preserved for future generations.

Consider talking to some of the following people: great-grandparents, grandparents, parents, other relatives, sisters and brothers and their childhood friends, neighbors, teachers, pastors and church members, medical doctors, coaches, music teachers, and anyone else who had contact with your family members through the years. Each person may have pieces of the puzzle you are trying to construct. Even if you can only get a few of the pieces, you may begin to see the overall picture. The more pieces you can locate, the more accurate your picture will be.

It's important to note that, at this stage, you are not trying to zero in on any abuse you may have suffered as a child. While that is very important and must be resolved, it is definitely not the only factor that influences who you are today. It is a part of the puzzle. Sometimes other pieces have more impact on us than the abuse that may have occurred. In any case, we need to look at the whole picture.

It's important to withhold judgment until you've assembled enough pieces to have a reasonable view of the whole picture. We must exercise extreme caution to avoid conclusions until most of the pieces are in place. We can still work on a few pieces, if that is all we have. But we cannot judge other people, or our entire lives on the basis of only a few pieces.

As children, we had no concept of the many factors influencing our treatment by our parents or others. Children assume that they bring about mistreatment because of their own bad behavior or their lack of desirability or worth. But as adults, we can place ourselves in the historical context. We can see the many, many factors that affected us and those around us. We can let go of the lies we have believed since childhood.

In this chapter, we will suggest specific ways to find and record personal memories and the recollections of our past by significant and knowledgeable others. There are many ways to do this; we will present two. We will continue to look at the lives of Greg and Melissa and their family as we explore these two methods.

The first method we will call *examining our heritage.* This involves a background study of: physical attributes, emotional characteristics, spiritual involvement, and intellectual abilities and achievements.

The second method is *tracing our development.* In this, we will use the Stages of Development set forth by well-known theorist Erik Erikson to examine personal history.

Examining Our Heritage

Physical Attributes

What's one of the first things people say about a newborn baby? Oh, she looks so much like her mother. He's the spitting image of his dad. She's got her mother's eyes. Look, you can see his father's strong chin.

As you search for pieces of your puzzle, perhaps the easiest place to begin is your physical heredity. Our unique physical attributes are a visible connection to the past.

As we look at Greg and Melissa, we see that Melissa looks very much like her mother and maternal grandmother, tall, with thin, angular features, large expressive eyes, and beautiful thick blonde hair. Jenny, their ten-year-old daughter, looks very like her mother and maternal grandparents. They all have a pretty, elegant demeanor. Lynn, now twenty-one, does not have the height or slenderness or blonde hair. Her eyes and mouth are clearly like her mother's, but her lack of makeup minimizes this.

Greg is a combination of both his parents, but he has the stocky muscular build and large features, including large hands and feet, of his maternal grandfather. He has the height and the facial angularity of his father. He has very dark hair and light skin, the contrasting coloring of both paternal grandparents. Tad, the twelve-year-old, looks like his father, muscular and athletic, but with the blue eyes of his mother and paternal grandmother. Tim, fourteen, has the slender build and height of Melissa's family, with Greg's dark hair and eyes and contrasting skin color.

As a result of all of these combinations, there is very little appearance of cohesion. This is not a family that looks as if they belong together. Jenny and Melissa look like a pair, Greg and Tad resemble each other, and Tim has some obvious characteristics from both parents. But Lynn often states that she looks "adopted."

Both Greg and Melissa come from active, athletic families. All of the children but Lynn also look athletic. Tad's muscular build has helped him excel in sports, surpassing his older brother, Tim. Physically, at least, it's Tad who is "his father's son," more than Tim.

As they researched their personal histories, Greg and Melissa checked into the general health of their ancestors. High stress times were accompanied by occasional ulcers, frequent high blood pressure, and even some heart attacks in Melissa's family. General energy level was average to above average, and they were generally healthy, except for bouts of depression and migraine headaches for some of the women. Greg's family was reported to be very physically active and healthy, although some weight problems occurred in adulthood.

None of Greg and Melissa's children have a history of serious illness. Tim had the most problems, with several broken bones, severe cuts requiring stitches, and numerous bruises. Lynn had a history of acne, severe headaches, and stomach ailments. Tad and Jenny were rarely sick. All had the usual childhood diseases.

Sexual development generally occurred early in Melissa's family, and about average in Greg's family. All of the children but Tim seemed to follow the early development. This was another area in which Tad surpassed Tim, causing further alienation. The younger Tad is quite popular with his classmates, especially the girls.

Life expectancy in Greg's family is very long, with his grandparents living to their eighties and nineties, and capable of functioning independently until the last year or two of life. Three of his grandparents died of strokes, the fourth died in her sleep at ninety-five. Melissa's grandparents died much earlier. Her grandfathers both died of heart attacks, at the ages of sixty-four and fifty-nine. Her grandmothers lived until seventy and seventy-six, one dying of a stroke and one of pneumonia. In Greg's grandfather's family, only two of seven children survived to adulthood, initially suggesting a sickly, physically weak heritage. However, he further explained the causes of death, such as smallpox, typhoid fever, and the like, all illnesses that were common and very often fatal at the time of their childhood.

Emotional Characteristics

An emotional profile, or better yet, a psychological evaluation of each of our ancestors would be intriguing. Since that is probably impossible to obtain, you will need to construct such a profile on your own. Some people have used a checklist of descriptive emotions and have asked others to check whatever describes the parent, grandparent, or other relative. It is helpful to use the same checklist in having others describe you. This should include both positive and negative traits. This makes it very easy to identify the common qualities in different categories.

There were similar characteristics for many of the men on both sides of Melissa's family: responsible, honest, hard-working, controlling, intelligent, proper, distant, and absent. In addition, Melissa's father and his father were both described as critical. The women on both sides were loving, giving, intelligent, proper, refined, somewhat unfulfilled, and moody in a quiet reserved manner. Melissa's father's parents were emotionally very unavailable, while her mother's mother was intensely involved with both her children and grandchildren.

Greg's male ancestors were described much like Melissa's, but were less critical and proper. The women were stronger, more emotional and expressive, as well as being intelligent, giving, and hard-working. Both Greg and Melissa were the oldest child in their families. Melissa has a younger brother and sister. Greg has a younger sister and two brothers.

Melissa's parents and extended family seemed to live friendly but somewhat distant lives. Her dad was often busy with work, sometimes critical and controlling of others. Melissa and her brother and sister had separate lives without much interaction. As adults, they rarely got together because they were too busy, but it was pleasant when they did find the time. Melissa was closest to her mom, except when Mom was sick, busy, or depressed. The death of Mom's mother, when Melissa was seven, created severe depression for Mom and Melissa, both feeling very alone and abandoned. Grandma was Melissa's frequent caretaker and the most loved person in both Melissa's and Mom's lives. There was little contact with extended family, who did not live in the immediate area and made rare visits, except for weddings and funerals.

Melissa's childhood family took yearly vacations that were expensive, fun, and pleasant, traveling to many different lovely places throughout the world. There were not many arguments; disciplining was by time-outs ("Go to your room") when they were young, and restriction ("You're grounded") when they were older. Generally, when family members got angry, they withdrew.

Socialization was primarily outside the home, with family members having their own friends. Most of the socializing within the home was for business purposes.

Greg's family was much more expressive. There were many fights, mostly verbal, occasionally physical. Spankings, hitting, and yelling were the primary means of discipline. Greg's mother was very affectionate and permissive when the children were young. The boys often stuck together, playing mostly outside or involved in sports. Both parents were proud and supportive of any sports accomplishment. Most holidays were spent with many relatives. These times were filled with fun and activities and food, but might become chaotic in the evening if the adults drank too much. By the time Greg was in late grade school, both parents worked outside the home, so the kids were alone often, with Greg assigned a lot of the responsibility.

Melissa's ancestors' history revealed no addictions, except perhaps work. They were upper middle class and had been financially successful for many generations. There were no divorces, and there was stability in jobs, homes, and relationships. They liked their elegant lifestyle, but the men worked hard to maintain it. Wives stayed at home, enjoying many creative endeavors. Unplanned pregnancies were infrequent, and resulted in marriage when they did occur. Early and unexpected deaths were traumatic throughout the family's history. Their ancestors, primarily English, with a little German on Melissa's father's side, have been in the U.S. for many generations.

Greg is a third-generation Italian, from a lower-middle-class home. His ancestors worked very hard, attempting to better their lifestyles. There are times of excessive drinking and overeating, especially at the frequent family gatherings. Divorces have not occurred, and unexpected deaths were rare. Unplanned pregnancies were common and, as in Melissa's family, always resulted in marriage. Moves were quite frequent as better job opportunities occurred or nicer homes were attainable. Most of the extended family stayed in the same general locale, really valuing the frequent contact with relatives. Large families, with four to nine children, were common.

Greg's family showed intensity, feelings, and spontaneity in work and play, and as the model for marriage and family interactions. It was inclusive of both immediate and extended family. Melissa's family had, for generations, modeled very polite and proper marriages and families that were controlled and opposed to open conflict or hostility, preferring intellectual debates. They were kind and giving, but not very close or spontaneous. They lived more independent, parallel lives.

Spiritual Involvement

Since spiritual heritage is often at the core of personal satisfaction, it is often helpful to know what role it has played in our families.

Greg comes from a long line of deeply devout Christians. Christianity was a central part of their morality as well as of their social lives. Greg experienced his spiritual influence as mostly positive. A favorite among both teachers and ministers, he really liked the church and the religious school he attended. Greg viewed God as expecting a lot, but also forgiving. His church was small and intimate, with a feeling of family that you could depend upon. He found his faith to be personally strengthening and directing, especially enjoying the youth group in which he was actively involved and eventually a leader. He enjoyed this so much that he considered a career as a minister.

Melissa's family was not religious. They did not attend church or have any spiritual interests. Morality was based on goodness, which required integrity, self-control, charity, kindness, truthfulness, and responsibility as the most important values. There were not any discussions in their home or family concerning the existence of God. One of Melissa's aunts was a church organist, and the family attended a few musicals. All comments that followed such events centered on the quality of the music. In high school, Melissa attended some social events at a church with a friend. This was her only exposure to any religion until she met Greg and his family. She was immediately very attracted to the fun and warmth and intimacy of both their family and their church.

Intellectual Abilities and Achievement

In general, our ancestors strongly influence us in the areas of intelligence, individual strengths and weaknesses, and the presence of inherited learning disabilities. Achievements, areas of enjoyment, the value of accomplishments, working, and responsibilities are all taught and modeled by our parents and extended family.

Melissa comes from a long line of very intelligent, highly educated professional men and women. The men were achievement-oriented and extremely responsible. They valued academic achievement for both men and women. Many of the men in the family became college professors. Others were business executives. The typical male in Melissa's heritage might be pictured as an intensely studious, reflective man in a neat suit or sport coat, with a pipe in his mouth, sitting at a desk and reading. The women were often volunteers in musical, dramatic, or community projects. As members of the country club, they clearly portrayed the lower echelon of aristocracy. The children were continually trained in orderliness, cleanliness, responsibility, proper manners, social etiquette, and trustworthiness. Hobbies were quite genteel, including art, music, drama, dance, golf, and tennis. Lessons of some type were usually the order of the day for much of their childhood.

Greg's ancestors were also intelligent and very hard-working, but not highly educated. Greg's generation was the first to attend college. They lived a more spontaneous life, with sports, playing cards, and outdoor parties. They enjoyed barbecues and dancing, working on cars, carpentry, and working around the home. But school and sports were the first priority. They frequently reminded the children of the necessity of a good education, in order to "make something out of yourself." The older generations worked hard first, and later they played hard.

There were no diagnosed learning disabilities for either Melissa's or Greg's family. Nor were there any known difficulties in pregnancy or childbirth, or any known birth defects.

While this study of Melissa and Greg's families is far from exhaustive, it does indicate areas of your heritage you might begin to examine. As you ask questions and listen, many other factors become evident. After looking at your heritage, you should look next at your personal experiences.

Tracing Our Development

Child development is a fascinating study with several prominent theories. As I have taught in this area, I have found the work of Erik Erikson to be especially helpful.[1] He describes the human life span in eight stages. At each of these stages, there is a choice to make and a turning point that will determine the quality of our future lives. We will look at Melissa and Greg in each of these stages so we can have specific examples. Any theory of development can be a helpful framework in which to organize our personal experiences.

Stage 1: Trust versus Mistrust (Infancy)

The infant's basic task is to develop a relationship with someone it can trust to meet its needs.

Both Melissa and Greg had loving, consistent caring the first year of life, and decided that it was safe to trust this world to meet their needs. They were fed when hungry, kept physically comfortable, held frequently, loved, and enjoyed. They were both the firstborn children and the firstborn grandchildren in their families, and thus received a great deal of attention from many adults.

Their daughter, Lynn, developed some early trust with women, although her caretakers changed quite frequently due to the fact that Melissa was working full-time after Lynn was six months old. She did not develop any trust with male caretakers. The other three children all experienced love and consistency from both Melissa and all four grandparents. Their interaction with Greg was positive, although somewhat limited.

Stage 2: Autonomy versus Shame and Doubt (Early Childhood)

In this stage, the child needs to establish that it's acceptable to be a separate person with some control over himself, without needing to control others.

Melissa's independence was strongly encouraged by her mother and grandmother, who ignored her temper tantrums, normal for this age. The birth of her brother, who had demanding medical problems, kept Mom preoccupied. Grandma continued to be the primary caregiver; she enjoyed and accepted Melissa's independence. However, when Dad became involved in her life in a controlling manner, Melissa reacted with anger and fear. Since he wasn't around very often, she established her autonomy quite well, with some shame and doubt from interactions with Dad.

Greg was still the darling in his family, as the only child and grandchild, and was given what he wanted. He appears to have had too much control over the family, not just over himself. He experienced no shame or doubt, nor sufficient self-control over his immediate needs. He learned to expect to receive whatever he wanted.

Lynn established very little autonomy. Even this early in her life, she was attempting to take care of her mommy and be exactly what Mommy wanted in order to avoid the possibility of abandonment. Instead of autonomy, she developed considerable self-doubt.

Tad went to the other extreme. As a strong-willed child who was very extroverted, he followed the history of his dad at this stage, dominating the entire family, usually in a delightful and charming manner, but sometimes through anger and threats.

Both Tim and Jenny were very successful at developing independence without controlling others. Tim was fairly quiet, loving mechanical toys. He demanded little that was unacceptable because of his introverted nature, and made almost no attempts to control others. Jenny was very social and verbal, eliciting love and enjoyment from everyone around her. Since attention and interaction were her major goals, she was rarely disappointed. Her beauty as a child also elicited positive interactions from strangers and acquaintances wherever she went.

Stage 3: Initiative versus Guilt (Preschool)

In this stage a child needs to be encouraged to initiate and choose his own activities, making as many of his own choices as possible. The basic task is to establish competence and initiative.

Both Greg and Melissa were encouraged to make many of their own choices. They both liked preschool and were well liked by their teachers due to their intelligence and creative leadership and initiative. Dad became less controlling of Melissa, and she became more relaxed about her autonomy and initiative with him. She developed friendships outside of the home. Her interactions with her brother were minimal, but positive. Her baby sister was born, and was allowed to be her "doll." Melissa loved to play with her, often dressing her, rocking and holding her. She was given choices in most areas of her life. She did not express much awareness or interest in childhood sensuality, or the attachment to her father which is normal for this age.

Greg received enthusiastic affirmation for new things he tried or accomplished. Parents, grandparents, and other extended family all thought he was the smartest and most athletic child ever. His awareness of sensuality was received in an accepting manner by both families. Greg's body awareness and flirting received positive attention, laughter, and playful teasing (perhaps too much attention). The birth of the first of his three siblings did not seem to affect him or take away his favored position in the extended family. Both Melissa and Greg experienced some difficulties during this stage, which will be presented later.

Lynn finally came into her own at this stage, although most of her initiative was directed toward her care of her mommy. But it was received very warmly. Her intelligence and interest in learning received very positive attention from all of Melissa's family. She showed no awareness of sensuality or attachment to any man.

Tim, Tad, and Jenny were all enjoyed as they were allowed to make most of their own choices. Tim showed the normal attachment to Mom and Jenny to Dad. Tad, however, seemed unwilling to let anyone but himself have much importance.

Stage 4: Industry versus Inferiority (School Age)

The main task of middle childhood is to produce things that are personally meaningful, gaining recognition and praise for accomplishments.

Both Greg and Melissa were very successful in school. Greg began having success in sports and Melissa in music, art, and dancing. They both clearly mastered this stage. However, for Melissa, her activities became an escape from the pain and depression following her grandmother's death. And for Greg, things became difficult at home with the birth of two more children. In this time period, Greg's mom began working later, and more was expected of Greg, with less appreciation and attention. Accomplishments outside of the home became the central focus for both Greg and Melissa.

This was Lynn's most successful stage. She did wonderfully in school due to her high intelligence and desire to please authority figures. She was usually the teacher's favorite. Tim was similarly industrious, in his quiet, unobtrusive manner. Sometimes he got lost in large groups in the classroom, resorting to projects of his own when he completed assigned work well before most of the other students. He didn't interact much with his teachers. Lynn and Melissa enjoyed him at home, both encouraging any projects he initiated.

Tad was very bright and capable of excellent work, but only performed well if he felt like it. In the younger grades he did quite well, but by fourth grade his rebelliousness was strong. His success occurred primarily in sports, where he was outstanding, praised by any coach who knew him. His occasional outbursts were tolerated better by coaches than by teachers. His coaches also had the power to prevent him from playing, and that really mattered to Tad. Nothing the teachers or the principal did had much effect. Tad didn't care if he got kicked out of school or sent to detention or even humiliated in front of the class.

Jenny was confusing to her teachers. She was delightful and cooperative, but she had a very difficult time *not* socializing, thus often not completing her work. Some teachers thought she was not as bright as the other children. She was clearly aware of this, but seemed happy with average grades. Melissa attempted several areas of lessons for Jenny, trying to find an area in which her daughter could excel, but Jenny didn't enjoy any of these activities.

Stage 5: Identity versus Identity Confusion (Adolescence)

The adolescent is trying to determine who he is apart from his parents, feeling very confused until he can come to a clear sense of self.

Melissa did not resolve this stage primarily because of her early dating, unplanned pregnancy, and disastrous marriage, all occurring by the time she was nineteen. She did not have the time as a teen to decide who she was apart from someone else's expectations of her. Her first husband was dominant, critical, and controlling. She began dating him when she was only fifteen, and from that time on he dictated her actions and even expressed her thoughts.

Greg did better at resolving this stage, but a lot of his behavior was unknown by his parents. He did develop his own personality, ideas, values, and interests, but he did it in secrecy to avoid conflict and his parents' criticism. As Greg grew older his parents expected that he would take more and more responsibility for the younger children, especially since his mother was working so much. The only ways to get out of this were academics and sports, so Greg spent increasing amounts of time away from home in these two activities. In both areas, he received recognition and acceptance.

Lynn's only identity was as a good student. She continued to be whatever Melissa wanted, except in the area of her appearance. This was her area of rebellion, a fairly obvious one since she did not look like Melissa, and other girls her age did not dress up either.

Tim is currently struggling with his identity. He knows he is intelligent and responsible, and more of an introvert than any of the other family members. But he does not have a place where he fits with his peers.

Tad is at the beginning of this stage and definitely needs some help before he self-destructs academically. Control over his temper and direction for his aggression will be essential.

Jenny has not entered this stage yet.

Stage 6: Intimacy versus Isolation (Young Adulthood)

The young adult is eager to form intimate relationships without his own sense of identity being threatened.

Melissa has not developed a confidence in her own identity. She also has a fear of intimacy stemming from the relationship with her father and her destructive first marriage. So she resorts to *achievement* or *industry*, the stage where she was so successful. This was also her previous method of escaping unpleasant abandonment feelings, which she now feels in her marriage to Greg. She's lonely, because her task at this stage is to develop intimacy. Having babies helped meet some of these needs, until the children began to gain some independence.

Greg developed his identity secretly, finding success outside the home and hiding some behavior from his parents. Now he continues that style with Melissa, receiving most of his value outside of his home. But he too is lonely and isolated. He also resorts to his successful achievement stage. Neither Greg nor Melissa knows how to achieve intimacy.

None of their children have arrived at this stage yet.

Stage 7: Generativity versus Self-Absorption or Stagnation (Middle Age)

Love, work, and play through parenting, career, family, and leisure are the tasks of this stage, which centers on guiding the next generation.

Both Greg and Melissa are excellent at work and good at parenting. However, they have never developed the intimacy of Stage 6, and their sense of loneliness increases. Melissa's solution is to work, to parent, and to have friends. Greg's answer is to work, to be involved in sports, and to have an affair. His parenting is primarily centered around sports, specifically involved with Tad. Greg and Melissa both moved into self-absorption, as they faced possible divorce.

Stage 8: Integrity versus Despair (Later Life)

The final stage should bring a sense of wholeness and completeness, with the feeling that a worthwhile, productive life has been lived.

Neither Melissa nor Greg have arrived at this stage yet. It still awaits them.

I often recommend to clients that they organize their lives according to age, and with events that are mostly positive on one side of the page and mostly negative experiences on the other side. Some people like to use Erikson's stages as segments of their time lines.

As you compile your personal history, you will find it amazing how some pieces fit together. "Oh, that's why I always do this!" Or, "Oh, that's why I thought that!" If there are memories of abuse that are beginning to surface, you may begin to see where these pieces fit in. You may have some gaps in your story, where you blocked out memories. And you may see some sudden changes that occurred in your own personality or relationships or activities.

Don't jump to conclusions! Now, with your personal history marked out, you have a framework for your memories, if new ones emerge. You can proceed to research the accuracy of your memories now that you have a better idea of who you are, and who you have been.

11

How Can I Check Out the Accuracy of My Memories?

When Melissa had the dreams of her father molesting her, she assumed this was a factual event. She also had the recovered memory of Dad yelling at her, saying, "No man can ever live with someone like you. Who do you think you are to demand your own way?" She also remembered him throwing the book he was reading, breaking a vase.

She immediately became anxious, angry, and preoccupied with these memories. It affected her moods as well as her efficiency at work and home. She wanted to cut off all contact with her dad, and never allow him to see the grandchildren again. She planned to contact her brother and sister, so they would also protect their children. She was angry at God, and felt the whole world was unsafe. These were obviously significant memories that needed to be either validated or dismissed.

Melissa also had a recovered memory of a neighbor man molesting her, along with his threat to hurt her and her family if she told anyone. She again reacted strongly, with fear and shame. Sexuality, which had been difficult before, became nonexistent after this memory was recovered. Melissa wanted no man even to touch her.

The first step in investigating recovered memories is to determine which memories are *significant*—that is, significant enough to dig into.

In therapy, Melissa related many memories that had not been repressed, and these did not fall into the "significant" category. These included positive, neutral, and negative memories of school, home, pets, her brother and sister, parents, grandparents, playmates. It included her kindergarten teacher, who had been angry and controlling. But Melissa had felt less fearful about her after telling Grandma all about it, and Grandma removed Melissa from that classroom. Melissa was believed, reassured it was not her fault, and action was taken to eliminate any repetition of this mild form of abuse. She had investigated her feelings about this teacher in previous therapy.

These "insignificant" memories do not continue to affect Melissa in her current choices and feelings. But significant memories do affect us deeply, in the following ways:

1. They change our self-concept.
2. They modify our view or trust of another person and/or God.
3. They alter our perceptions of our world.
4. They elicit strong emotional reactions.
5. They interfere with our ability to cope and function.

Throughout this chapter, we will review significant memories recovered by Melissa, Greg, and their daughter Lynn. We will also look at the story of Marilyn Murray. We will follow their search for truth and their attempts to validate or disprove these memories.

List Facts and Feelings That Support or Disprove a Memory

Many therapists believe the memories of their clients because the clients come in with symptoms that so obviously match the specific memories. I see this regularly in my work with children. As they play, abused children will often repeat the actions of the physical trauma they went through.

Dr. Lenore Terr describes this in her book *Too Scared to Cry*. She focused on twenty children for whom she had documented evidence of trauma.

Examining their repetitive play, she noticed that their actions often matched the trauma they had experienced, even when the child had no conscious awareness of the trauma. The body memory was being played out, even when the conscious memory had blocked it.

In many cases, parents notice the unusual content of their children's repetitive play and its obsessive nature. It's often morbid or frightening or startling in some manner. They may not know what it is or where it comes from, but often they'll remember it.

"Post-traumatic play is so literal that if you spot it, you may be able to guess the trauma with few other clues," writes Dr. Terr. "In other words, by hearing about the play and by knowing little else about the child, you can postulate a certain traumatic event."[1]

As you piece together your memories, consider whether you exhibited any odd playing behavior. You might ask your parents or siblings or childhood friends if they remember any unusual repetitive actions on your part. Think back also to any unusual fears, habits, or dreams you had as a child. Other symptoms of trauma include nightmares, a change in personality, and a sense of doom or futility for the future.

If you were traumatized as an older child or an adult, you could expect to have nightmares or flashbacks, or emotional reactions in which you fear that the trauma is reoccurring. When the trauma has been repressed, you may be able to verbally describe the trauma you "see" happening, even though you may have no conscious memory of it happening to you.

Melissa was prayerfully seeking the truth of each memory. As she considered the scene of her father's angry outburst—throwing the book, breaking the vase—several things came to mind. That scene started with Melissa needing something and asking for it. Instead of attending to her need, her father got angry. As Melissa thought through her years of childhood and adulthood, she realized that she felt anxiety whenever she needed anything from a man, but felt comfortable when she needed something from a woman.

Prior to marriage counseling, she had often said that she needed nothing from her husband. She did not know why she was depressed around him. She had learned to suppress even her own awareness of anything she might desire from a man. If Greg was mildly irritated, she became frightened that he would start breaking things. Despite the fact that he had never raised his voice or thrown anything, she remained fearful. What she liked the most about Greg was his even disposition, and the fact that whenever he felt angry he left until the emotion subsided.

So does that prove that her memory of her father's outburst is factual? Not so fast.

Melissa also remembered her father as being controlled and proper. This outburst would be quite out of character. Neither of her parents tended to show anger. None of her children felt any fear of their granddad. They had never seen him express anger—except with tightened lips as he walked away. As Melissa considered this side of the evidence, she concluded . . . that nothing was conclusive.

What about her memory of being molested by her father? She knew she did not like him to touch her, not that he ever did it much anyway. She often felt shame when she was around him. She struggled with sexuality in her marriage, often feeling anxious when Greg approached her. But, on the other side, she never saw Dad look at her or at anyone else with any sexual desire or interest. He seemed to ignore her most of the time. He was so controlled and proper and good that it didn't seem to fit with his personality. On one occasion, Mom had described their sexual relationship as regular, planned, scheduled, and pleasant, with her desiring more frequency than he did.

Evaluating this memory, Melissa seemed to find more evidence against the sexual abuse by her father, but this was also inconclusive.

The third memory she investigated was of being molested by the neighbor. On a conscious level, she had no memory of him, although he had lived next door for eleven years. She also had no memory of his house from her younger years. She only remembered the house from the time when she was older, when he was no longer living there. This could suggest that she had blocked some incident, she figured, but the specifics were uncertain.

Melissa had no memory of her play as a child, except when she was with Grandma. She recalled lots of pleasant, normal play activities then, such as coloring, Play-Doh, dolls, hopscotch, reading, and learning interesting skills and information. She remembered age five and age seven as being very difficult years. She assumed the fear at age five was related to her mean teacher, although she did not remain in her class very long, only a few weeks. Age seven was Grandma's death, a very painful time for Melissa.

Lynn had several recovered memories under hypnosis. They involved sexual abuse from her biological father when she was three and four. She had complete confidence in the accuracy of the memories, and wished to find him to confront him. Her parents did not know why she had decided to contact her father. Since she was unwilling to discuss it with them, they felt she needed someone else to help her evaluate her plan and prepare for any reactions following the contact. They urged her to come into our clinic before contacting him. Although Lynn felt it was unnecessary, she acceded to their wishes, and decided we might be able to help her with the confrontation.

Lynn was encouraged to list anything that supported or disproved her memory. She resisted at first. After the therapist stressed the importance of being open to all the options, Lynn managed to come up with a few ideas supporting the molest by her father. These included her lack of dating, anger at men, dislike of touching from men, and general negativity toward all boys and men. She didn't remember much play, except repeated play with her dolls, making sure they were never left alone. She recalled that, in preschool, if she was planning to be gone from "her babies," she left a big teddy bear in charge of them. She fantasized that the bear held her dolls and comforted them and rocked them to sleep when they cried. She recalled no personality change in herself.

As for Greg, his memory was just a flash in his mind. He saw a momentary scene of being beaten by his parents. He had no other details. Through visualization, Greg again pictured this scene as it flashed before him. He prayed for truth, and the picture began to change.

He hears loud voices, his parents fighting. It appears that they've been drinking. They begin hitting each other, and Greg runs into the room, trying to stop it. Mom pushes him away, screaming, "Stay away or you'll get hurt!" Greg lands against the wall, falls to the floor, curls up, covers his head, and feels as if he's getting hit. He hears the door slam. It's quiet. Then Mom comes over and picks him up. She's crying as she carries him up to his bed. He is about four years old.

As Greg tried to evaluate this memory, it was very confusing. He had no memory of either parent becoming physically violent with anyone. He knew they drank too much occasionally, getting loud and argumentative. He was very aware of how much fear he had of anyone's anger or drinking, and of his instinct either to run out of the room, or at least to cover up his head.

His play was typical for boys. Mostly he and his friends played war, sometimes with little figures; sometimes he and his friends were the soldiers. He made lots of caves and places to hide from the enemy—for himself and for the toy soldiers. There were usually several countries at war. He liked to play the role of the negotiator or the neutral country that tried to make peace between the nations and stay out of the cross fire.

Greg remembers two personality changes. One occurred sometime before first grade, when he recalled feeling withdrawn, sad, and fearful. The other change occurred in early adolescence with a major shift into secrecy and sneakiness.

As Greg evaluates all of the information, he remains uncertain about his memories.

Look for Physical Evidence

If the memory involves anything that could have left scars or marks, have these medically evaluated. If the supposed abuse occurred at an age when you were writing or drawing pictures, look for diaries, pictures, or stories. Examine photographs of yourself at the appropriate age for the memory, comparing other photos from different ages. Take special note of anything shortly before or after the trauma in question. Check out report cards before, during, and after the targeted time. Note any variations in school achievement, behavior, absences, and teacher's comments. Teachers' evaluations are often quite valuable. They take into account age-appropriate behaviors and attitudes, and are able to point out areas that are out of the norm, since they have the advantage of seeing so many children of the same age.

For Melissa, there were no scars or physical markings involved. But photographs from age five and age seven (her troubled years) were striking. At age five, Melissa looked frightened in some pictures, and angry in others, not what you would expect for that age. Melissa's second grade pictures again looked angry and sad. By late second grade, she looked numb, her eyes looked dead. School reports were glowing for preschool, then very negative in kindergarten. Even after Melissa changed classes, the kindergarten reports were of a withdrawn, quiet, nonparticipating child. First-grade reports described her as more optimistic, outgoing, and achieving. Second-grade reports reverted to the withdrawn, quiet child, who now seemed to resent any control. Depression and sadness seemed to increase as the year progressed.

What a change was reported by third grade! Now Melissa had excellent grades, was highly motivated and successful, but not very social. She did not like recess, preferred to stay inside and work on projects. Throughout the rest of grade school, her report cards were outstanding, and she was consistently described as extremely bright, responsible, cooperative, and a pleasure to have in class. By fourth grade, she seemed to have many girlfriends, and was quite popular.

There were many pictures of Lynn, especially at her grandparents' house. Lynn was most interested in the pictures prior to age six. In most of these she was playing with either Grandma or Grandpa. She looked quiet and peaceful, but never free, spontaneous, laughing, or happy. Melissa also had pictures of Lynn. In many of these pictures, she was alone, looking sad and forlorn. There was no medical evidence of abuse. Lynn's report cards, beginning with preschool, were very consistent: She is very bright, learns easily, completes tasks assigned, is overly helpful and very anxious to please, and seeks the teacher's attention (by offering to help, giving her a picture or special treat, or bringing a little gift, like a wildflower). She had one male teacher (in fifth grade), who described her as very withdrawn and impossible to reach, despite his many attempts.

Greg found many pictures of himself with both sets of grandparents, his parents, and with other relatives. He was often pictured laughing, showing off, very happy. There were also pictures, beginning at age five, where a change was noticed. He looked serious, and the sparkle in his eyes was missing, but there were no dramatic, discernible changes. His reports from school were consistently of a bright, responsible, hard worker, with excellent coordination and skills in sports. He was described as pleasant and very popular with his classmates, but not very communicative with any of the adults. He had a good sense of humor, teachers said, but he never got into any trouble.

Evaluate Your Experience as the Memory Was Recovered

Melissa was in therapy when the memory of the neighbor's molest occurred. She felt young and small. It was as if she was there, living through it for the first time. *She sees the neighbor, his house, and herself in vivid detail. She hears his words, his breathing, and her heart pounding. She smells the mustiness of the house, and cigarettes and alcohol on his breath, odors she has always detested. She feels his touch and feels her skin crawl. She hears the screams inside of her and hears his threats, and feels the fear they elicit. She experiences herself leaving his house. She feels a numbness as she sits on her steps at home for a long time. Then she starts crying and runs up to her room. When Mom comes in, Melissa holds her breath, terrified she will tell what had happened. In fear, she yells at her mom to leave.* All of this felt very real to her.

The second event, her dad's anger, was equally vivid to all of her senses, until the vase broke. Then she saw herself leave her body, and watch the rest from a distance (dissociation). Now it was happening to another little girl, not to Melissa. When she experienced what was happening to the other little girl, the face of the man changed. It looked like the man next door, then changed back to Daddy. She felt the terror and the confusion. The memory continued with a faceless man at times, and other times the face alternated between Dad's and the neighbor's. There was a sense of unreality and detachment from this memory, once the vase broke.

Understanding that dreams are rarely interpreted as factual, Melissa prayed for the truth about her dad's possible molest. During her intensive therapy, the memory of that night flooded back. *Seven-year-old Melissa is having a nightmare about being trapped. Then Daddy comes into the room, and she's terrified that he will hurt her. But the face keeps changing between Daddy and another man, who looks like her recovered memory of the man next door. She sees and hears her screams as she watches from a distance. Then Daddy leaves and Mommy comes in. Mommy holds her and comforts her, as Melissa clings to her. She feels so confused.*

Melissa considered the method by which the memories returned. None of the memories had occurred as a result of hypnosis or drugs. She was fully aware of what was occurring as they emerged. She did not feel there was any external influence to produce any memories. There were no leading questions, and she was genuinely surprised about where the memories led. She could not think of any internal reasons for the memories either, other than the possible need to explain her sexual problems in the marriage. She had been praying for the truth.

It did occur to her that the dream of the molest by Dad could be indicative of her fears of him and of all men. She did not see him molest her, but it seemed like he was going to do that. As a child, she had no close relationships with any men. Dad and the neighbor were both controlling and demanding. They both had those scary eyes, and when they got angry, they seemed to merge into one.

For Lynn, the memory of the hypnosis was quite clear. She remembered picturing her biological dad in the bedroom with her. She saw what they both were wearing. She recalled seeing her father just as he looked in a photograph before she was born. She was dressed as she had been in a picture at age four. She could see details of their house. She pictured her father sexually touching her, and then walking away. *Three-year-old Lynn is running after him, pleading with him to stay and be her daddy. She says she'll do anything he wants, "just don't leave me." Then Dad is touching her, and has her touch him. She willingly does whatever he wants, with no resistance. Then Dad leaves. Four-year-old Lynn is sitting there all by herself.* Lynn had heard that hypnosis does not necessarily produce accurate memories, but she doubted that her memories were false in any way. It did seem so real. She has no conscious memories of her father, so she assumes that something traumatic must have happened in order for her to block it all out.

As Greg evaluated his memory, he found it difficult to believe, although it felt very real. He did not view himself as very susceptible, nor did he feel that he had been influenced by others. He did not know what to think. When the flashback occurred, he was not looking for any memories. Later, as the memory emerged, he felt as if he was there. His body hurt as he hit the wall. During therapy, he curled up on the floor and covered his head, feeling very young and terrified. He felt overwhelming fear and sadness as he pictured his mommy carrying him to his bedroom.

Go Back to the Scene of the Memory

Research on memory demonstrates that our clearest and most accurate retrieval occurs at the place where the event transpired, under conditions that are as similar as possible to those of the original event. Sights, sounds, smells, tastes, and touches may all elicit blocked memories. The more of these that occur together, the greater is the likelihood of recall.

Has this ever happened to you? You start to go into another room to do something, but you can't remember what you were going to do. What do you do to remember? You go back to where you started. When you return to the place where the thought originated, the thought often returns to your mind.

Melissa went back to the neighborhood where she grew up. When she saw the neighbor's house, she could feel the panic and the tears and hear the screams inside her head. The woman outside allowed her to come in when Melissa explained that she used to live next door. Although the house looked somewhat different inside, the layout was as she had remembered it, except that everything seemed so much smaller. (When we are young and little, everything is much bigger in comparison to our size.) Her feelings were a powerful barometer of the events that had taken place there so many years ago. The details seemed very clear as she stood quietly in the room where it had all transpired. It was difficult for Melissa to even move; she felt trapped and frozen in fear.

Melissa also went next door, to her old home. Floods of memories of all kinds washed over her, but none with the terror of the neighbor's house. She mostly had a feeling of self-control and quietness. She had the full range of feelings, from laughter and delight to sadness, pain, anger, fear, and contentment. The most frightening place was where the book had been hurled, and the vase had broken. The saddest area was the window seat where she and Grandma sat and read, and where she sat missing Grandma after her death.

Lynn, with Melissa's help, found the apartment where they lived during her preschool years. With considerable difficulties, they finally managed to go inside, at a time it was vacant, accompanied by the owner/manager. Lynn had few feelings about this place. She had little awareness she had ever lived here. The visit was uneventful and disappointing.

Greg's relatives had bought the house where his family lived when he was four. It was easy to visit them without any explanation. But he pictured this event occurring in his parents' bedroom. He visited a couple of times, but found no convenient way of entering the bedroom. He felt uncomfortable giving his relatives any explanation. But a few months later, some unexpected circumstances put him in that bedroom, all by himself. He felt terror. He felt very young. And he felt driven to hide in the corner and cover his head, although he resisted the impulse.

Melissa was with him on that trip. She observed that when he came out of the room, he was white and shaking. He was shocked at his reaction, and didn't know quite how to understand it all.

Ask Anyone Who Might Have Knowledge Related to the Memory

Melissa thought that she was around five when the incident with the neighbor occurred, and in grade school when both incidents with Dad would have happened, probably second or third grade.

She talked with her brother and her sister, two and five years younger. Obviously, neither remembered her when she was five. Her brother said she was very upset when she was in second grade and he was in kindergarten. He recalled that she would not walk by the house next door, but ran as quickly as she could. She had explained that a bad man lived there, though she never said what made him bad.

Melissa's brother also reminded her of her fear of her father, which he always thought was so silly. Dad played with him frequently, and they had a great time.

He mostly talked about how upset both Melissa and Mom were the year Grandma died, and how lonely and depressing it was at home for a long time after that.

Melissa's sister did not remember much from that time, except for Melissa's very stern and threatening admonition that she was never to go near the neighbor's house.

Melissa had a best friend all through school—Anne, who lived across the street. Melissa contacted Anne, who knew most everything about Melissa's life. They talked for many hours about all their memories. Relevant ones for this discussion included both Melissa's dad and the man next door. Anne remembered strong fear and anger that Melissa had for both men. The feelings seemed quite similar, although she knew that Melissa always avoided the house next door. She assumed it was because he was a child molester. Anne said that her own mother wouldn't let her go near that house either.

Melissa was stunned. She could not recall her parents telling her that the neighbor was a molester. Anne said that she and Melissa had never discussed it; she just assumed that was why Melissa was so afraid of him. She did not know any specifics about Melissa's dad, except they never asked him for anything. If they couldn't get what they wanted from Anne's parents or Melissa's mom, Melissa gave up. She adamantly refused to ask her dad for rides, money, the car, or even permission to do something. Anne was unable to recall anything positive that Melissa ever said about her dad. Melissa frequently said how mean he was, and that she hated him.

Anne also talked about the games they played as children. She commented on a game that Melissa created and wanted to play again and again. She called it "Escape." It involved one of the kids in the neighborhood wearing a frightening mask. The mask was from Halloween, a very ugly, scary-looking man. All the other kids got as close as possible to the masked man and then ran away. If the monster caught you, he could hold you down, and you could try to get away. If you couldn't escape, you were out and sat on the porch until a new monster was it. Melissa rarely seemed to get away, screaming loudly every time she got caught. As a result, everyone thought it was fun to catch her. Melissa had forgotten about this game, but remembered it as Anne described it.

Anne did not remember much about Melissa at age five. She did recall Melissa's major change in second grade. Suddenly, Melissa wanted to be alone, rarely coming outside to play. Anne was very lonely, feeling she'd lost her best friend. Anne's mother finally talked to Melissa's mother, who started forcing Melissa to go out and play again.

Next Melissa mustered up the courage to contact Mom. She did it in the context of an autobiography she was writing, which is how she referred to her journaling. Mom was helpful. She knew that the man next door was a child molester, though she admitted that she had never told Melissa. She assumed it was sufficient to tell her never to go over there. When Melissa told Mom about the molest, Mom immediately believed her, and was supportive, loving, concerned, and apologetic. Over the next few days, Mom searched her mind for other details, recalling Melissa's difficult kindergarten year. Mom pictured a time Melissa came in from playing outside and was crying with deep sobs, but would not say why. Melissa had gone directly to her bedroom, but when Mom followed her into the room, Melissa screamed at her to get out, so she did.

Mom also described Melissa's screaming and crying if Dad tried to pick her up. She thought it might have started after the crying incident, but she also knew that Melissa was never close to Dad, as the other children were. Mom didn't understand why, but asked permission to discuss this issue with Dad.

"Did you ever notice anything unusual in the way I played or acted?" Melissa asked her mother. Mom immediately reminded her of how mean she was to her dolls. She often said they were bad, doing things like tying scarves across their mouths so they "wouldn't say bad things" or do bad things.

"When I asked you what kind of bad things they had done, you told me that they didn't obey Mommy and Daddy. You also left those dolls around without any clothes on. Even when I would put the clothes back on, the next time I'd see them, they'd be naked again." As her mother described this, Melissa began to recall her feelings of anger at her dolls for being bad by disobeying, and fear of their saying bad things.

The personality changes at both ages five and seven were very apparent and troublesome to Mom. Grandma had thought that she had taken care of the problem at age five by removing Melissa from the mean teacher's classroom, but Mom said she always felt there was something more to it. She assumed something horrible had happened with the teacher, but Melissa had denied it when Mom questioned her. Grandma had said Mom was being foolish, and shouldn't worry so much.

Mom also expressed deep regret over her unavailability when Grandma died. She knew Melissa was devastated; she was too, and had nothing to give her.

A few days later, Mom called and said that Dad had some interesting information. Would Melissa be willing to come over and talk with them? With curiosity and apprehension, Melissa arrived the next evening. She was prepared to just listen and try to avoid hostility toward Dad. He began by talking about his recollections of Melissa at age five. With his usual incredible memory for details, he described the day in question. He remembered that she was extremely upset and that she began to have nightmares that night. He came in to comfort her, and she pushed him away, looking terrified. He heard her say, "I didn't tell. Don't hurt me." As he tried to comfort her and awaken her from the nightmare, Melissa became more frightened, to the point of panic. He called her mom, who was able to comfort Melissa. But he perceived that she was never the same after that day. Although they had never been close, she seemed frightened of him after that night. Her nightmares continued nightly for a while; sometimes she would sleepwalk, as if she were trying to run away from someone. He said it was really frightening to observe. He knew something was wrong, but Grandma said it was just the teacher at school and she would handle it.

Then Dad said there was something that had always bothered him, and he needed to apologize. He described the incident in which Melissa asked him for help. He couldn't remember the details of her request, but he knew he was very frustrated with his studying, and that he yelled and threw his book that broke the vase. He said he knew he was wrong, and had always felt bad about it. He could still see Melissa's face of terror. That night she had another of her nightmares, and he went in to try to comfort her, desperately wanting to fix what had happened. She screamed in terror, the same words as at age five. He never dared approach her again after that day and night. She told him the words she remembered. He verified that he had said those words, but certainly didn't mean them. Melissa almost laughed with relief—at least she wasn't crazy and hadn't just imagined all of these stories.

It wasn't until weeks later that she asked him about her dream of his molest. He was visibly shocked, denying any such actions or even thoughts. But he did remember going in to comfort her that night, feeling so remorseful and concerned about his angry outburst earlier that day. He remembered her look of terror as she saw him, and he felt that his anger had done that to her. He also recalled the personality changes, especially at age seven, because he blamed himself. Grandma's death only intensified the withdrawal that had already started with his outburst of anger. Melissa believed his innocence about the molest. She did know her dad to be a very honest, forthright person, who had always admitted blame readily. Even when she was afraid of him as a child, she always believed what he said, which is why his harsh words had such power. Melissa also talked with her mom about the question of Dad's molest. Mom remembered the nightmare at age seven, because of the intense terror Melissa demonstrated. Mom recalled running into Melissa's bedroom just seconds after Dad, because the screams were so terrifying. Mom assured her that Dad had no time to molest her even if he had been capable of that kind of behavior, which Mom could not even conceive.

Lynn talked with her mom about the memory of her father's molest. Melissa knew that Lynn was dealing with some memories, but was shocked that this was the memory Lynn had. She informed Lynn that Lynn had had no contact with her father after she was three months old. So it obviously could never have happened, at least as she pictured it. Both Lynn and Melissa sat in stunned silence.

Greg struggled with the possibility of talking with his parents. Although the family was very expressive in most ways, Greg had not been very open or communicative since late grade school. He was encouraged to begin by approaching the past in general terms. He requested that Melissa go with him. She agreed.

Greg's dad wasn't interested in these discussions. A few minutes after the discussion began, he retreated outside. Yet Greg's mother was very open. She loved talking about those wonderful years with her delightful firstborn. They asked her for any information that might help Greg understand himself better, especially his withdrawal and extreme fear of anger. She knew of the marriage problems Greg and Melissa were experiencing, and wanted to help in any way she could.

She continued talking with them over the next few weeks, recalling that Greg had been afraid of anger since starting kindergarten, while all the other family members seemed to feel comfortable hearing and expressing anger, which she described as fairly frequent (several times a day) but of short duration. She did remember that Greg rarely got angry and that he was "overly sensitive" to the normal arguments of their family. Greg finally asked her about the specific incident at age four. She had no memory of it, but agreed to ask her husband about it as well. He also had no memory of it. Both acknowledged that the verbal fighting between them was frequent when they drank. As a result, they both had quit drinking. Neither could imagine beating Greg, but they could imagine yelling at him and pushing him out of the way.

Give the Memories Time and Prayer

Now Melissa felt that she had gathered the evidence she needed. She let it settle, as she continued to pray for the truth. She felt absolutely confident of the incident of her dad's yelling, throwing the book, and verbal attack. He had verified that.

She also came to believe that probably the neighbor had molested her in pretty much the manner in which the memory unfolded. Although she did not have validation for the details at the neighbor's house, both parents had given her enough information about her reactions at home to create a high level of certainty. She was also given information from Anne's mother that enabled her to find the neighbor's court records where he pled guilty to an earlier child molestation. His previous conviction involved events that were similar to the ones Melissa remembered. All of her behaviors, along with the reports of Anne, Mom, Dad, and her brother, seemed to fit together.

For the third memory, she came to believe that her father had not molested her, but that her traumatized mind had merged the neighbor and her father into one. His angry eyes must have looked like the molester's eyes, and she must have feared that he might do similar things. Whenever Dad was angry and controlling, he reminded her of the man next door, who did trap and hurt her. She realized the helplessness and the shame she felt with both men, even though their behavior had been different in many ways.

How tragic it would have been if Melissa had continued to believe a lie! She would have brought extreme pain and loss to her parents, to herself and her family, and to her brother and sister and their families. To a lesser degree, the ripple effect would have included those people close to anyone in Melissa's extended family.

Lynn accepted that her memory of abuse by her biological father was simply not true. She wondered whether it might have been someone else who molested her, but eventually decided that was not the case. She concluded that this memory had been influenced by the group, due to her suggestibility and her need to belong. This memory had also been less painful than the truth, that her father had chosen to have no contact with her. It was a way to express her anger at his abandonment and her wish for any kind of contact with him, even negative touches.

Greg concluded that he would probably never know the truth of what happened. But he did know that his parents' anger terrified him as a child. He believed that the incident was likely, except for the beating, which seemed to be emotional and not physical. This memory did provide the framework in which he could experience and release his fear, hurt, and anger toward both of his parents for their drinking, yelling, and fighting.

Marilyn's Search for Truth

The person whom I know personally who has done the most extensive search for the truth is Marilyn Murray, who tells her story of repressed childhood trauma in her book, *Prisoner of Another War.* Marilyn is a nationally known speaker on child abuse and a therapist at the McDonald Therapy Center. But prior to 1980, the possibility of sexual abuse never crossed her mind. She was raised in the Bible-belt of Kansas, and described her life as "the perfect childhood." Her only problems were physical. Severe asthma, allergies, leg pain, and frequent nightmares began when she was eight.

In 1980, Marilyn was a very successful, highly functioning business woman who owned an art gallery in Scottsdale, Arizona. She also was the cofounder of an organization of support groups for Christian women that quickly grew to over 350 active participants. But Marilyn had severe headaches, and even the huge amounts of medication she took daily gave her very little relief. She also had many other physical problems including leg aches, TMJ, and back and chest pain. After consulting many doctors, all of whom said they could not help her, she reached the point of desiring death to escape this torturous sentence of continual pain.

A friend, who knew of Marilyn's depression and suicidal thoughts, insisted that Marilyn seek therapy. The friend gave her no choice; she put Marilyn on the plane and sent her to California to a psychological counseling center. It was not long before Marilyn's "volcano" erupted. The memory of abuse by a group of soldiers erupted into her consciousness, as she describes so vividly in her book:

> The torment continued for several hours as my body released its horrifying secret. . . . Eight years old with my nose in a book, I had missed my bus stop . . . Getting off in a strange part of town, I walked . . . massive arms grabbed me suddenly and violently . . . lots of soldiers, laughed and jeered . . . I was thrown, tossed, dropped, . . . kicked . . . blur of lights . . . brutal hands . . . peeled away my clothes . . . violently yanked my head

> backwards . . . forced my mouth open. . . . next attacker . . . one last burst of energy, a final effort at survival, I fought back and was knocked unconscious . . .[2]

Later, when she regained consciousness, "frantically I searched for my shoes." The eight-year-old made it home, telling no one, because she was bad and didn't want to make her mommy cry or her daddy mad. The asthma and the nightmares started that night.

Marilyn continued in therapy, with more details of the repressed memories and the many intense repressed feelings eventually released over a seven-month period. She did not accept the truth of any of this readily, and became like a detective, trying to prove that none of this could have happened. She had never heard of repressed trauma, and it all seemed too unbelievable. Her search for the truth will be organized according to the process described in this chapter and previous chapters, rather than the time sequence in which it occurred.

Evaluate if there was an external influence to believe the memories. For Marilyn there was never any external influence. She had read nothing, seen nothing on television, knew no one who had been abused, and was not very suggestible. It was 1980, prior to all of the attention on child abuse. Marilyn lived in a world where no one talked about topics like that, even if something had happened. Her therapist was psychoanalytically trained to be a listener, never giving the slightest hint or leading. She had never been in any group where sexual abuse was even mentioned.

Evaluate if there are any internal reasons to create a false memory. Marilyn did not want to go to therapy. She was forced there by a friend who believed Marilyn would not live unless something drastic was done. She seemed to have many needs met in her life, with numerous people who were loving, giving, affirming, and helpful. Financial success gave her many of her material desires. An exciting job brought travel, friendships with successful artists, respect, and fun. The memories did enable her to express feelings, but the violence and terror are way beyond what a person would unconsciously select to release everyday anger and hurt. She certainly wasn't trying to please others. In fact, many of her friends and family were very critical of her staying in California instead of being at home where she belonged. Some of the minor details could be confusing imagination or fear with facts, but not the central features of this memory. There were no developmental factors that were relevant.

Consider the impact of the specific method used to recover the memories. No method was used when Marilyn's "volcano" erupted. She was by herself and was not in any therapy session. Nor had it been suggested to her that this might happen. She was stunned and terrified.

List facts and feelings that support or disprove a memory. One of Marilyn's most unusual obsessions was her "unquenchable need for shoes . . . owning no less than one hundred pairs, to compensate for the panic of needing to find my shoes before I could go home. . . ."[3]

Her only paranoia was of being smothered, or of anything that had the capability of smothering. This is certainly the experience of many children who are orally raped. They cannot breathe and fear they might die.

Marilyn has always had an excellent clear detailed memory of her childhood, except age eight, of which she had almost no memories.

Light hurt her eyes and made her feel fearful. In her memory, the soldiers had a cigarette lighter and threatened to burn out her eyes.

As an adult, Marilyn found herself seeking out people who would protect her, becoming very upset if they were unavailable. This did not fit with her picture of herself as a strong, competent businesswoman. It seemed so childish. And it probably was the eight-year-old child who desperately needed protection.

Look for physical evidence. Asthma for Marilyn started at age eight, and occurred only in cold climates. Asthma is viewed by many doctors as often psychologically caused. It could be her body's repetition of the oral rape, with the coughing, choking, and inability to breathe. In her memory, the rape and asthma felt the same. It has never reoccurred in the fourteen years since her therapy.

Since age eight, Marilyn was often sick in cold weather and was very allergic. If cold weather triggers any memories, even though not at the conscious level, the adrenaline is secreted until depleted, leaving one very susceptible to other illnesses and allergies. Since therapy, neither her susceptibility to illness nor her allergies have returned.

Marilyn had weakness, pain, and numbness in her legs since eight. The soldiers had held her down on the frozen ground. After therapy she began walking and could soon walk three to five miles daily. She also began ballroom dancing and became successful competitively. There has been no more numbness, pain, or weakness in her legs.

Her headaches seemed to be related to the oral rape when the soldiers had held her by the hair and hit her head on the ground. In seeking treatment for headaches as an adult, an X ray revealed a concussion and a misplaced bone in the back of her skull. The doctor said this would have been caused by a severe blow. She was never in an accident and had no memory of head injury until she recalled the soldiers hitting her head on the ground, knocking her unconscious. The headaches stopped after her therapy and have not returned.

She also had severe TMJ and severe chest pains—symptoms that are not unusual for people who have always been conscious of an oral rape. In these cases they are often associated either with the need to tightly hold one's mouth closed to keep everything out, or with the pain of the oral rape itself. The chest pain could have resulted from someone pushing on her and sitting on her chest to hold her down. Both stopped after therapy.

One thing Marilyn did wonder about: Wouldn't her mother have seen bruises? But as she thought about it, she realized that oral rape leaves no marks. Most of the time she was held down by several grown men, so certainly couldn't move around much. If she did have any bruises they might not have been noticed. She was eight, so she bathed and dressed herself, wearing long sleeves and long pants in the cold winter of Kansas. It is likely that enormous emotional and physical shock occurred, and she unconsciously "decided" to keep it a secret to avoid hurting her mom and irritating her dad.

Photographs existed and said a million words. The life had gone out of the eyes of that eight-year-old little girl in Wichita, Kansas. She didn't look the same as the younger pictures, with the smiling bright eyes and the open mouth smile. Marilyn felt fear and foreboding when she saw the photo of this eight-year-old at the beginning of her therapy, before any of the memory had surfaced. It certainly seemed that something had happened to this little one.

Evaluate your experience as the memory was recovered. The eruption of the memory came so unexpectedly, with the full force of the feelings, both emotional and physical. It felt like it was really happening right then. Each time an additional piece of the memory surfaced, all previous parts stayed consistently the same. Her body moved and made sounds outside of her control; she did not understand what could be happening. For example, Marilyn reports that the first time she saw a client in a regression session who had always had conscious memory of her oral rape, but who had blocked all feelings, the client's head went back and the noises and reactions were the same as Marilyn had experienced. In true regression, the adult steps aside, and does not know what is coming next. In Marilyn's therapy, she experienced the splitting, choosing to stay as the eight-year-old, although the adult could be there at will. She found she wrote and ate and thought and behaved as an eight-year-old. Her body even began to act as an eight-year-old, losing body hair and speaking in a young voice that was slow and stammering.

Go back to the scene of the memory. Marilyn carefully and anxiously planned to revisit Wichita, Kansas, doing so three years after her therapy. She obtained a map of the city in 1944, the year she was eight. She located and talked to an old bus driver who remembered the bus routes driven during this time. She located the "bad house" where she had lived at this age. She found the church where the choir practice occurred, taking each possible bus route home, but could find nothing. Missing a turn,

> suddenly, my breath caught in my throat. An invisible fist slugged my stomach. Immediately in front of me, I could see the skyscrapers of downtown Wichita, looming as large as I had seen them once before—when I put down my book after reading on the bus. I had missed my stop—the tall buildings were supposed to be far in the distance. The memory of the sight burst over me. The attack happened on the way to choir practice, not on my way home! . . . my eyes were seared by hot tears . . . a scream from deep within . . . hysterical . . . keep my trembling body from disintegrating . . .[4]

She could see the area where it occurred. There had been an abrupt change from the White, middle-class area of her residence to a poor, Black area. She later checked, and found this area had always been segregated. In her therapy she saw her attackers as Black soldiers, but previously couldn't understand what a group of Black soldiers would be doing in a White community, and why someone wouldn't have seen them and been suspicious. But they, and little Marilyn, were in the Black community. Another puzzle piece fit.

Ask anyone who might have knowledge related to the memory. Marilyn talked to a doctor who knew her as a child. He recalled that she had very poor self-esteem. Another friend, who lived next door to their next home after Wichita, reported that Marilyn often looked so sad. But the most confirming report came from Marilyn's mother. She listened to a tape of one of Marilyn's therapy sessions, and was shocked to hear the same screams she had heard so often in Marilyn's nightmares that had started at age eight. Mom also said that the content of the nightmares, as Marilyn had told her at age eight, was that Marilyn was drowning in white glue, unable to get away, with sticky stuff on her face. The time of the beginning of the nightmares and asthma was easy for Mom to confirm. She remembered they had begun when Marilyn was eight, because they had occurred in a house where the family had lived for only six months.

A woman who had heard Marilyn speak called her, having read a letter in an advice column in a newspaper. It was from a soldier in World War II stationed in the Midwest. He said he participated in a gang rape in which a little girl was killed. He was never arrested, but always lived with the torment of that event. Could this have been one of Marilyn's attackers? She was probably left for dead when she lost consciousness.

Give the memories time and prayer. Marilyn has a very deep trust in God, repeatedly pleading for these memories to be false. But the more she prayed, the more the pieces fit together. She continued praying and searching for several years after concluding her therapy. It has now been fourteen years since the memories returned. Marilyn is about 98 percent certain of the truth of these memories. However, she always leaves room for information that might disprove them, even after all the research and evidence she discovered.

Summary

Redbook magazine, in a January 1993 article, "Unlock the Secrets of Your Past," asked the question, "So how can you tell if a memory is accurate?" The writers gave the following answer:

> "While there's no foolproof way, the more detail and sensory information you recall, the more likely a recollection is to be true," says Steven Ceci, Ph.D., professor of developmental psychology at Cornell University. He also suggests asking witnesses to verify what you remember. But that doesn't mean you should let others convince you that your memories are incorrect. "There's a fundamental integrity to our recollection," says New York City psychiatrist Mark Epstein, M.D. "Though the details may be distorted or inaccurate, most of our memories contain a nucleus of truth."[5]

There are methods to assist us in determining the truth of our memories. After we have evaluated the influence of external sources, as described in chapter five, and internal motivations, as described in chapter six, we also apply the information we have learned about the method employed to recover the memory.

As we next list facts and feelings that support or disprove a particular memory, we may find some unusual and unique behaviors and feelings that have never made sense before, but now fit, if the memory is true.

If the memory is such that physical evidence is likely, this can be one of the strongest validations. Photographs, medical records, school evaluations, and diaries are all potential sources of physical evidence, as well as any physical damage or scarring.

As we evaluate our experience as the memory was recovered, we may become aware of something that really occurred, as opposed to something that we imagined. We can have strong emotions to fantasies that are not true, and it is possible to have no emotion to a trauma that did occur if we dissociated. Rarely is that true for the initial trauma, but more likely for repetitive, inescapable events.

The place where trauma occurred will most likely elicit very strong feelings, similar ones to those associated with the trauma. Revisiting these places has assisted many clients with further understanding of the truth.

It is often amazing to hear reports of our childhood that we never knew before. Many people have excellent observations and intuitive feelings about our life, even if they did not know the details. Others actually saw events or were told about them. Sometimes we may even have told someone about a trauma and forgotten we shared it.

Ascertaining the truth of any memory is so important, we cannot stop until we have turned over and examined all available evidence.

12

How Do I Recover from Traumatic Memories That Are True?

When we have determined that our memories are accurate, it is important to continue the healing process until recovery occurs. In this chapter, we'll briefly walk through some of the steps that promote healing. Each of us is unique, and so the steps may occur in a different order. But each of these steps is important. For most of the process, we need the guidance and assistance of a well-trained and experienced therapist.

This chapter is not in any way intended to replace the professional therapy needed. It is more like a checklist, to make sure you're not forgetting any of the important steps. It is not meant to be definitive or complete, merely a brief outline of the basic components of therapy which promote recovery from repressed trauma.

Identify the Form and Severity of Splitting

Almost everyone who has been traumatized, even in adulthood, experiences some form of splitting at the time of the trauma. It is God's method of giving us a temporary numbness in order to cope. If it is a trauma that has just occurred and if we are willing to face the pain, the normal process of grieving, repetitively talking about the event, and expressing our feelings will generally bring about the healing and integration.

There are excellent books written on the topic of splitting and dissociation. It can become very complicated and intricate. I can only introduce the topic here, offering a very basic, simplified primer.

If your trauma occurred in childhood, you will need professional help to identify the splits or dissociation. This does not mean you are a multiple personality, as some people fear. Almost everyone learns to have a minor form of conscious splitting. We may refer to this as level one, the necessity of putting on our "business side" and getting serious, or we may express relief that we can let down our hair and relax. Or we talk about different roles we play, as we put on our parent hat or act the dutiful daughter. This serves us well in lives that demand a wide range of behavior.

On a more serious level, we may have learned that our society or our families have certain standards regarding our feelings or behaviors. Some things are acceptable; some aren't. We learn to hide specific feelings from others, perhaps anger for women or crying for men, pretending that everything is just fine—this is level two.

You're in a social situation and someone asks, "How are you?" You may be furious or frightened or hurt, but you smile and say the perfunctory "Fine." You're not trying to deceive anyone. You're just putting on your public face, because you know that's what the other person wants to hear.

Some keep that public face on most of the time. They never reveal to anyone certain awful events that have occurred in their lives. They haven't repressed these memories—they know very well what has happened—they just hide them from others.

A third level of splitting involves the hiding of feelings or past events from ourselves. This is *blocking* or *dissociation* or *repression,* and it comes in a wide variety of forms. Some might have amnesia for one event, while others block out everything about their lives, even their names and identities (though this is very rare). In milder forms, a person might block out a certain feeling for a particular person. In more serious forms, a person might block out all feelings (also rare).

The final level is the multiple personality disorder that became popularized by the movie *Three Faces of Eve.* In this dissociative disorder, a person has more than one personality. These personalities alternately take over complete control, with no conscious awareness of another part or parts.

In the healing process for all levels, each of the *splits*—or parts that are "not acceptable"—will need attention. There's a story behind each part of a person who has gone through any level of splitting, and those stories need to be told—along with the associated feelings. Although it sounds easy, it's a serious business. At levels three and four, professional expertise is essential.

Greg had the least amount of splitting. He is an example of the second category. He clearly knew his own feelings and behavior, but he learned in adolescence to hide from others. He wanted acceptance, not criticism, so he continued to be secretive, if necessary, in order to get his needs met. He knew when he felt anger, but withdrew and did not express it directly. He also knew he was afraid of other people's anger, and protected himself. The memory that he recovered would fall into the third category, repression or dissociation.

Lynn and Melissa were quite similar. They both represent the third category. They had both learned to split off awareness of their needs and their feelings. Melissa had also blocked out three specific events.

Cindy, who had the recovered memory of sexual abuse by her grandfather, as well as other severe trauma, was diagnosed as having a multiple personality disorder. There were periods of time in her adult life where she had no awareness of what she had done. She has clothes that are very seductive that she cannot recall buying, and she doesn't know when she has worn them. She occasionally meets men who act like they know her and refer to their times together, giving information that's true about her, but she has no recollection of them or the events they're describing. She only became aware of her dissociation when her husband followed her and discovered the other personality. (Very few details of Cindy's life or recovery are presented because of the complexity of both the abuse and her therapy, which are beyond the scope of this book.)

Release the Feelings

Many books present information concerning the emotional reactions to trauma. In *Psychological Trauma and the Adult Survivor,* Drs. McCann and

Pearlman summarized the research, revealing a variety of response patterns that are common among trauma victims.[1]

Denial

For almost everyone, the initial reaction to any trauma is denial. "NO! This can't be happening!" We can't take it in. We don't want it to be true. Generally, as soon as people are there to take over for us and to do whatever has to be done, the denial lifts. Even then, the denial may come and go as needed for coping. Throughout therapy, there needs to be a place for this denial to be expressed, and for the memories to be questioned, even if they are true.

Greg struggled with the denial of the physical abuse, eventually deciding it was not true. Melissa experienced the denial as she doubted that she could block an entire memory such as the molest from the man next door. She came to believe that it had occurred.

Cindy had the strongest denial. Part of her knew all about the abuse by Grandfather, as well as other abuse which was very frightening. But most of the time, she had no awareness of periods of time, of places, of activities, and of people.

Sadness and Grief

Other intense feelings follow, often in an isolated form. The sadness and grief will come through deep sobs and tears. If it's in reaction to an early painful event, the feelings may seem childlike. Most people seem to have a limited amount of tears. So, the more time we can spend releasing the pain, without interruption, the quicker we move past it. Often the emotional intensity is similar for many different events, but in general, the more severe and extensive the pain, the longer the grief lasts. The grief work usually begins with the pain of the past, but we also need to look at the present and the future losses to ourselves, our families and friends, our children, and our careers—losses that have resulted from the earlier trauma.

The first feelings that emerged in Greg's therapy were his sadness and his fear of his parents. For Melissa, it took longer to feel the hurt with both her dad and the neighbor. It was even more difficult to feel how much she needed and wanted her dad's love and acceptance. Melissa and Greg also grieved over the present losses, the impact on their marriage and their family, as well as their relationships with their parents. Lynn had difficulty, but persisted until she could allow herself to feel and release the deep pain she felt from needing both a mommy and a daddy. She grieved over the intimacy she did not have with friends and family, and the spontaneous fun she had missed as she assumed the caretaker role from early in her life.

Cindy had no negative feelings about her grandfather. They were pushed deeply into her unconscious. Eventually, she had to face the pain and to grieve the incredible damage done to her marriage by Grandpa's abuse and other events.

Anger

Anger may also occur, aimed at anyone we might be able to blame, including ourselves and God. But instead it needs to be directed toward the cause of the pain, in a manner that is age-appropriate for when it occurred. It can be very freeing to release your anger, if you have a safe place and method of doing so. I often tell clients that I see anger as similar to food poisoning: We must get it out of our systems in order to recover and feel better. It's not appealing and needs to be done in private. It's not a spectator sport. Persons who are objects of our anger should not hear it; anger work should be done in the therapy office or a safe private place at home. We need to face that anger within us, admitting it to ourselves and to God. Don't worry—he already knows about it and isn't shocked. God wants to be allowed into that place that we've kept hidden.

Our anger can be the source of our protection when used in a healthy manner. It's where we find the strength to say that abuse is not acceptable and that we won't be helpless victims anymore. We learn to protect ourselves rather than needing others to take care of us. Through our anger we learn to intuitively sense danger and take appropriate precautions.

Melissa and Lynn were both comfortable with their anger toward their fathers, and released it easily. Anger was the first reaction they experienced. The anger toward the neighbor was also easy for Melissa. For Greg, the hurt had been easier. He struggled with the anger, because he feared feeling or acting out of control. When he finally expressed it, he was relieved and surprised. He expected it to be much bigger and more explosive than it was. Melissa, Greg, and Lynn all practiced expressing anger with each other in the counseling office, learning acceptable means of release and communication.

For a long time, Cindy felt no anger. As with the hurt, it was deeply buried. Eventually she began to feel anger at Grandpa, while still loving the good things about him.

Loneliness and Loss

The loneliness and reality of loss will at times be overwhelming even for someone surrounded by loving friends and family, but their presence helps tremendously. The primary reason we repress trauma is because we are alone, or feel that we are. No one is there to comfort us, to take care of us, to function for us when we're overwhelmed. This is why a support system needs to be in place before uncovering repressed trauma. Without support, we feel helplessly alone in the abuse again. With spiritual, physical, and emotional support, we can make it through all of these feelings.

Ironically, Melissa, Greg, and Lynn all felt alone. They learned to be there for each other in a loving, supportive way. It was especially touching to see both Greg and Melissa hold Lynn as she sobbed about the rejection from her father and the aloneness when her mother was working or exhausted. The intimacy being established was beautiful and deeply needed by all three of them. Later, the other children were also involved in some family interactions of support.

Cindy's family was upset and angry at her accusations against Grandpa, except for her aunt, who had also been molested by him. Cindy's husband was angry, hurt, and distrustful. They had gone through extensive marriage counseling, so he tried to be there for Cindy, but he was also working on his own feelings. Most of her support came from two close friends, her church, her aunt, and her therapist.

Fear and Anxiety

The fear and anxiety surface intermittently, but are often the shortest part of the therapy. *Safety* is usually not a concern for adult survivors of abuse (unless we are in abusive relationships currently). In most cases, the perpetrator is no longer present, and adults have many more options for defense and protection. Occasionally, anxiety will center around *overwhelming feelings* and the belief that we cannot handle them. As the feelings are released, the anxiety usually disappears. A third source of the anxiety is *telling the secret.* But as soon as it is told, even to one person, the fear begins to decrease. With each retelling, there is more reduction of the fear, if the reactions are empathic and caring. The fourth cause of fear is the *threats that were made* by the perpetrator concerning the results of telling. The most common threats are: no one will believe you; they'll think you're crazy; they'll know you're bad; it's your fault; I'll hurt (or kill) you or someone close to you. When the threats are known, the rational adult can usually release the fear through various means of physical or emotional protection.

Melissa's fear of telling and being hurt by the neighbor was short-lived, since she's had no contact with him for almost forty years. She felt greater anxiety over asking for what she needed from her dad and from Greg. She informed both of them of this fear, and requested they work with her on the issue. Both gladly agreed. Over time, she learned to express needs and wants, even when they were irritated with her requests.

Greg's anxiety was also brief, as he realized how large and capable he was to protect himself from someone else's anger or physical abuse. He had ample opportunity to practice within his family. His relatives were all very expressive, and he was finally free to observe how comfortable everyone else was with anger, and that it never resulted in physical violence.

Lynn feared abandonment. As the intimacy with her mother and Greg grew, the fear decreased dramatically.

Cindy's terror was intense. The abuse had been quite painful at times. But other times Grandpa was very loving, the most wonderful person she knew. She feared the pain. She feared trusting, never knowing when the person she trusted would change. These feelings were the most exhausting part of Cindy's therapy, but were shortened considerably through EMDR.

EMDR, the eye movement therapy discussed in a previous chapter, is often very helpful at assisting us in areas where the anxiety persists or reaches the terror level. It also helps identify different anxiety-producing events that have been associated neurologically. It is theorized by Dr. Shapiro, the developer of EMDR, that it works in a similar manner to REM (Rapid Eye Movement) sleep, in which our dreams work to resolve the unsettled conflicts of the day. EMDR is helpful in anxiety reduction of past events, where there is no current cause for the anxiety to remain.[2]

Shame and Guilt

Shame and guilt are often the most difficult emotions. For some people, these are so overwhelming suicide seems the only option. In such cases, of course, these feelings must be resolved immediately. Victims of sexual abuse may not experience the shame until they become teenagers and understand the sexual nature of the touching. At earlier ages they may have felt emotional discomfort or physical pain but guilt and shame can hit them hard in adolescence.

The release of the shame and guilt involves two steps. We must *identify the guilty party,* giving the shame and guilt back to that person, where it belongs. And we must *forgive ourselves,* accepting God's forgiveness for anything that was legitimately our fault.

Melissa had disobeyed her mother and had gone next door, where she was abused. So she felt it was her fault, that she had been bad. She needed to forgive herself and accept that there may be some consequences when we disobey. It's important for Melissa to trust that there is a good reason for limits and laws. They were in her best interest and needed to be obeyed. But she did not deserve to be abused even if she did disobey her parents. The neighbor was totally responsible for that behavior. She probably did deserve a reminder or a minor consequence, but she also should have been told by her parents why the man was not to be trusted.

Greg did not feel shame or guilt. He knew it wasn't his fault.

Lynn felt some shame over having needs at all, as well as badness—that she wasn't lovable enough to make her father stay with them.

Cindy's shame and guilt were pervasive, especially as she became aware of her promiscuous behavior. The split existed because of her inability to accept sexuality, and then she discovered that she had been behaving in a way that was contrary to everything she believed. Cindy also felt guilt over her anger at Grandpa. Her healing process cannot be described in a simple manner, but it did require self-forgiveness, understanding, and changes in her behavior.

Betrayal

The feelings of betrayal are devastating when any abuse occurs at the hands of a trusted caretaker. Our parents or caretakers are the people we should be able to trust to protect us from abusive people or situations. When they are the sources of pain, trust is shattered.

Melissa felt some betrayal from her dad, although she had never felt much closeness or trust. Lynn's issue was abandonment, with a very minor sense of betrayal, which came from the belief that all parents should be there for their children. Greg experienced betrayal only in the moment of being pushed away. Otherwise, he knew it was his parents' fight, and it had nothing to do with him.

Cindy felt profound betrayal from her grandfather. She knew he loved her. She seemed to be his favorite person. Yet he also hurt her. This betrayal shattered her trust—and her personality.

Helplessness

Helplessness is another feeling that inevitably results from abuse that occurs more than once. If we are able to figure out some method to avoid it after the first incident, we do not feel this powerlessness. But repetition leaves us feeling like helpless victims; no matter what we do, we are not safe.

Greg avoided some of the helplessness by walking away from angry people, thus protecting himself from physical abuse. However, he did continue to feel helpless to handle anyone's anger, and his childhood home was rife with anger. Both Melissa and Lynn felt helpless to get their needs met from a man; Lynn had some of these feelings toward women as well.

Cindy felt totally helpless as a child. The abuse was repetitive and from the person she loved the most. It occurred at night when no one was around. The only method of coping she discovered was dissociation, where all the uncomfortable feelings were totally split off, and even the knowledge of the events completely blocked.

For all of them, specific training and strategies were developed to teach competence in their areas of helplessness. With these behavioral changes, over time the powerlessness was conquered.

Confusion

Confusion is common. Most children cannot make any sense out of a world in which they are abused or neglected. In an attempt to do so, they often prefer to believe it is their fault, that they did something bad to deserve it. It's easier to believe that and feel some hope of escape by changing their own behavior than to feel the overwhelming helplessness of trying to change an abuser.

Melissa and Lynn learned to stay out of the way, and to need nothing. Greg learned to run from anger and become secretive about anything that might elicit anger.

Cindy's massive confusion was handled by splitting the conflicting thoughts and feelings into other parts, with no awareness the confusion even existed.

They all felt incredible relief as they began to make sense of their own behaviors and feelings. As the puzzle pieces connected, they were able to see the whole picture. Their lives became simpler and more focused.

Detachment

If any of the emotions listed so far are missing, the reason may be threats or frightening experiences. For example, some children are abused more if they cry or get angry. Thus they learn to dissociate or detach in such a way that they can control their reactions or feelings even if they have intense pain. This makes it terrifying to experience those feelings again.

Anger was harder for Greg to feel and express than pain, while the reverse was true for Melissa and Lynn. All three of them were able to deal with all of the feelings involved in a relatively short time period.

Cindy's task was much harder and demanded more time and support.

Depression

Depression is a feeling experienced by almost every victim. It is usually the result of other unresolved feelings combined, most commonly anger, sadness, loneliness, and helplessness. There may be added physical components resulting from exhaustion, poor nutrition, and stress. Generally, when the other feelings have been resolved, the depression lifts. Sometimes medication is needed to break the pattern.

Body Memories

Body memories are also released, and may occur before, during, or after the time when the memory is being recovered. In these body memories, the victim reexperiences the pain of the trauma wherever it occurred in the body. This usually lasts for only a short time after the memory has been completely recovered.

Dissociation from the body is very common in physical or sexual abuse, as a way of escaping from the physical pain. Many clients describe watching the abuse to "another little child" from somewhere else in the room. This splitting enables a person to survive the experience, but causes a feeling of separateness from the body. When this occurs, people may neglect the care of their bodies, or even intentionally abuse themselves. People who have severe dissociation often describe the feeling of "renting" a body that doesn't have much value to them, except for its immediate use. Part of the healing comes when we reclaim our bodies, taking responsibility for proper and healthy care and protection.

Greg and Lynn did not have body memories, other than those associated with feelings of anxiety. Melissa felt the asthma, as the memories returned, as well as many other physical signs of stress.

Cindy had many body memories, including choking, suffocating, the inability to breathe, pain on her arms where she had been held down, and feelings of sexual arousal. None of her personalities took responsibility for "the body," so proper eating, rest, and treatment of illness was sporadic and unpredictable. This became an important task in her therapy—choosing responsible, healthy behavior.

The quickest resolution of these feelings usually comes through an intensive therapy program in which a person can stay with whatever reaction is emerging, rather than cutting it off to go back to work or back home to his or her family. When the feelings are interrupted and not allowed expression, it is difficult to return to them. People who discontinue therapy at this point are generally worse off than if they had never begun. The faster this part is completed, the better it is for them.

Greg completed this part of his therapy in one week of intensive work, and Melissa in two weeks. Lynn had three days of intensive therapy when she was considering the option that someone else had molested her. All three of them continued in weekly therapy after this time, sometimes alone, sometimes as a couple, and occasionally as a family.

With the severity of Cindy's abuse, considerably more therapy was required. Over a two-year period she had weekly sessions, and several weeks of intensive therapy at times when the feelings were overwhelming.

Identify the Lies Believed

The events that occur to us as children strongly influence our conclusions about ourselves, others, God, our world, feelings, and so on. These thoughts and convictions are the invisible but destructive scars of the abusive event. A major requirement for healing is that we identify the specific lies we have believed and replace them with the truth. This includes any programming that has occurred from pedophiles or sadistic abusers.

Lies about Ourselves

Certain negative beliefs about ourselves and our value are very common for victims of child abuse. They include the following:

"It was my fault. If only I had (or hadn't) . . ."
"I'm bad. I deserved it."
"I'm not lovable."
"I'm helpless. I can't protect myself."
"It's useless to fight back. I'll get hurt more if I cry, or yell, or struggle."

Lies about Others

We also learn negative messages about others, and generalize thoughts like the following:

"No one is safe."
"Everyone hurts children. All men (or women) do this to children."
"No one cares. People know what's happening and they do nothing."
(Most young children believe that all adults know everything.)

"No one will believe me."
"No one will help me. They think I'm bad, or crazy, or at fault."
"They'll blame me."

These beliefs obviously interfere with satisfying social relationships and intimacy with friends and family. As these change, many of our normal needs and desires for closeness can be met.

Lies about Our World

Conclusions about our world often are based on whatever our childhood world was like (our home, primarily, or significant others). These might include thoughts like:

"Life is always scary. There's no safety anywhere."
"Life is full of pain, and then you die."
"Life is not worth living."
"Life is aloneness and not mattering to anyone. My needs will never be met in this life."

Lies about God

Perhaps the most destructive lies we come to accept are those concerning God:

"God doesn't exist."
"God doesn't love me."
"God's mean and wants little children to be hurt."
"God's indifferent. He's absent."
"He loves others, but not me because I'm too bad."
"I can't trust a God who allows little children to be hurt. The abuse is God's fault."

Replace Lies with Truth

This process of therapy can, and usually does, take time. In this phase, the traditional weekly therapy works well. Each of the lies needs to be replaced with the truth. Guided imagery is often helpful in this area, as we visualize the truth about God, ourselves, and others. This is an area of therapy where positive suggestions have a very productive place. Those who are most suggestible often make quick and lasting changes during this part of therapy.

Cindy did some good work in identifying the lies she had been believing about herself, and replacing them with God's truth. Here are samples from the list she came up with.

Lies I Believed	What God Says
"I'm bad."	I am the righteousness of God in Christ (see Phil. 3:9).
	"Blessed are the pure in heart" (Matt. 5:8).
	I am being conformed to the image of God's Son (see Rom. 8:29).
"It's not OK to cry."	"Those who sow in tears will reap with songs of joy" (Ps. 126:5 NIV).
	"Jesus wept" (John 11:35).
"It's not OK to feel."	The Word of God is a discerner of the thoughts and intents of the heart (see Heb. 4:12).
	Jesus was filled with compassion (see Matt. 9:36 NIV; 14:14; Mark 1:41; 6:34).
	"Blessed are those who mourn" (Matt. 5:4 NIV).
"I must be quiet."	"Speak the truth to each other" (Zech. 8:16 NIV).
	Speak the truth in love (see Eph. 4:25).
	"I pour out my soul" (Ps. 42:4 NIV).

Lies I Believed	What God Says
"This isn't happening."	By constant use of the Word I can learn to discern good from evil (see Heb. 5:14 NIV).
"I'm a loser."	"We are more than conquerors through Him who loved us" (Rom. 8:37 NIV).
	God always causes us to triumph in Christ (see 2 Cor. 2:14).
"It's unacceptable to be me."	I am accepted in the beloved (see Eph. 1:6).
	I am God's workmanship (see Eph. 2:10).
"I'm fat and ugly."	"I am fearfully and wonderfully made" (Ps. 139:14 NIV).
"I'm weak."	His strength is made perfect in weakness (see 2 Cor. 12:9).
	In quietness and trust is my strength (see Isa. 30:15).
"I'm useless."	"For it is God who works in you to will and to act according to his good purpose" (Phil. 2:13 NIV).
	"I can do everything through him who gives me strength" (Phil. 4:13 NIV).
	"I am the vine, you are the branches. He who abides in Me, and I in him, bears much fruit" (John 15:5 NKJV).
"I'm an emotional cripple."	I have the mind of Christ (see 1 Cor. 2:16).
"I'm too vulnerable to succeed."	I have the full armor of God (see Eph. 6:11–18).

Lies I Believed	What God Says
	No weapon forged against me will prevail (see Isa. 54:17).
"No place is safe."	"He is my refuge and my fortress" (Ps. 91:2 NIV).
	I can dwell in the secret place of the Most High (see Ps. 91:1).
"I'm all alone and abandoned."	"He (God) Himself has said, I will not in any way fail you nor give you up nor leave you without support. I will not, I will not, I will not in any degree leave you helpless, nor forsake nor let you down, relax my hold on you—assuredly not!" (Heb. 13:5 AMP)

The church can take an active role in the healing of someone with abuse, not only by presenting the truth, but (more importantly) by living the truth, as members relate to victims of trauma.

See the Whole Picture

Cindy had justifiable anger at her grandfather. But as she continued her process of healing, she learned more about him from her aunt.

He had grown up with a very loving, adoring mother and a brutal, abusive father, who forced his mother to give the sons beatings when they were disobedient or disrespectful in any way. If she refused, he beat her and the boys in violent anger and with a barrage of vicious words for all. Grandpa's mother believed that if she administered the beatings, her children would be safer than if she enraged her husband. She expressed her fear that he might kill all of them, so she cowered in obedience. Grandpa was also sexually abused by older relatives, in repeated "games" where he was

> restrained in a fairly playful manner. Grandpa had learned to associate love and abuse, and he saw beatings as a protection from something worse—death.
>
> This does not lessen the grandfather's responsibility for what he did to Cindy. But it does explain the context of his behavior, that he was acting out of his own needs and pain. He was a victim as well as a victimizer. It wasn't about Cindy or who she was as a child.

When we've worked through the previous steps, we need to enlarge our vision. We need to see our childhood in larger terms—there was more than just the abuse. We need the broad picture, including an appreciation for the positive aspects of our childhood. Focusing only on the negative will rob us of many of the joyful memories of those early years.

We also need to see the perpetrators in the whole context of their lives. This will not be easy. We may need to ask God for the strength and compassion to do this.

If the perpetrator was a stranger, like Melissa's neighbor, we need not expend much effort in researching his early life. But when the abuse has been committed by a relative or family friend, the issue is, quite literally, closer to home. It's common to demonize the perpetrator, to see the person as being totally bad and to erase any good memories of time spent with that person.

The problem is that this can keep us from being whole. We are editing out memories of our lives. We are canceling out relationships that, at certain times, we found enjoyable, although at other times they were destructive.

We can love and hate the same person. They can have wonderful and terrible characteristics. We can continue relationships, even if there has been destruction in the past, as long as certain conditions exist—repentance, forgiveness, security. We must honestly examine all aspects of our relationships with the persons who abused us.

Then it is helpful to find out whatever we can about their childhood. It is incredibly freeing to see the little child in our perpetrator, and often the tragic abuse he or she experienced. We then begin to see that our abuse did not have much to do with who we are. It's much more about the angry, frightened, acting-out child inside of the perpetrator. This does not make the abuse acceptable. But it helps us have a different perspective of ourselves, the people who hurt us, and the people who didn't protect us. Often we can even feel some pity for them and the pain and guilt with which they have lived.

As Melissa learned more about her dad, she became aware that he grew up in a critical home with extremely high expectations. He was frequently shown how he could do a little better. When Melissa's mom got pregnant before marriage, his parents were angry and rejecting, declaring that he had ruined his life and now would never be a success. Melissa's dad was determined to prove them wrong. With no help from them, he finished college and worked full time to support his new family. He continued to drive himself, to prove that he could succeed. And he did. But he was often irritable and tired in the process. Melissa was able to talk with him about this, and to hear his regrets over never being able just to relax and enjoy her.

Melissa's father committed himself to finding time weekly for Melissa, Greg, and his grandchildren. During the following year, they went fishing, golfing, and camping, relaxed around the house, and took part in other special interests of each of the children. This was especially healing for Tim, the more reserved grandson, who matched his grandfather in personality. These two began spending time together playing golf and tennis, sports that Tad, the athletic brother, did not play—thus avoiding the brotherly competition, where Tim lost.

For the first time, Lynn found out about her biological father. He grew up without a father; his mother was rarely available, either physically or emotionally; and he suffered from severe neglect. He put on a tough exterior, but when he met Melissa, he let down his defenses. He became very needy and extremely controlling, demanding that she meet his every need. Melissa found his attentiveness very appealing, and his control similar to the way she pictured her dad. Their insecurities matched, although they would not have married if Melissa had not become pregnant. But when Lynn was born, Melissa showered all her attention upon her little "doll," as she had done earlier with her baby sister.

Lynn's father felt neglected by Melissa. This touched off severe feelings of neglect from his childhood, so he closed up emotionally and became the tough guy again. Soon he left the area. This required Melissa to go to work to support herself and young Lynn, and she was also continuing in college. She followed her dad's modeling—a driven, work-first lifestyle—but she felt conflict because of her strong attachment to Lynn and her desire to be a full-time mother. Lynn obviously felt her mom's love, and she sensed how overwhelming Melissa's life was, so Lynn learned to be the rescuer very early in her life.

Both of Greg's parents came from very expressive families, both loving and angry. It was normal for them to yell, hit, laugh, hug, cry, and express any other feeling that occurred. The role of alcohol, however, exacerbated this behavior, resulting at times in extreme volatility and aggressiveness.

As Greg looked at Melissa and the kids—and all of the extended family, he saw clear distinctions between his heritage and Melissa's. Lynn and Tim had the quiet personalities of Melissa's people, and they had bonded well with their maternal grandparents.

Tad and Jenny, on the other hand, were both more like Greg's side of the family, with their extroverted, expressive personalities. And, as you might expect, Tad had developed a closer relationship with Greg's parents, who loved all of his sports and were not threatened by his anger. They were the ones who began to get through to Tad concerning the importance of school "to make something out of himself," and to use a more acceptable expression of anger. Tad was able to identify with them and learn from open discussion of their mistakes of cruel, improper anger.

Look for the Positive

Can anything good come out of abuse?

Surely there are many negative results of abuse. But every experience has both positive and negative consequences. And there is a time to leave the negative past behind us. We can do that, in part, by looking for the positive results that have occurred.

As Melissa looked for the positive with her dad, she was grateful to realize his example of success in work, responsibility, and academic achievement. She also saw three of her four children following this example.

She knew she had inherited his high sense of responsibility and his drive for achievement. She knew she needed to learn to play and relax more. But what if it were the other way around? What if she had learned a lifestyle of relaxation and now had to learn responsibility? It's probably easier this way, she thought.

Even her response to her father's rare angry outburst had yielded something positive, she now realized. Because she had been so frightened by his anger, she had been very aware of showing kindness toward her own children. And in her reluctance to ask for things from men, she had learned self-sufficiency and competence, qualities that were greatly admired in the business world.

The biblical story of Joseph is one of the most dramatic examples of good coming from abuse (Gen. 37–47). His brothers sold him into slavery, and he was taken to Egypt. He became the chief slave in his household, but his master's wife falsely accused him of rape and had him thrown in prison. There, he demonstrated his ability to interpret dreams. When Pharaoh, the ruler of Egypt, had a troublesome dream, Joseph was called to analyze it. Pharaoh was so impressed that he made Joseph second in command, responsible for storing up enough grain to get the whole region through the terrible famine predicted in the dream. When Joseph's brothers came to Egypt begging for grain, they were shocked (and scared) to see Joseph in charge.

Yet Joseph expressed to his brothers a principle that can change our whole outlook today. "God turned into good what you meant for evil, for he brought me to this high position I have today so that I could save the lives of many people" (Gen. 50:20 LB).

Philippians 4:8 instructs us to focus our minds on the good and true and pure and lovely things. Research has demonstrated the power of a positive focus and the destructiveness of worry and negative thinking. We can trust God to use even the bad things that occur in our lives for our good (Rom. 8:28).

Consider Confrontation Issues

Some therapists insist that a victim must confront the abuser and end the relationship. I disagree. There are many concerns that need to be evaluated.

Safety

The first consideration must be safety. If you are dealing with someone who has chosen evil and is violent, do not even consider any form of confrontation. It puts you in danger. If someone is currently physically or sexually abusing you, and you can find no way to protect yourself, stay away.

What are you saying by running away or staying away? You are demonstrating that you are incapable of dealing with that person, that he or she is still stronger than you are. *That may be true,* especially in cases with a violent perpetrator. If that is true for you at this point, it is necessary to acknowledge that. You are wise to get away from your abuser and to stay away. A confrontation could only hurt you more.

Timing and Purpose

But if violence is not a danger, should you directly confront the perpetrator? It depends on timing and purpose.

Whatever your relationship was in the past with this person is likely to be repeated. If the perpetrator has generally been kind and open to your opinions, the risk in confrontation may be low. However, if the person was usually very angry, defensive, or verbally and physically abusive when you were a child, expect the same response. So you must ask yourself:

Am I ready, at this time in my life, to handle all of the possible outcomes of such a confrontation? What is the worst that can happen? Am I ready for that?
Is it a risk I want to take at this time, or do I need to heal more first?
Will I ever want to confront this person?
Why is it important for me to do this?

Are you planning a confrontation as a way of dumping your anger on the person? If so, it's not appropriate. This needs to be done in therapy before you are ready to consider a confrontation. Otherwise, you would become what you hate. You would go from victim to victimizer. Empty out your own anger first. Don't use a confrontation as a way to resolve it.

But when you remain upset with anyone, it generally means you are still looking to that person for something—your validation, your self-worth, permission to say no, agreement, acknowledgment, love, acceptance, protection. If your desire to confront your abuser is based on something you need to get from them, be careful. Will you get what you need from the person who abused you? Probably not. Often people go into confrontations seeking to make it all better, assuming that now, finally, they will get the love or affirmation they missed as children. They usually come back disappointed.

Rarely will a perpetrator admit what he has done. He usually does not want to risk whatever legal or family consequences might arise. Most of us are reluctant to admit any wrong behavior, even things that have no legal consequences. If you go into a confrontation looking for an admission of guilt or verification of your memories of abuse, you are unlikely to receive it.

Given the likelihood of denial, do you still want to confront? Are you prepared to be called a liar? Our clinic has worked with many perpetrators and almost all of them have initially denied their guilt. Denial only changes with an external event, like getting caught, or with something internal, like a spiritual experience or overwhelming guilt feelings. At this point, you have no control over either of those factors. Denial is a brick wall you can't smash through—you'll only frustrate yourself, and maybe hurt yourself, in trying.

If the abuse occurred within your family, you may have difficult choices. Cut yourself off from your family, go on pretending that nothing happened, or find a way to confront the issue. In such cases, with proper precautions, confrontation may be the best option. But don't expect instant satisfaction. Rarely does a family want to admit the truth of abuse unless it has been so pervasive and so openly known that hiding it is impossible. Confrontation may mean that you are rejected by your entire family. Are you prepared for that? Are you willing to take that risk?

There are many good things about families. These are the people who probably know you best. They can offer love and support in ways that others can't. It's hard to be a whole person without a good connection to your family. But, for many of those same reasons, families can be devastating when things go wrong. Family members know how to hurt you if they so choose. They can shake your identity and challenge your sense of self-worth like no one else can.

So, if your confrontation will affect the whole family, you must weigh the rewards and the risks. What are the chances that things will turn out well? How strong are you to deal with a family that falls apart or turns against you?

We gain our greatest freedom when we can feel good about ourselves and act in a manner we admire in the presence of those who have threatened or abused us. As an advertisement used to say, "Living well is the best revenge." It may take a long time to get to the place where you no longer feel threatened, where the perpetrator no longer has control over you, where you can look the person in the eye and say, "You hurt me, but I'm going to be all right now. With God's help, I forgive you." That kind of confrontation can be healing, but it doesn't come easily. Don't rush it.

How to Confront

If you decide to do this, how should you confront your childhood abuser?

If there is any danger of physical violence, you still might achieve a confrontation by phone or letter. Or perhaps you could meet in a public place, preferably (but not necessarily) with trusted friends present.

If someone is verbally abusive, those options still exist, but make sure you have the freedom to discontinue conversations when they become destructive. Be willing to hang up the phone or to walk away. You have no obligation to keep listening to someone who is tearing you down. You need not be polite if you're being abused.

It's often a good idea to keep the confrontation short, depending on your own level of strength. You might be able to handle only two minutes with the perpetrator. Then plan for that: speak, listen, and leave. Consider the support you will need from friends before, during, and after such a confrontation. They will help you gain the strength and clear thinking you need to protect yourself.

Melissa had decided that she did not want to confront her dad, that she didn't trust him to be honest. She feared his anger, and she feared rejection from the rest of her family. She did feel safe asking for information from her mother. It was an amazing surprise to her how the events unfolded, how open her dad was, and how she was able to learn about the sexual abuse that did and did not happen.

Greg felt differently. He knew that most anything could be discussed in his family. The worst that would happen is anger, and he did fear that. But he needed to get past that fear. He felt confident of his ability to protect himself physically. And if it got too bad verbally, he could leave. After training in anger management and releasing childhood anger, he was now quite confident that he would handle his own anger in a constructive way. An angry confrontation, if that should occur, would not mean rejection in his family. People got over it, and still seemed to like each other as much—sometimes they were even closer after yelling it out. Greg was very pleased with the interactions with his mother, and felt that he had finally taken down his wall that had kept her at a distance. Eventually, he also talked with his father. That went all right, but was more factual. It did open the door to better communication between them.

Lynn's intention to confront her father came at a time when she would have dumped all her anger on him, even anger that belonged to Melissa and to Greg and to anyone else who had ever rejected her. It would have been an attack for some things he didn't do. She now feels settled about her relationship, or lack of one, with him. She still may contact him someday, but doesn't wish to do so at this time.

Cindy attempted to talk with her sisters and brothers about Grandpa. They were all very angry at her. How could she possibly accuse such a wonderful man of such horrible behavior? Something was obviously wrong with her, not him. If she ever mentioned it again, she would not be welcome in their homes. She attempted to express her hurt to their reaction, but the conflict only escalated.

In following the biblical direction on how to confront (Matt. 18:15–17), Cindy decided to try again to resolve the hostility with her siblings. They all respected and liked her aunt, who acknowledged that she too had been molested by Grandpa—her father. She agreed to go with Cindy to attempt to broach the subject again. This interaction was calm, although Cindy's family still doubted the truth of either of their accusations. Cindy eventually decided to discuss this indirectly with her grandfather. They talked for some time about forgiveness and repentance and clearing the air—and Cindy's love for him, no matter what he had done. She told him her need to know the truth and her desire to continue a relationship with him. After many hours over several weeks, her grandfather was finally willing to ask for forgiveness, alluding to the abuse, but not clearly defining it. Cindy persisted in a loving manner. He agreed to come into therapy with her for a few sessions. After several more weeks of patient talking and listening, they began to discuss the specific events that had occurred. Some of Cindy's memories were accurate, and some of them seemed to come from pornography that Grandpa had. Cindy's healing came quickly from this point on.

Confrontation is not always advisable. If you anticipate a close, loving, trusting relationship with the perpetrator, then you will need to talk it through with the person, and come to a point of resolution and forgiveness.

Melissa and Greg were able to do that, and all the relationships were dramatically improved. Lynn and the three other children all communicated many hurts and frustrations and needs with Melissa and Greg, with open and honest patterns of sharing established among all of them.

Know the Legal Options

People often ask if we recommend lawsuits against perpetrators of childhood abuse. Only in rare cases. We do recommend criminal prosecution of pedophiles in order to protect other children from being abused.

A second type of case, child custody, usually goes through family court services. These are cases where the truth is sometimes difficult to determine. Some innocent parents are faced with the frightening task of proving innocence, and are deprived of contact with their children. Other times children are forced to continue visitation with a parent who is abusing them. Evaluations should always include psychological testing of both parents and all children as well as individual and family interviews and observations.

It's only been since the early 1980s that adults who were abused as children began suing their perpetrators in civil actions. There are a few therapists who do encourage lawsuits.[3] The stated purposes have been: to establish publicly the perpetrator's guilt; to regain power over the helplessness the abuse created; to recover financial losses due to therapy and career limitations caused by the abuse; and to defy the threats against telling the secret, by speaking the truth in the courtroom.

It is my opinion that lawsuits against families by adults who were abused as children rarely belong in the legal system, but in the counseling office. It's appropriate for clients to work through in therapy something that they believe might have happened in childhood. But certainty and corroborating evidence are required before a lawsuit should even be considered. Even then, I believe that it is emotionally and financially too costly. It prevents the resolution of the past. Instead, it keeps all parties focused on the abusive events of the past long after they should have moved on to successful and happy lives in the present.

Because our court system is designed to be used only after every other means has failed, it is an adversarial system. Anger is rarely resolved, but only increased. Lawsuits polarize the parties, and make them look for the worst in each other and the best in themselves, denying any of their own wrongdoing. Lawyers on both sides may overstate and exaggerate in order to make their points and to provide room for negotiations. Rarely is there any chance of restoration or resolution or healing of the family after it has been torn apart by the deep hurts and anger caused by a lawsuit. The courts should not be the place to resolve anger. Anger work needs to be done in counseling.

Rarely does a lawsuit provide a sense of regaining power and control. Many people express that they have rarely felt less powerful than in court, especially when cross-examined. They are cut off, interrupted, challenged, and disbelieved. Every attempt possible is made to discredit them, to make them look like liars. Every questionable event of their lives is put in the worst light imaginable. In such an environment, it is nearly impossible to regain a sense of power and control. Humiliation, yes. Control, no. Empowerment is most likely through family counseling, where direct confrontation can occur.

Often both sides experience severe destruction to their reputations, since everything is done to discredit the opposition. Family members and friends, who would otherwise be helping to reconcile the parties, are forced to take sides. This is usually devastating to those who are called as witnesses. It is especially embarrassing for children who are still in the home. They face the teasing, rejection, and humiliation by other kids who have heard about their parent, "the pervert." Their lives may be severely damaged. The financial cost often becomes astronomical, sometimes destroying a lifetime of saving for the future. No one wins. Everyone loses.

> George Carson, a retired engineer from Bloomfield, said that his 30-year-old daughter sued him in 1992, charging she had suffered sexual abuse that began when she was three years old and extended into adolescence.
>
> Mr. Carson, who denies abusing his daughter, said that his lawyer advised him to settle out of court because of the financial costs and emotional trauma. He said the ordeal cost him nearly $21,000 in court costs and attorney's fees and that he advises other parents in his situation to try to settle the problem in mediation. If it then goes to court, he said, the findings of the mediator should be made part of the court record.[4]

Susan Fink, a lawyer from Naugatuck who specializes in child sexual abuse cases, "discourages adults who have recently recalled memories of abuse in childhood from taking legal action against the perpetrators—also because of the costs and the amount of corroborating evidence needed to prove a case."

My perspective, as well, is expressed in her statement that: "What's new is the move from therapeutic to forensics and alleged false accusations. A therapist's tools in validating a patient's recall for recovery purposes, for healing, are far different than burden of proof in a legal forum. Now we're talking true or false, guilt or innocence. That's what this controversy is really about."[5]

Choose to Forgive

Should someone who has abused a child ever be forgiven? If it happened to you, it's more than a theoretical question. Can you forgive the person who abused you?

Some recovery books suggest that forgiveness should not occur, that it would be saying that the abuse was acceptable. That misses the whole point of forgiveness. There is no need to forgive behavior that is acceptable. There is no apology required when we do things properly.

Every one of us needs forgiveness, not only from God (Rom. 3:23) but from many of our friends, family, and acquaintances. If we come to face our own badness or selfish mistakes that have injured others, we become much more willing to forgive. If we do not forgive, we remain bitter and defensive and unable to have intimacy. It is likely to cause ill health, career difficulties, and conflict in our present families. It's not worth it, no matter how we feel about the perpetrator. We must forgive.

Perhaps you would like to forgive, but simply cannot. How can you change your feelings?

Forgiveness is not simply a statement of "I forgive you." Forgiveness is a process. Dr. David Augsburger in his excellent book, *Caring Enough to Forgive,* presents and explains five steps in the forgiveness process:

1. Realizing the wrongdoing
2. Reaffirming love, or seeing that you have value because you are created in God's image
3. Releasing or letting go of the past
4. Renewing repentance
5. Rediscovering community, or restoring the relationship[6]

You can take the first three steps on your own, totally independent of the other person. But the final two steps depend upon that person's repentance. Jesus made it very clear in Luke 17:3–4: "If your brother sins against you, rebuke him; and if he repents, forgive him. And if he sins against you seven times in a day and seven times in a day returns to you saying 'I repent' you shall forgive him" (NKJV).

Restoration requires repentance. But even without that, you can release your desire for revenge and let go of the past, freeing yourself from the consequences of not forgiving. The relationship, however, is not restored until repentance occurs.

On the *Maury Povich Show,* the topic was "Trying to Forgive the Unforgivable." David Blevins appeared, who had been viciously attacked by Fred McDonald. David was being a Good Samaritan to Fred and his wife. After finding them beside the road with no place to go, he took them to his apartment to clean up and eat. Fred hit David in the face with an electric heater and stabbed him seven times, leaving him for dead. David believed it was an act of God that got him outside where a neighbor could spot him and get him the necessary medical help. David testified against Fred at his trial for attempted murder. It concerned David that he was becoming mad at the world. Fred, speaking from prison, admitted the brutal attack, although he said most of his memory of it is blank, probably due to his drinking. He asked for David's forgiveness, and wants to compensate him in some way when he is released from prison in three years. David's response was, "I have already found it in my heart [to forgive him] . . . God enabled me to get through this."

The second crime occurred within the Gagnon family. Sherry and her sister were sexually abused by their father and were threatened, "You never tell what goes on in this house." But they finally did. Norman Gagnon pled guilty to sixty-six counts of sexual abuse, facing up to eight hundred years in prison. From prison, he talked with his two daughters, sobbing so deeply he could hardly speak. Sherry stated, "I don't want him to die in jail. He can't undo what he did . . . but he can get help . . . and get better." Sherry's sister said, "I still love my dad. . . . He's sick in the mind. . . . What good is it going to do for me to go through life angry and bitter, I have four little kids to raise." Through his sobs, Norman repeated, "I'm so sorry, I'm so sorry." The daughters both told their dad they loved him, and were proud of him for agreeing to go into a group for sexual offenders. Maury Povich expressed his response, "I don't know if I'm amazed or bewildered. I've done more shows on sexual abuse within families, and I've never seen this kind of forgiveness." Sherry immediately responded, "I get my strength through God."

Obviously, none of us is perfect. We frequently make the same mistakes again. But repentance requires that our intent must be to change our behavior.

My mother's favorite story about my childhood involved a lack of repentance, despite my words. I had taken my sister's doll. My mother told me to say that I was sorry. So I begrudgingly said, "I'm sorry."

"Now give her back her doll," my mother said.

"Well, I'm not that sorry," I replied.

In order for a relationship to be restored, the person must be genuinely sorry, with the plan and intent of changing the behavior.

Augsburger also mentions the following occasions when the forgiveness process may not be completed:

1. When forgiveness puts you one-up
2. When forgiveness is one-way
3. When forgiveness distorts feelings
4. When forgiveness denies anger
5. When forgiveness ends open relationships[7]

Forgiveness is more than words, and it isn't easy. To understand specifically how to proceed in the forgiveness process, study Augsburger's book and other books devoted to that topic. Completing your part of the forgiveness process may be the most important thing you do in the entire healing process.

Greg easily forgave his parents. It was more difficult for him to forgive himself for his affair and the pain he had brought into his marriage.

Melissa could quite easily forgive her father. It helped that he voluntarily told her about the anger incident and apologized. Their current relationship continues to reveal his intention not to repeat the verbal explosion. (It actually has never happened again since that one time when Melissa was seven.) They have also talked about his unavailability when she was very young. He is attempting to be more generous with his time and his emotions, although it doesn't come easily for him. But he has found a soft spot in her heart through his genuine love and enjoyment of Tim.

Lynn has forgiven both Greg and Melissa for their unavailability and distance. Many changes have occurred for them as they developed intimacy, openness, and honesty. Lynn has taken the first three steps with her biological father, but since he is unavailable, she cannot move any further without contact with him.

Cindy was in the same position with her grandfather. At first he did not admit any of the abuse, so she could only take the first three steps of forgiveness. Eventually, they were able to move toward specific feelings and actions, resolving the pain, anger, and guilt. She struggled to forgive herself for the promiscuity, but finally did come to understand the intense need for touch and love, and the connection between sexuality and badness created by Grandpa. As the promiscuous Cindy could understand the moral Cindy's desire to avoid sexual affairs and to make her marriage work, she came to accept her. Over time, Cindy was able to embrace all of her feelings. Integration into one person, as God intended her to be, eventually occurred. Cindy was able to have a reunion of the shattered parts of herself.

Move On to Wholeness

We must move on, regardless of what our past has been. Certainly that's easier for some people than for others. How long will the healing take? It depends upon three factors: the severity of the destruction in the past; the opportunities in the present; and the possibilities for the future. But move on, we must.

It has been said that the '70s were the "me" decade and the '90s are the "not me" decade. *Victimization* has become the all-inclusive word for all of our helplessness and unhappiness. We've begun to use the word *survivor* rather than *victim,* and that's a positive change. But as we heal, we need to leave that behind, too, and start to live fully in the present.

The recovery process is important. But we can make it more difficult on ourselves than it needs to be. We've probably all known people who continue to stay in their physical or emotional pain to the point of provoking impatience and irritation in others. Pray to find a balance that allows healthy grieving without wallowing in the pain. Throughout all of the therapy process we need to have fun, laughter, and enjoyment. Some of us have to learn to play, just as we would learn other skills. We cannot survive living only in the pain. Sometimes it means forcing ourselves to have fun. We need music, and laughter, and friends, and play throughout our lives, but never is it more needed than when we are dealing with the pain from our past.

Risk Trust

Cindy found it very difficult to trust people. Grandpa was always very spiritual, as close to God as anyone she knew. But he had betrayed her trust and had shattered her ability to trust anyone, especially God. As she healed, she began to tell God that she was willing to trust him, but that he would have to reveal to her his trustworthiness. Again, the process moved slowly because of her deep devastation. But Cindy stuck with it, step-by-step, and eventually the healing and restoration came.

Abuse shatters trust. Many victims of abuse learn a pattern of suspicion and emotional defense. It's hard to let others love them or be truly intimate with them. Love is risky. They might get hurt again.

Trust God

If you find your own trust shattered, you need to take some risks. Small ones at first—don't rush it. It needs to begin with trusting God, for he is the only one who is totally trustworthy. Getting to know and to trust God is an essential process for rebuilding a firm foundation for the rest of your life.

You also need the support and encouragement of a group with whom you can grow spiritually. There are many different churches because people have different needs in this area. Various types of music, worship, socializing, and teaching appeal to different people. Pray that God will reveal himself to you and that you'll find a place where you can learn and grow.

Greg did not have much repair work to do in the area of trusting God, both because of his positive Christian childhood, and the fairly good relationship he had with his father (except when Dad was drunk). Lynn and Melissa both had father issues to resolve and viewed God as similarly unavailable. As Melissa grew closer to her father and Lynn to Greg, both of them also experienced greater trust in God.

Trust Yourself

We must also come to trust ourselves again. Having been so devastated by the pain we may feel we cannot risk going through something similar. We are sure that the next betrayal will kill us.

But perhaps exactly the opposite is true. Because we survived once, we already know the path to recovery. We'll never again be the helpless little child. We can and we will cope with whatever occurs.

We may also distrust our judgment, especially if the abuse occurred as a result of choices we made. We may now be fearful of making wrong choices. The fact is we will make wrong choices. And we will be hurt again because of our wrong choices. But we're durable. It's like riding a bike. We get up again and again, regardless of the bruises and cuts. We are made to heal! Count on it. The tragedy of biking is not the scraped knee or even the broken arm, but the bike that stands unused in the garage because the rider gave up.

Greg learned quickly that he could trust himself to handle anger, both his own and others. He also developed a trust in his openness as he committed himself to ending the secrecy of his life. His affair had been so painful he knew he did not want to repeat that again.

Melissa and Lynn began to trust themselves to listen to and value their own needs, and then to take the risk of expressing these needs. They are also trusting themselves to express their feelings in appropriate ways.

Cindy's trust has come to include the ability to face her actions and feelings without dissociation. She trusts the integration and the commitment to stay present. She desires intimacy, and trusts her willingness to work toward that with her husband and friends.

Trust Others

We must risk again with friends and family, giving them a chance to love and care about us. We must believe that intimacy is possible, that we are capable of having healthy, rewarding relationships. We must be able to evaluate the ways in which we can trust each person. It might be in consistency, or honesty, or kindness, or wise advice, or spontaneity, or good cooking. We all have areas where we are more trustworthy than in other areas. As we learn to observe others, we will begin to see who each person is, rather than what we would like them to be.

Greg, Melissa, and Lynn are all doing well in evaluating the ways in which they can trust each individual in their lives. They often compare notes so they can check out their observations and intuitions. They are developing healthy, open relationships with family and friends, expanding their choices, and experimenting with new kinds of relationships.

Cindy and her husband continued in counseling, and have begun to develop trust in each other. She is also attempting to observe people and the areas in which they are trustworthy. Since this was a skill almost totally lacking in her, she's still at the early stages of developing it. She checks out her own observations with both her friends and her husband. There is very little trust with her family right now. She is beginning to look at their positive qualities and ways in which they can be trusted even though they still do not believe her report about Grandpa. He is considering the possibility of telling them the truth, but has not done it so far. He has written a letter, stating the truth, which can be shared after his death. He is aware that he holds many of the keys to the restoration of the family.

Trust the Abuser

Finally, we must evaluate the ways in which we can risk trust again with the abuser. Certainly you don't want to set yourself up for a fall. If there is any physical danger or serious emotional danger (verbal abuse), take proper care. We must evaluate the good qualities of the abuser, even if we are not in an ongoing relationship. Otherwise, we will have no way to relate to anyone who reminds us of that person. This is one of the most difficult aspects of trusting again. It is also one of the most freeing. As we find that strength to relate in some way with this person, we give up the victim role, even if we do not like him or her. We leave the fear behind and take away that person's power to intimidate.

Greg again has the easiest task, readily trusting his parents (and, in general, any people who are angry). He is aware of the impact of alcohol and has a realistic caution around those who are drinking.

Melissa is growing to trust her father and Greg more and more, and men in general. She is expecting them to consider her needs and not to become furious if she asks for something they do not wish to give, or if she asks at a bad time. Several times she has even persisted with a request when someone was angry at her need.

Lynn is coming to identify unavailable, rejecting people, not trusting them to meet her needs. She is also learning not to take it personally, but to let it be their problem. She is asking for more of what she wants and needs, as well as receiving emotionally from her friends and family. She is starting to become comfortable with looking attractive and has taken many positive steps in this direction with her weight, exercise, clothing, makeup, and hair style. She and Jenny have begun to enjoy shopping and helping each other "be beautiful," as Jenny says.

Cindy is learning to identify the men who seem absolutely wonderful, but who have another side to them that is abusive. She is no longer allowing herself to be drawn into affairs with them. In general, she's learning to be more discerning about people.

Dream New Dreams

In the midst of our pain we often feel utter hopelessness. I remember a powerful letter of encouragement I received from a dear woman at my church, when I cried through the church service Sunday after Sunday for a full year. It included a thought based on Isaiah 61:3: "God will bestow a crown of beauty instead of ashes and the oil of gladness instead of mourning." Many days I repeated this, and carried the letter with me, with little hope or faith. Soon it came to be true, and the pain subsided.

Let yourself have dreams again. When we're in the depth of pain or grief we usually believe it will never pass. But we do heal. I recall that, in my darkest time, someone encouraged me to pray for a new dream, so I did. Within a month or two my prayer was answered. Leaving the past memories and feelings behind us, we really do begin to picture possibilities.

I felt clearly directed by the verses in Isaiah 61 that had brought me hope:

> The Spirit of the Lord God is upon me, because the Lord has anointed me to bring good news to the suffering and afflicted. He has sent me to comfort the brokenhearted, to announce liberty to captives, and to open the eyes of the blind. He has sent me to tell those that mourn that the time of God's favor to them has come, and the day of his wrath to their enemies. To all who mourn . . . he will give beauty for ashes; joy instead of mourning, praise instead of heaviness.
>
> Isaiah 61:1–3 LB

Melissa and Greg shared the new dream of intimacy and joy in their immediate family first, and then with their extended family. Lynn's dream was for the same intimacy, including a husband and children of her own. Her career dreams changed to include working with needy children in some aspect. She began to investigate the options.

Cindy's dream was intimacy with her husband and friends. She also began to dream about a career as an artist.

Set and Reach for New Goals

For many people, it's necessary to take out a new option on life. Schooling or training for either a career or a new hobby are common. Start with small goals that you can quickly accomplish, such as one craft class where you'll be trained to arrange flowers or a weightlifting class where your progress is very measurable by the increase in weights. Do things that are tangible, seen and enjoyed not only by you, but by others as well. Try hobbies you've never done before, especially creative outlets. Consider painting, drawing, pottery, or any artistic mediums. Try music, interior decorating, gardening, writing, wood carving, raising dogs, sports. Open up your world to adventure, to travel, to new and different activities like sailing or skiing. Start asking others what they do for recreation or fun or relaxation. Write these ideas down. See if there's a way to try them, even once. Learn to have fun. Perhaps the most critical aspect of recovery is learning to enjoy life. If we do everything else, and miss this, we will still be unhappy. It is not enough to eliminate the negative. We must replace it with the positive joy of life.

Melissa and Greg began to explore the world of fun. Over a period of time, the entire family tried tennis, golf, dancing, and sailing lessons. They planned relaxing family vacations to new places. Each family member planned a special day of fun. These included music concerts, plays, trips to the beach and amusement parks, parties, roller and ice skating, skiing, camping, hiking, biking, and more. Melissa and Greg each also picked one thing to do without the other. For Greg, it was learning to fly. Melissa went parasailing.

Cindy also set new goals. She returned to college, beginning with one class in art. She was told she was very talented and should continue. She did, and eventually graduated. She also became a clothing designer and painted watercolors in her spare time. She met her goal of mounting her own show and selling her paintings. Dance and music had always intrigued Cindy, so she learned to play several instruments and took dance lessons in ballroom, western, and ballet. She and her husband set goals for fun and enjoyment. He joined her in the western and ballroom dancing. She joined him in athletic interests, such as handball and biking. They set a goal together for a family, and had two children.

We can find healing from the abuse that we have endured. Do not give up until you reach it. The length of recovery and the intensity of the pain will vary for each of us, depending on many factors: the severity and frequency of the abuse, the age it began and ended, the closeness in relationship and daily living to the perpetrator, the level of trust and obedience to God, and the general strength of the personality and health.

As you proceed through the steps briefly examined in this chapter, your therapist can assist you in understanding unique areas of recovery for you personally, as well as in finding the methods that work for you. I repeat: This is not meant to be a self-help chapter that replaces professional, individual counseling. But I hope it gets you started and encourages you to continue moving through the process.

13

How Do I Recover If My Memories Are False?

Remember Samantha? Into adulthood, she was still overly dependent upon her parents, calling them daily and counting on them for everyday needs. When she tried to gain some independence, pulling away from them emotionally, toward her husband, she felt terribly guilty.

Then the dreams came, dreams of abuse. Though the thoughts of being molested by her loving parents caused pain, in a way these dreams were just what Samantha needed. If her parents had abused her, then she felt justified in pulling away from them. After all, she needed to protect her children. She couldn't trust anyone who would be abusive and then lie about it.

After Samantha came to our center, we revisited her memory of abuse by both of her parents, after she prayerfully asked for truth. The memory changed. The same event occurred, but this time the abuse was from a couple who had lived down the street. As a child, Samantha believed it was her fault, that the abuse had occurred because she hadn't been with her parents. If only she had stayed at home that day, like they wanted her to do, none of this would have happened. She should never have gone against her parents.

Now she was shocked and horrified at her mistaken accusation. She felt she should immediately seek restoration with her parents and confront the true perpetrators. Since it was her impulsiveness that created much of this chaos, she was encouraged to wait a few days, continuing to pray for the truth. As she waited, she felt confident about this memory, but was also willing to seek external evidence before jumping to another wrong conclusion.

All of us have had false memories. We may have distorted events that occurred ten minutes ago, especially if we were in conflict with someone or were very stressed. We may have distorted events from our past and our present. We have failed to remember things accurately both about ourselves and about others. We have forgotten things we've said and done, even promises we've made. These have included insignificant facts or feelings, as well as ones that are very consequential.

Understand That No One's Memory Is Perfect

The first step for recovery is to accept the fact that none of us has a perfect memory. It is not realistic to expect our memories to be perfect. If we cling to the fantasy that any perception is totally accurate, we'll be dogmatic, rigid, and sometimes wrong. People who remain open to correction in any area of their lives are admirable. It's not the end of the world to have a false memory. We all do. We can use this experience to understand ourselves better as we consider the cause of the false belief. We can then discover the necessary steps to heal from the effects of believing misinformation as well as from the cause that created it.

Understand the Reasons the False Memory Occurred

We have already considered possible reasons for false memories. In order to heal properly, we need to understand where the falsehood came from. That may help us resolve our underlying need, and keep distortions from surfacing again.

Were You Influenced by an Outside Source?

Did you allow someone else to determine your reality? No one should ever be given that power. That does not mean you stop listening to others' points of view. But if anyone can convince you to believe a lie, you are obviously too susceptible to outside opinions. We try to teach our children to think for themselves, not to blindly follow the advice or actions of others. We know that if they are too easily influenced someone can lead them into trouble.

Do you need to gain strength in this area? Look at your past history to determine your susceptibility to outside influences, to examine the frequency and the manner in which it has occurred. Ask others for their input about this, too (but avoid those who might take advantage of your suggestibility). Psychological tests can also determine your suggestibility.

Were You Fooled by an Enemy?

Are you shocked when people turn against you or betray you? If it's a frequent occurrence, you should evaluate the relationships you choose. Sometimes we like to believe in the goodness of people. We view our world as free from enemies, but this is not true. The two extremes—paranoia and total naive trust—are neither healthy nor realistic. Sadly, most people are selfish and will do whatever is in their best interests. Pray for wisdom and discrimination to see the truth about each person in your life. None of us will ever be perfectly accurate in discerning the intentions of others, but we should be continuing to grow in our wisdom and judgment.

During their separation, both Jack and his daughters were influenced by his wife, Carol, to believe he had molested the girls. After the truth was determined and Jack was exonerated, the girls' perceptions and fears had to be reversed to see the truth about their dad. Jack investigated his own willingness to believe a horrible lie about himself. He related his childhood experiences of continual badness. He described his parents as critical, and his belief that they were right. He was often in trouble, doing something wrong. If he denied it or defended himself, he got into more trouble. But if he admitted it, he was usually off the hook, and the consequences were minimal. Jack could see that he had followed the same pattern, expecting bad behavior from himself and quickly admitting it, even when he had no memory of the event, in order to avoid worse consequences.

Jack's therapy involved seeking the truth about himself from God's perspective, letting go of the lies and expectations of bad behavior, and learning to defend himself when he was innocent.

Did You Go Along with Friends or Recovery Groups?

We are probably all influenced by our friends in many ways. In fact, we should seek friends who will influence us in positive ways. "As iron sharpens iron, so one man sharpens another" (Prov. 27:17 NIV). It is to be hoped that our friends will influence us to become more healthy physically, emotionally, and spiritually, and will challenge us intellectually. But even though our friends have certain beliefs, we are accountable for our own beliefs, and must take the responsibility to find the truth for ourselves, especially the truth about our own childhood.

Are you influenced if several people agree on the same opinion? Do you find yourself unquestioningly believing what the group believes? If you came to believe a false memory because of a group's influence, you need to learn to take protective precautions so you won't be unduly swayed by group mentality. Many of us are followers and naturally do whatever our peers are doing—or believe what they are believing.

Lynn had been influenced by her group to believe that her father had molested her, based on the similarity of her symptoms to the symptoms of those who knew they had been abused. She was also told by group members that it was "obvious" to them that she had been abused. As discussed in previous chapters, Lynn learned very early to ignore her needs and do everything possible to meet her mother's needs. She became an extension of Mom, rather than an independent person with thoughts and needs of her own. She became angry and depressed when she assumed the mother role in their home during Greg and Melissa's impending divorce. Her group was an oasis in her desert, a place where feelings were accepted and her needs were expressed. This made her very vulnerable to their thoughts and opinions. She didn't listen to her own reality, but gave more validity to the group's perceptions.

Were You Influenced by Books or Media Presentations?

Books, newspapers, magazines, and television are viewed by some as authoritative sources of truth. They automatically see an author, writer, or television personality as an expert. We all need to assess our susceptibility to what we read or what we see and hear on radio and television. We need to question and prayerfully think through the assumptions and opinions of others, no matter how confident and informed they may seem. If you were influenced in this manner, consider the reasons for your naivete in this area.

Melissa was initially convinced that all of her family had been sexually abused. Why? Because of a book she read.

Remember that her upbringing had been primarily intellectual. Her family gave great value to academic knowledge. Melissa's own thoughts and opinions, and especially her feelings, were of little importance. It's not surprising that she believed the printed word. Her therapy included learning discrimination, seeking information supporting both sides of an issue, and acknowledging the value of her own needs, feelings, and thoughts.

Have You Been Influenced by a Nonprofessional?

Many of us believe what anyone tells us as long as they seem sure of themselves. We often fail to question the qualifications of the person giving information—even if it's information about ourselves! But why should we accept that person's perspective? We put ourselves at risk by non-thinking compliance.

Barry was told he was sexually abused. The message came from a respected Christian leader who had no specific training in this area. The real issue for Barry was his abandonment at age four by his mother, but he chose to accept the theory of an untrained observer who said what Barry wanted to hear. Somehow Barry considered it less painful to blame abuse for his problems with women than to face the devastation of abandonment by his mother. As he considered the cause of his false memory, he acknowledged that he preferred victimization to nonexistence.

But that choice wasn't left up to him. The abandonment happened. It didn't help him to believe the wrong thing about his past. He had to take that difficult step of being willing to face the truth. There was pain and fear in acknowledging his abandonment, but comfort and healing could only come after he addressed the real issue. If you have pneumonia, it doesn't help to put your arm in a sling.

It was Barry's fear of abandonment that made him keep women at a distance. As he dealt with the abandonment issues he found the strength he needed, as well as a group of caring friends.

Then disaster struck—Barry's wife left him. This was exactly what he had always feared—being abandoned again. But instead of retreating into self-pity, Barry learned that he could live through abandonment. He wasn't four years old anymore. He was no longer as alone or needy as he had been back then. Instead of pulling back into himself, he pushed forward into intimacy. He decided to risk opening his heart to his estranged wife, to try to put their marriage back together on more intimate terms. They eventually reconciled, and Barry continues to experience the newfound enjoyment and challenge of closeness.

Norma received the revelation from a well-meaning church woman: Norma must have been abused as a child. Wanting to be a "good girl," Norma went along with the woman's suggestion, producing false memories to comply with what God had supposedly told this woman.

In therapy, Norma recalled the verbal humiliation that occurred for her as a child, whenever she wasn't "good." She recalled her determination to always be good, which meant compliance to authority. Obviously, there's nothing wrong with being genuinely good, but she was granting extreme power to her parents and other authorities to determine how she would live. Even as an adult, she had tried to please everybody, being overly compliant. As she began to step out from the shadow of her parents' judgment she began to risk genuineness and honesty. She sought to place her life in God's hands, seeking *his* goodness, not the behavior that everyone else desired.

Norma will probably always be a cooperative person. That's one of her strengths. But she also gave herself permission to be different from others' expectations, to have a mind of her own, to have values and behavior that seemed right to her.

Have You Been Influenced by a Therapist?

Before Carol accused Jack of sexually abusing the girls, she sought counseling. After a few sessions, the counselor accurately perceived Carol's anxiety over sexual abuse. She concluded that Carol knew that Jack was molesting the girls, but did not want to admit it. As the counselor continued to question, Carol wondered if it might be true. After all, at that time she could not see anything good about Jack.

When the counselor mentioned the need to protect the children, the light went on for Carol. This was the way she could gain full custody of the girls and move out of the area with her new boyfriend. Besides, it might be true. All men were like that, in her opinion, just like her stepfather, who had molested her. And if a therapist thought it was true, it must be.

She then brought her girls to the counselor, who quickly confirmed the suspicions of abuse. Time and investigation revealed that this counselor had been abused herself and was beginning her own therapy. It is not uncommon to misperceive others when we are in a place of pain, and to see them as we view ourselves, but the counselor was apparently unaware that her perspective was skewed by her own pain. She was unwilling even to consider the possibility that Jack had *not* abused his daughters, despite the fact she had done no psychological testing, had not met Jack, and had never seen him with the girls.

Carol's anger at her stepfather and at Jack, combined with her motivation to leave the area, made her susceptible to believe the false leading of a therapist. In Carol's therapy at our center, she admitted her tendency to stretch the truth to accomplish her purposes and her irrational generalizations from her stepfather to all men. She faced her tendency to manipulate in order to meet her needs. Over time, she resolved her anger at her stepfather for sexually molesting her, and learned not to generalize this experience to all other men. Both Carol and Jack progressed well in their individual counseling, as well as in marriage counseling. The family was eventually restored.

If you have been influenced by a therapist to believe a false memory, what can you learn from that? Does this indicate high suggestibility on your part? Does it extend to all people in authority, or only to specific roles or types of people? When and how did it begin? Is there something that you need from people that gives them too much power? It's easy to trust a therapist to solve the mysteries of your murky mind, but you must learn to establish your own identity and truth. Get expert help when needed, but allow an advising role only, not a controlling or dictating role.

Were You Influenced by Internal Factors?

We have just examined how to begin eliminating our suggestibility to external sources. Now we also need to understand the internal motivations. They are often interrelated. We are generally susceptible to influence by outside sources because they offer to meet an internal need.

Were You Seeking to Gratify Unmet Needs?

This might include the need for attention, belonging, acceptance, intimacy, independence, or something else. When we have identified the need, we can usually find alternative ways to meet it. When we are unconscious of our needs, we are most susceptible to cults, to false information, or even to betrayal of our own values and conscience. The intensity of the deprivation in any area determines the degree to which we are willing to give up honesty, truth, and even reality. The tragedy is that unconscious needs lead us into further destruction and pain. If we are starving emotionally, we'll do anything to meet that need, just as a baby will scream to be fed regardless of how much that irritates the parents, or just as a starving person will eat food from a garbage can even if it might be contaminated or spoiled.

Are you lacking support in your present life? Are you looking to others for the care that you're not giving to yourself? If so, you'll never find it. Or if you find some support, it will never be enough—because there is some nurturing that we have to do for ourselves.

We must care for ourselves physically by proper eating, rest, and exercise. We can't look to anyone else to do that for us. Friends may cook for us or take us to dinner, but it's still our responsibility to care for ourselves physically. In the same way, we must find methods to deal with our spiritual and emotional needs. Many people refuse to care for themselves in these areas, believing it's selfish, but then they feel angry and hurt when others don't meet their needs.

In his book *New Choices, New Boundaries,* Rich Buhler describes ways we can emotionally and spiritually nourish ourselves and others. It is very helpful in beginning to identify the obstacles that keep us from being nurtured, as well as specific steps to take to begin to meet our needs.[1]

Lynn had many unmet needs: intimacy, acceptance, belonging, attention, and care. She learned very early to act independently, expressing few needs or wants, and taking care of her mother. She learned to hide feelings, especially anger and hurt. She felt no support in her home during the threatened divorce. Essentially, Lynn became the functioning parent for the rest of the family.

Lynn's group experience opened the door to her feelings, her needs, and her wants. It was a safe place to discover who she was apart from her mother, and to try different methods of expressing feelings, gaining attention, disagreeing, asking for needs to be met, and accepting care and nurturing. Lynn's individual therapy centered upon discovering these needs and feelings that were often hidden from herself. Because of her entire family's involvement in therapy, she also learned communication with each of them.

Penny had some of the same needs. She suffered severe neglect as a child. As an adult, she was unable to make friends. A wonderful world of support from a therapist and a group opened up to her, *if* she had been abused. Under those conditions, it's not at all surprising that she created a false memory.

As it turned out, even after Penny concluded that she had experienced no abuse, the group continued to welcome her. Yet some of the group members had difficulty understanding her pain, thinking it would be wonderful to be left alone, rather than hurt. Others, who had experienced both neglect and abuse, were more empathic. Penny was encouraged and taught to develop relationships outside of the group as well. Eventually she did develop other close friendships and interests, no longer needing the group. And after she left the group she continued friendships with several of its members.

Were You Justifying Unacceptable Behavior?

We all have done things in our lives for which we feel shame and guilt. Guilt is healthy when it promotes a change in harmful behavior. Welcome it as a friend, just as you might welcome a fever that indicates a physical illness. Neither guilt nor fever feels very good, but both do us a service by alerting us to a greater problem.

One of the most admirable qualities in a person is a willingness to admit fault. Without it, we force ourselves into denial, defensiveness, anger, self righteousness, or projection of blame elsewhere, none of which are very endearing qualities. A person who can admit wrongdoing and then learn from the mistake continues to grow in self-regard as well as in the esteem of others.

Pointing the finger of blame is not new. In the Garden of Eden, Adam blamed Eve for his disobedience, and Eve blamed the serpent. Things haven't changed so much: Even today, few people are willing to take responsibility for their actions. It's the "not me" generation. Someone else is at fault. Despite our childhood or current circumstances, we will never be free until we become responsible. Until then, we remain the helpless victims, waiting for others to change.

> Penny initially sought therapy because of her guilt over her promiscuity. When she heard that sexual abuse often caused acting-out sexual behavior, she latched onto that as a justification. If she was a victim, then her promiscuity could be blamed on someone else. She wouldn't have to feel so bad about herself. This created a second motivation (besides the group pressure) for a false memory.
>
> But Penny's promiscuity did not change when she recovered her false memory of abuse. It was only as she began to meet the underlying need—intimacy with both men and women—that it became controllable. She also perceived the emptiness of her sexual behavior and its destructiveness to both herself and her partners.

If your behavior is out of control in any area you need to look for the underlying driving force. But be careful. We all like easy answers. We'd all like to find one event that explains all our problems—but it seldom works that way. And if you lock onto the wrong answer, the likelihood of resolving or ending the unacceptable behavior is very low. If your false memory is a way of justifying unacceptable behavior, you probably need a counselor with a broad understanding of behavior who can help you sort out the real reasons for your actions and help you chart a new course.

My son's baby-sitter, Ginny, taught me something important about dealing with bad behavior. "We need to allow children to make restitution for their mistakes," she said. Mistakes are made. Children disobey. But there is a certain relief that we all feel when we can clean up our messes, pay for what we've damaged, or remedy the problem we've created. We gain a healthy self-respect by working through the problem and learning from it. It's true of children and it's true of adults. If there's some bad behavior that you seek an excuse for, ask yourself why you need excuses. Face up to it and change your ways. Blaming won't get you anywhere, especially if it involves a false memory.

Were You Seeking a Framework for Expressing and Accepting Feelings?

Lynn was adept at hiding all feelings until she pictured abuse from her biological father. Though false, that freed her to express feelings toward both him and her mother. The amount of hurt and anger Lynn felt toward him seemed more appropriate if he had molested her than if she were "only rejected and abandoned." As she expressed the feelings associated with the perceived sexual abuse, she felt much better. This also led to hurt and anger toward her mother, for not protecting her. Finding a place for all of these feelings was very freeing for Lynn. Although the memory was not accurate, it did open the door to her unexpressed feelings. It initiated the tasks necessary for her healing and wholeness with others and with the Lord. Since she had not confronted the alleged abuser, nor had she terminated any relationships, there were no fences to mend. The false memory was abandoned when it was no longer needed. By this time, Lynn could face the truth of her past, the pain of her father's abandonment and her mother's unavailability. She also expressed her anger at Mom for not giving her the loving daddy she needed.

Are there feelings within you that you cannot accept? The most frequently rejected feelings are anger, sexual desire, hurt, revenge, jealousy, and terror. Perhaps you have strong feelings like this and do not allow yourself to express them or even feel them. As in Lynn's case, such feelings may come out in false memories of abuse.

If you have already determined that the memory is false, you still need to deal with those buried feelings. Accept the fact that you have those feelings and try to find appropriate ways to express them.

Often expression is the hardest thing. People around us may not understand how deeply we feel. Or we may have trouble putting our emotions into words.

There's a helpful strategy presented by Gary Smalley and Dr. John Trent in their book *The Language of Love*. They suggest painting a "word picture" that communicates your feelings to another person. If you have trouble finding the right words to say, try picturing your feelings. What do your emotions look like? Are there everyday objects or events that describe the way you feel?

Smalley and Trent give an excellent example, a teenage girl's letter to her father, expressing her devastation over his decision to leave the family. She put it in terms of a car accident. These are a few excerpts, but it is well worth reading her entire letter, and the book.

> I feel like our family has been riding in a nice car for a long time . . . over the years, the car has developed some problems. . . . We feel real secure with you driving and Mom beside you. . . . But last month, Mom was at the wheel . . . we all looked up and saw another car, out of control . . . the impact sent us flying off the road and crashing . . . Dad, just before being hit, we could see that you were driving the other car. . . . Sitting next to you was another woman. . . . It was such a terrible accident that we were all rushed to the emergency ward. But when we asked where you were, no one knew. . . . Mom broke several ribs . . . one almost pierced her heart. . . . Brian is in so much pain and shock, he doesn't want to play with anyone. . . . I was hurting so much myself that I couldn't help them. . . . I wondered if any of us would make it. . . . The doctors say . . . they can help me get better. But I wish it was you helping me, instead of them. . . . The pain is so bad, but what's even worse is that we miss you so much. Every day we wait to see if you're going to visit us in the hospital, and every day you don't come. . . . Are you hurting from the wreck? Do you need us like we need you?

After receiving the letter, the father returned home.[2]

In essence, Lynn's false memory of abuse by her biological father was a word picture—or a mind picture—that expressed how she felt. Even though the abuse never happened, she felt abused, and this picture was her mind's way of letting the feelings out.

> Dennis as a child experienced verbal attacks from his father. He simmered with terror and rage, but never expressed these feelings. Instead he had regular bouts with depression. As an adult, Dennis envisioned his father beating him. It was a false memory, but it, too, was a mind picture, allowing Dennis to get his deep feelings out. It was as if his father had beaten him physically, though the attacks were actually only verbal. In his therapy, Dennis learned to accept and express his feelings and needs. The depression left. Changes occurred in his marriage, his job, and his family.

If you, like Lynn and Dennis, have found that framework for emotional expression through a false memory, then it has played a very valuable role in your life. But instead of letting your mind distort reality, learn the art of painting word pictures that will communicate your feelings both to yourself and to others.

If you have not taken action against the falsely perceived perpetrator, then you can take steps on your own to let go of the false memory. Some people can dismiss it easily; others need assistance to find freedom from the intrusive pictures of the memory. If the latter is true, find a counselor who deals with that specific problem. You need not be stuck with a false memory, or the associated feelings.

Were You Seeking to Please Others?

Do you have a strong need to be accepted and liked by others? Is that need so strong that you have sacrificed the truth?

We all want to be liked and accepted. But this need can become pathological and destructive. We may have to examine our worth apart from the acceptance of others.

Dr. Larry Day, a psychologist in Oregon, has written an excellent book, *By Design in God's Image.*[3] In a clear and interesting manner, it leads through many issues and solutions to poor self-esteem. It includes specific personal growth exercises and suggested readings. The foundation of our self-worth must be established in order to achieve any stability.

Even our best friends will at times fail to buoy us up. If that is their constant task, they will become weary and resentful. We must instead lay the foundation of our own self-esteem in the esteem God has for us. That is the only thing that will not change.

Penny would do anything to be liked, including sexual involvement with men she hardly knew. The severe neglect from her parents left her with feelings of worthlessness. As she learned to accept God's value of her, and as her intense needs for caring began to be met, she became less susceptible to this need to please others.

Have You Confused Facts and Fantasies?

Visual memories and fantasies are stored in the same area of the brain, thus possibly creating difficulty in distinguishing between the two. It is not surprising, then, if we confuse them. Your fantasies, not only the facts of your childhood, are important. As with dreams, they may be symbolic of fears or unmet needs. Consider their significance further.

Melissa's confusion over her neighbor and her dad vividly illustrates the blurring of fact and fantasy. It was easy for her to understand the confusion the day her father frightened her by his anger. The bewilderment was even more profound during her nightmare and half-awake state. Since Melissa had spent most of her life living in her thoughts and intellect, she is beginning to enjoy the world of imagination and fantasy. She knew it might occasionally be difficult to distinguish between fact and fantasy, but found the challenge interesting. She determined that, as long as no actions were taken that were based upon these fantasies and they weren't used to escape, they did not pose any risk in her life.

For many years, psychology students have been taught about conditioned responses in learning theory. When we pair a neutral event with a frightening event, we are conditioned to fear the neutral event as well. Say that every day after school Nice Nathan and Bully Bob come over to your yard and Bob beats you up. One day Nice Nathan comes over alone and you respond with fear. Why? You've paired him with Bully Bob. Generalization may then extend this conditioning even further. You may extend your fear of Bob to everyone named Bob or to everyone who's big or to all boys in general.

Our emotional reactions frequently demonstrate this conditioning, whether our conscious minds agree or not. You may know that Nice Nathan is harmless but you may still feel the fear.

One of the central goals of therapy is to free each individual to act appropriately in the present rather than overreacting from past conditioning. The Nathan-Bob analogy may be pretty silly, but there are children who duck, from beatings, whenever a hand is raised, and adults who hate eggs, since getting the flu after eating them years ago, and a number of women who fear all men, because of the abuse from their fathers. There are probably no adults alive who do not have some example of a conditioned fear in their own lives. These fears can seem irrational, but they feel real. And, as we have seen, they can easily distort our memories. If your false memory of abuse has been mingled with some conditioned fear, you may need to confront that fear and unlock that bond.

Were Your Memories Recovered by an Unreliable Method?

No method is totally reliable. I know of no method of memory recovery that is reliable enough to produce evidence to convict someone. Recovered memories do not belong in the courts, but in the counseling office. No memory should be accepted as factual without corroborating evidence. The purpose of every method of memory recovery should be to promote our emotional health or recovery. Obtaining a factual history of our childhood may come in time, with our additional research.

Sometimes we jump to conclusions without seeking adequate information. We need to slow down, to question and research, and to develop more objective, logical thinking skills.

Jack was unaware that the accusations of child abuse against him were not supported by what is known about child development. Carol and her therapist reported that the girls presented detailed accounts of his molest and verbal threats, which allegedly occurred when the children were one to two years old. Carol and the therapist did not report any behavioral evidence. The girls were three and four at the time of the accusation. Children do not have complete verbal memories much earlier than the ages of three or four because of brain development. The only way they can give a detailed verbal account of something occurring when they were one or two is if they have been told this by someone else. In this case, Carol admitted that both she and the therapist had suggested options to the girls.

Lynn entered hypnosis with the expectation of finding abuse from her father. Since she has already demonstrated her high susceptibility, it was not surprising that she could easily imagine the scenario of the molest. Although it was difficult to determine, it also appeared that the hypnotist asked leading and suggestive questions. Both Lynn and the hypnotist were very surprised when they discovered that the recovered memory could not have been true.

The specific memory is only a minor part of therapy. The goal of therapy is not to find the memory. The goal is to deal with all aspects of our lives, bringing restoration and reconciliation, both within ourselves and in our relationships.

Accept and Forgive Yourself

If you have created a false memory, does that mean you've done something wrong? Does that mean you're a bad, deceitful person? Or worse, does that mean you're crazy, losing your grip on reality?

No.

As you've been following along in this book up to now, you've probably identified one or more reasons for your false memory. And beyond those specific distortions, our memories are just plain fallible. You are fortunate to realize that now. It may save you many conflicts in the future—those fights where you try to prove that you're right and someone else is wrong because you think you remember specifically what went on. Always take your memory with a grain of salt.

No, you're not bad or crazy. However, you may have been unwise if you jumped to conclusions and cut off relationships with people based on your false memory. If so, that's understandable. We're dealing with highly emotional issues here. It's easy to make some bad choices along the way.

Before you try to make up with others, you may need to make up with yourself. Can you accept and forgive yourself for your own errors in judgment?

It was very difficult for Samantha to accept herself when she realized that she had deeply hurt her parents by falsely accusing them. It certainly taught her to question her memories, and not to jump into any confrontational actions without careful and prayerful consideration. She also evaluated her impulsiveness and its past consequences in other relationships and in other areas of her life.

It is important to see the positive results of the process you've come through, the ways in which you've benefited. You probably have a better grasp of your internal needs. Perhaps you have come to understand that you're highly suggestible to external influence. You may have learned about your brain's functioning, and the process and reliability of your memory. You may be more aware of childhood pain, and the healing process. You may have built new friendships with other hurting people, and learned listening and empathy skills. You may even have confronted areas within your childhood family that needed attention. We all tend to think of our experiences in black and white, good and bad. But try jotting down the positive and the negative things that have come out of this experience. I think you'll find a balance is there.

Lynn was grateful for her group. She loved being where she could openly discuss anything, where all feelings were acceptable when expressed appropriately. She really needed a family like this. She learned to express anger and hurt toward both her father and mother. The group had been helpful in identifying realistic needs. As a result, Lynn could focus on her feelings of isolation and rejection, and find ways to change this. As her parents continued in their own therapy, they were also able to develop greater intimacy with Lynn and their other children.

There were also good things that had occurred for Samantha through the false memory. She had finally made the emotional break with her parents and allowed herself to need her husband. She could now understand this extreme dependency upon her parents and the fear of going against their wishes. When she had acted independently as a child, she was physically and verbally abused by the neighbors. Independence as an adult no longer carried the same threat.

Seek to Restore Broken Relationships

Perhaps you've decided that your memory is false, after examining the evidence, or the lack thereof. But your feelings may not go along with that conclusion. Because you have paired so many pictures of abuse with a parent (or other supposed abuser), you may continue to have a conditioned emotional reaction to this person. So you may think you should restore your relationship with the person, but you still feel ill at ease with him or her. This may require one of the desensitization therapies to break this connection. EMDR has been very successful in this type of treatment. After we have released the emotional reactions created by the false memories, we are ready to attempt to repair broken relationships.

It may feel as if your relationship with your family has been irreparably shattered, but you must take the first step toward restoration—*acknowledge the truth.* Sometimes it needs to start with the statement, *I was wrong*—the hardest words in the English language. You need to be specific about the ways in which you were wrong. It might be that you believed a lie, that you refused to listen to their perspective, that you didn't give them a chance, that you did a poor job of confrontation (even if the memory had been true), that you condemned without telling them why.

Samantha felt total humiliation approaching her parents, and decided to do it by letter. She explained the entire situation, beginning with "I was wrong about you."

Dennis felt differently. He was wrong about being physically abused himself, but he had seen his dad abuse his brothers, and both parents had verbally abused all of the children. Yet he also wrote a letter after several attempts at phone conversations ended in screaming matches.

The second step is *asking for forgiveness*. Remember that forgiveness requires repentance—or genuine sorrow—over your behavior, as well as specific intent and plans to change that behavior in the future. You need to express that sorrow and your plans for change. It is usually important to explain how and why you have come to believe that the memory is false. It is also helpful when you include what influenced you to believe the false memory in the first place. Then, ask specifically for forgiveness.

The response may take some time, depending on the degree of shattered trust. We need to allow the time without pushing for an answer. Both sides will need to hear and be heard. Counseling at this point has been essential and invaluable for many families. Some parents need about one minute, no matter what the devastation has been. Others approach restoration cautiously, needing to talk the entire incident through first.

Families are different. You will learn more about your family's uniqueness through this difficult experience. Neither way is wrong. Building bridges takes time. The span between the two sides, the number of workers, and the number of hours per week they work will all determine the time required to complete the bridge. We have found the intensive therapy to work the best in building a bridge after the bomb of a false accusation has family members hunkering down for protection on each side of the wide gulf between them. At this point, you must find a therapist who is excellent at building bridges.

It took Samantha's parents a heartbeat to respond positively to her letter. They immediately called her, in tears, and said they forgave her, asking if they could come and see her. It was a wonderful reunion. Samantha's depression immediately lifted. They did still come into therapy with Samantha and Jim, so they could all discuss the best way to proceed from this point. They were all able to express their feelings and hear each other's reactions. Because they had a very close, loving relationship, with good communication, restoration of the relationship came quickly and easily. Together they decided how their relationship would be in the present.

Dennis's family was very different. No one listened. Yelling, sarcasm, put-downs, and criticism were the norm. In counseling, they first learned to listen, a very difficult task for this family. Then the

> entire family became involved in several deep, painful issues, as will be described in the following chapter. The gulf between Dennis and his parents was very wide and deep, caused by many years of erosion of trust. Thus, the building of the bridge was long and difficult. But it did get built.

We all have distorted perceptions and need to realize that our memories are not perfect, and never will be. We need to go through a recovery process from false memories, the associated feelings, and their impact on others. We need to understand the reasons the memory occurred, whether from outside sources of influence, our internal needs, or the method of recovery.

Even though we have created a false memory, self-forgiveness and acceptance are possible and necessary. Appreciating the positive results that have occurred is as important as facing the destruction. As we seek to restore any broken relationships, we must seek forgiveness and rebuild bridges of understanding and communication.

14

How Do I Survive a False Accusation?

To be falsely accused is very painful. We feel so helpless when there is no way to prove our innocence. It is especially devastating when we are accused by our own children or grandchildren. Almost all parents do what they consider best in raising their children, but we all make mistakes. Sometimes in retrospect we can see we made huge mistakes. Whatever errors we have made with our children, most of us have also given an enormous amount of love, time, and money to them. Any parent who has been rejected by a child of any age is usually shocked, hurt, angry, and defensive.

As we have worked with parents who have been falsely accused, we have found that some things cause further alienation, and other things bring about reconciliation. This chapter will discuss those actions that have promoted restoration of broken relationships. Although this chapter refers primarily to parents, the same principles apply to anyone who has been falsely accused and is seeking resolution and restoration.

(In order to simplify the wording, the term *child* will be used to refer to accusers of all ages, including adults, since usually the issue is alleged abuse and conflict with parents or adults in authority when the accuser was a child. The pronoun *she* will be used since the majority of the false accusations come from women, although the same principles apply to men.)

Chuck Swindoll, president of Dallas Theological Seminary, recently spoke on his international radio program, *Insight for Living,* on the topic

"How to Do Right When You've Been Done Wrong." The ideas are based on the life of David as reflected in Psalm 26, giving excellent psychological and spiritual guidelines that will be included in this chapter.[1]

Pray for the Dismissal of All Charges

First, pray for the dismissal of all charges. The ideal outcome is the immediate withdrawal of all false accusations. In Psalm 26:1 (LB), David prays with his request and statement of innocence, "Dismiss all the charges against me, Lord, for I have tried to keep your laws and have trusted You without wavering." He also affirms his trust in God, despite the false accusations. David was being chased by King Saul's men; Saul intended to kill him even though he had done nothing to deserve death. Yet David maintained his unwavering faith in God.

Look at Your Own Behavior

David continues his prayer with openness before the Lord (v. 2): "Cross-examine me, O Lord, . . . test my motives and affections." He's asking God to scrutinize him, to open up all the closets and to examine him. Are we that courageous, to look first at ourselves?

Whenever we have conflict with anyone, we need to look at our part in the difficulty. Even if only 10 percent is our fault, we need to acknowledge that part. Sometimes we don't know what our errors have been. Like David, we believe we are innocent. Parents who have been willing to seek spiritual and psychological counsel to understand their responsibility in the conflict have not only found support and encouragement, but have also gained respect in their children's eyes.

Denial

Denial is usually our first reaction to any accusation. We do not want this negative behavior to be true about us. Even if it is true, we certainly do not want anyone else to know about it. Just as in other kinds of trauma, the anxiety of an accusation, true or false, results in denial as the first step. Dr. Snyder, psychologist and author of *Excuses: Masquerades in Search of Grace,* discusses how we all deceive ourselves, generally by exaggerating our positive behaviors and minimizing our negative actions, intentions, and feelings. He reports that men are more likely to engage in "denial excuse-making" than women, with the common response of "I didn't do it." Women are more likely to admit their actions, but then justify it, with the response, "Yes I did, but . . ."[2]

Research with known molesters, rapists, and pedophiles has illustrated that most of the time they verbally and even mentally deny their abusive behavior, instead of justifying, minimizing, or rationalizing.[3]

Self-Deception

The second step may be to deceive ourselves. We want to see ourselves in a good light. In fact, most of us really try to be good people. So when our behavior is not in line with that self-perception, we often try to deceive ourselves by thoughts or comments like, "It wasn't that bad. . . . It didn't really hurt him. . . . She asked for it. . . . He had it coming. . . . If they hadn't . . ." We are all masters at denial, minimizing, and blaming others. We do not want to be wrong.

Sometimes, we can use denial so extensively that we can even change reality—or our understanding of it—to be more in line with what we wish it to be. Many individuals guilty of unacceptable behavior forget what they have done, or actually block it out of their awareness.

Certain people are experts at denying their own behavior. Eating disorders (anorexia, bulimia, and obesity), alcoholism, drug addiction, sex addiction, or any other addictions often serve the purpose of hiding from painful realities or feelings. Anorexics and bulimics generally believe that they are always too fat, disregarding the scale, mirrors, and other people's opinions. A bulimic may deny the visible evidence of the binges and purges, even to the point of death. Alcoholics and drug addicts lie to themselves, diminishing the amount, frequency, and destruction of the addictions. Many family members also want to deny the addiction and its impact. No one wants to talk about the "elephant in the living room."

Memory integrates the past with the present: desires, fantasies, fears, even moods can shade the recollection. People have a tendency to suppress unpleasant experiences and embellish events to make themselves feel more important or attractive, as psychologist Dr. Loftus observes:

> People distort their own memories in systematic ways. For example, people tend to remember themselves in ways that are favorable. They tend to see themselves as more honest or more creative than the average person. When they work on a joint task, they tend to overestimate their own contribution to the task. Married couples tend to overestimate the extent of their responsibility for household chores. Those who engage in conversation tend to overestimate how much they contributed to the conversation. People remember themselves as having held a higher-level job, received higher pay for work, purchased fewer alcoholic beverages, contributed more to charity, taken more airplane trips, and raised smarter-than-average children.[4]

Addictions

Because we all have the tendency to deny our wrong behavior, and because the likelihood of denial is greatly increased for addictive personalities, it's important to consider whether we have problems with drugs or alcohol or other addictions. Some people are unaware of their behavior when under the influence of drugs, including alcohol, prescription and nonprescription drugs. The most common results are lowered inhibitions, increased sexual behavior and comments, and an increase in verbal and physical anger. Parents who have been willing to consider that they may have done something in the category of the accusation, while under the influence, even if they do not remember it, leave the door open for discussions. Most of us have had unpleasant experiences with people who've been drinking and acting in very inappropriate ways. We realize the embarrassment they would feel if they were sober and fully aware of what they were doing. Many people have little or no memory of this drunken behavior, or at least the extent of it. Many of the recovered memories of incest come from a parent or stepparent who is drunk.

Offensive Behaviors

Here's a second area to consider: Some of our behavior might feel acceptable to us because it is what we experienced as a child, but it might be very offensive to our children. An example of this might be nudity. Reactions to this vary from the two extremes: those who join nudist colonies; and those who are uncomfortable even changing clothes in anyone else's presence. Other examples include sexually oriented jokes, seductive clothing or comments, sarcastic comments, and expressions or intrusive touches that feel angry or seductive.

I recall one mother who brought her very angry son in for therapy. In creating a complete history of his life, one of the questions concerned how he had been disciplined. The mother responded, "He gets the belt about a dozen times a day, no more than average." Both her and her husband's childhoods had been very abusive, and she honestly believed that it was normal to beat a child with a belt a dozen times a day.

Even if we are not beaten, any time we are touched when we do not want to be touched or forced to do anything we do not want to do, we feel intruded upon. Every child has experienced this sort of thing. In fact, it occurs quite often in early childhood. It's just part of parenting. Most of us have hugged and kissed our children when they did not want to be touched. Many of us have grabbed them in anger and frightened them. Probably all of us have yelled at them, and said things we wish we had not said. Our relationship with our children is also very "sensual," in a positive way. If we expressed the same behaviors and feelings toward another adult (holding on our laps, snuggling, kissing), it would be described as extremely seductive. Yet with our children, it's not only normal, but it's required for healthy development.

Pornography is a frequent cause of discomfort for children. When they find this in their home on television, in magazines, or books, they associate this behavior with the owner or perceived owner of the pornography. This can also become a source of accusations of sexual abuse, especially if the child is of preschool age.

> Because Melissa was so rarely touched by any man, including her father, hugs became associated with the trapped feeling she felt with her neighbor. As her father tried to comfort her during the nightmare, and on the same day he had been so angry at her, Melissa's unconscious mind quickly combined the touches of the two angry men, and translated this touch into sexual abuse.

In working with children who have been molested, I warn the parents that, when children become teenagers and comprehend adult sexuality, a sense of shame or "dirtiness" usually hits. Earlier, most children react to other aspects of the abuse—pain or threats or pleasure. But in adolescence, all touching gains this new sexual meaning. I wonder if that's behind some accusations of incest—teenagers or adults looking back at childhood touches through their new adult lenses of sexuality. They might even be reinterpreting angry outbursts or control issues or gentle hugs from their childhood in newly sexual ways. It is not surprising that children could combine all of these in their memories, especially loving touch and anger, and have symbolic memories of some form of incest.

If you have been falsely accused, start by looking at yourself and any possible behaviors that may have created pain for the child in question, even if it is not the specific behavior of which you have been accused.

Samantha was unaware that her parents sought counseling after her accusation of physical and verbal abuse. They were encouraged to give her a little time, while continuing to send cards and gifts to her and her family, as they had done in the past. Her counselor encouraged them to prayerfully consider any reasons she might want or need distance from them. They did see her as overly dependent upon them, and realized that her mother was too needy of her. They really wanted to support her independence, even though it hurt Mom to lose her "best friend." They were also encouraged to consider if anyone else might have abused her in the way she described. So they were not surprised by her letter.

Listen and Mirror What You Hear

If we want to understand our children of any age, especially adult children, we must commit ourselves to listening, not interrupting or correcting, not criticizing or giving advice, and not defending ourselves. We need to learn the art of becoming mirrors—of reflecting back to our children the essence of what they are expressing. It is one of the hardest things we ever do. In fact, most parents don't. I have promised parents that if they will learn this ability to listen, and do it with genuine caring and interest, their children will start talking. I have never seen it fail to get to the bottom of the problem, if parents can continue to listen patiently.

Problem solving cannot occur until the problem has been identified. Sensitive children will not reveal what the problem is if they are anticipating negative reactions. Instead they will withdraw, sometimes to the point of ending a relationship with the parents, rather than facing a confrontation. These are some of the same children who consider lawsuits in order to have a powerful advocate (an attorney) fight for them. They usually do not feel equal to their parents, even if they've been adults for many years. They do not feel heard or understood.

When Linda Lizotte, forty-three, sued her father, Don Howard, sixty-seven, for allegedly sexually abusing her as a child, she agreed to settle out of court after one day of testimony. Her attorney said that Linda had "wanted to make her father really listen to her and to take back power and control." She felt she had accomplished what she set out to do.[5]

One of Dennis's biggest frustrations in working through his false memory was that his parents wouldn't listen. It was their verbal abuse that lay behind his unfounded memories of physical abuse. And when he tried to apologize, the verbal abuse continued.

Dennis eventually involved his family in his therapy. But it was still his greatest challenge to get his parents to listen and reflect. They had indirectly heard of his memory and were furious. They came to set him straight once and for all! Before they all met together, the therapist spent several sessions alone with Dennis's parents, listening to their pain and anger. After they felt heard, they were able to comprehend instructions on reflective, caring listening, as they had just experienced. They were now willing to listen in order to identify the problem that had caused this false accusation.

In Dennis's memory, his dad's beating occurred when both parents had been drinking. In fact, their behavior did change under the influence of alcohol, becoming argumentative and angry. When Dennis discussed this with his parents, they became defensive over the drinking issue. Dennis pursued it one more time at their home, when his sisters and brothers were also there. As it turned out, all of the children shared the same concerns for their parents' drinking. All expressed their dislike at being around them when alcohol was being consumed. They requested that they try having the next family gathering with no alcohol. The parents angrily agreed.

Dennis felt relieved to discover the support and agreement of his siblings. This opened up a new level of communication among them, which they all chose to continue. Dennis began to experience options and power in relationship to his father, rather than feeling like the frightened, withdrawn little boy. And the communication with his brothers helped Dennis to feel that he was "one of the boys," and affirmed his masculinity.[6]

Understand the Need behind the Accusation

> My feet stand on level ground;
> In the great assembly I will praise the Lord.
> Psalm 26:12

Dr. Swindoll explains this last verse of Psalm 26 as David standing on a level or even place, a plateau, where he could have a commanding view of the whole picture, an objective panoramic view. It goes against our instincts to stand patiently when we are under attack. We want to fight back, not just pray for understanding. We want to focus on our own wounds rather than watch the horizon.

We parents experience a false accusation as a cruel attack on our love, our good motivations, and our characters and reputations. We feel unappreciated by someone to whom we've given all we could give. We're shocked, hurt, scared, angry, and depressed. In that context, it's difficult for us even to consider what this accusation might be saying about our children's needs. But we must and we can. We've demonstrated throughout our lives the ability to temporarily put aside our needs for the sake of our children. We must do that again, if we want the relationship restored.

Needs Related to Genuine Abuse

Some of our children's needs may relate to genuine abuse. The cases of Melissa and Samantha seem to be fairly common—they *were* sexually abused, but not by their parents. Their memories had the right events, but the wrong perpetrators.

When the memory of abuse begins to emerge, the identity of the perpetrator is often unknown. Many people who have been raped even as adults do not want to see the faces or know the identities of their assailants. It seems to provide some distance and safety to keep them faceless. A child is very likely to do this in order to continue functioning in her world, instead of being afraid of her abuser every time she sees him.

In some cases, it's strange to say, abused children would prefer the abuser to be the father or a relative rather than some stranger. It's easier to avoid one identified person who knows her, than the world of men in general. If a stranger did this, for some random reason, she must be afraid of everybody she meets. But if it's someone she knows, the fear can be neatly attached to that person, often with a specific reason that she imagines. Then it makes at least *some* sense. And she only has to watch her behavior with one person in order to be safe.

Melissa was a good example of this. She had superficial but good relationships with her outside world of men, because she had attached all her fear to her dad. She did have some emotional fear of him anyway, so it made this connection very easy to make.

Samantha recovered a legitimate memory of abuse by the couple who had lived down the street, but she had erased their identity. When, as an adult overly dependent on her parents, she needed to blame Mom and Dad for something, she slid them into the role of abusers. It's like the child on the hijacked bus who remembered her mom as one of the kidnappers, because she had a fight with her that morning. The events are there. The villains are interchangeable.

So if you, as a parent, have been wrongly accused of sexual abuse, it is quite possible that your child *was* abused, though not by you. When you get through your defensive maneuvers, try to focus on the child's real need. Even when you are cleared, the child may still have to recover from some real abuse.

Need to Express Fears and Feelings

The second common need is an attempt to express childhood fears and feelings. Many clients have experienced total frustration in their attempts to describe their pain to a mate, friend, or family. These attempts are met with responses such as: "You shouldn't feel that way. That shouldn't bother you. Why are you so upset at nothing? You're overreacting. You're crazy!" They do not receive empathy or understanding. They are told that in some way they are wrong and should change.

The only way you can make some people understand your pain is to paint a picture of an event that would hurt the listener in the same way that you felt the hurt. But this is when exaggerations of the truth can occur on an unconscious level. It makes us less crazy when we can find a reason big enough to match our feelings.

The previous chapter describes a word picture painted by a teenage girl to express the intense pain she was experiencing as a result of her dad's actions. Obviously he did not hit them with a car. She consciously painted a word picture in order for him to understand her feelings. This is what your child may be doing in her attempt to communicate the intrusion or control or trapped feelings she experienced with you. Look at her false accusation in this light. What might she be trying to tell you?

Dennis's anger toward his dad did not seem justified if Dad had only verbally abused him. In Dennis's evaluation, his feelings were too strong for just that. In the past, when anyone had tried to talk to Dad about the verbal abuse, he made fun of that person's sensitivity and weakness, sarcastically responding with, "Sticks and stones may break your bones, but words will never hurt you."

Only by intensifying his memory of abuse could Dennis express his depth of pain.

So if you have been falsely accused of abuse, consider what your child may be trying to tell you. Consider the feelings of pain and disappointment that may have sparked the false memory. Do not minimize any of the feelings that are expressed, even if you are being criticized. Listen, accept the feelings as real to your child and important, and talk together about what needs to be done.

Need to Deal with Depression

Your child might also be looking for answers to deal with depression or worthless feelings. If this is the case, consider the possible sources of this poor self-worth or depression. Have you contributed to it in any way, even through a biological or heredity problem? Or did your perfectionism and overcritical spirit rob your child of self-esteem? Did you neglect to praise or affirm your child? Or did you fail to show physical affection?

I'm not trying to make you feel guilty as a parent, but to help you identify hurtful patterns in your parenting. If you have contributed to poor self-esteem in your child, learn from this false memory. Take opportunities to build up your child, to undo some of the damage you may have done earlier.

This was definitely the case with Dennis and his parents. He never felt good enough. Mom's perfectionism and constant criticism left him feeling unsuccessful in everything she evaluated. Dad's anger brought his withdrawal and desire to be invisible, without any needs.

Need to Deal with Dependency

Dependency and the need to please are also characteristics of some of the people who have false memories. If an adult child is unable to break her need of her parents, an effective way to do it is to view them in a very negative manner. Then anger provides the strength to cut the cords.

Have you held on to your child too tightly? Visualize physically holding on to a child. Now picture the child trying to get away. The tighter we hold on, the more violent the child must become to achieve independence. Some children will break away no matter what parents do. But sometimes children enjoy the emotional closeness so much that they get lulled into a comfortable bondage—they don't want to achieve independence, even though it would be healthier for them. They make small efforts, but because of the love and closeness, never break away if conflict or hurt is involved. Yet there is a part of each of us that wants to grow into a healthy, self-sufficient adult, thus we might create a reason to do away with this closeness.

Parents often develop interdependent relationships with their children. It is always hard to let go. But adult children must be released to grow on their own. Consider whether your child's false accusation was actually a cry for independence. If so, honor it. Forge a new relationship with appropriate boundaries.

Samantha's false memory of physical and verbal abuse by both parents was her ticket to break her dependency. She was held too close by love and friendship and the ease of the relationship. Interacting with her husband required more giving, more talking, and more work. It wasn't as comfortable. Her parents were too good, too ideal, and Samantha enjoyed them more than she enjoyed her husband. Her false memory let her make a necessary break with her parents.

Need for Attention

Another common need is attention. Most children will do anything to avoid being ignored. For a child who has had very little interaction with a parent, abuse might be more tolerable than neglect. When children are neglected, they can come to question their very existence or their right to be alive. Abuse sends the message that we are bad and need to change. Change is something we can do—there is hope. But being unwanted leads to hopelessness and helplessness.

Lynn found the abandonment by her father to be more painful than her false memory of abuse. At least in that picture, she knew she mattered to someone for some reason. To realize that he made no attempt to see her at all after she was three months old felt devastating.

Penny also preferred the picture of abuse to the reality of the severe neglect from both of her parents. At one point Penny asked herself the question, "If your own parents don't want you, why should you even be alive?"

If you have neglected your child, see if you can find ways to pay attention. Your efforts may be resisted at first, but as you prove yourself sincere and consistent, you can heal some of the damage for your grown child.

Seek Family Counseling

When a false accusation has occurred, the chaos is generally beyond repair without assistance. Find a therapist who accepts both sides of the debate, the existence and recovery of repressed memories and the existence of false memories. Without that, one of the parties will not feel represented, and probably will not agree to therapy. The therapist must also be supportive of reconciliation and forgiveness. We're seeing many families restored in an atmosphere of safety and acceptance for both sides, and a listening environment.

Falsely accused parents must not attack the therapist; most clients will feel forced into defending the counselor. Remember how you learned not to attack your child's friends, because your child would then immediately rush to their defense? Instead, offer a neutral third-party therapist, presented as a second opinion.

Expect the therapy to take time. Intensive therapy is preferable because both sides have stored up so many feelings. When either side begins to open up, it's best for both sides to have the opportunity to be completely heard, and to have all their questions answered, rather than waiting for next week's appointment to continue the conversation.

But how can you handle your own feelings through all of this? That will be a huge challenge for you as falsely accused parents. You are the victims of an overwhelming trauma, inflicted upon you by your beloved child. It is natural to be stunned at first, numb with disbelief. Then the other feelings come plummeting upon you like hailstones, beating you to the ground. The hurt, terror, and confusion alternate with the anger and meager attempts to cope. If you have support and love as you talk through the trauma, you will survive. But it is a hellish experience! Many parents wisely seek counseling to survive the pain and grief. Somehow, we do survive, each in our own way, not always in the best way possible.

Dennis and his family weathered some stormy times as they all learned to listen with their ears first, and finally with their hearts. It was a difficult road for all concerned. Many sensitive issues had to be resolved. They stayed in intensive therapy for a week, opening up many old issues. Dad was confronted by all of the children about his alcoholism and he reluctantly agreed to enter a treatment program. A couple of months later, the family returned for a second intensive week. They made excellent progress, beginning to find resolutions that did not require, or even permit, verbal or physical abuse.

In most cases, both sides wish to begin with the truth of the abuse. The accuser wants the alleged abuse admitted. The accused wants the accusation recanted. Rarely does that work. More frequently, one or both sides need to address some of the other issues first. Often, when these are resolved, the alleged abuse becomes a minor issue. Neither side can push or demand. Patience and listening skills are required.

Dennis's parents wanted an immediate retraction of Dennis's memory, even before they had heard the specific details. Only with great difficulty did they agree to put it aside, with the promise that it would be addressed later.

Those families that have been willing to remain in counseling through the pain and confusion have not only found reconciliation, but have emerged stronger and more open and honest, with an understanding of each other that never existed before. We can't quit. We can't give up. The family unit is too important to throw away. There is hope and we must do everything possible for restoration!

Dennis and his family did openly consider the possibilities of what his memory meant. None of them expected that they would ever reach this point of rationally and patiently looking at the physical and verbal abuse within the family, as well as the rejection experienced from withdrawal. No family member was innocent. Each contributed to the conflict and chaos the family had experienced for so many years. Each one came to perceive clearly how their changed behavior could begin to build a safe and trusting family unit.

Avoid Lawsuits

If a lawsuit is threatened, request family counseling. For many falsely accused parents, that is very difficult to do at the point of a possible lawsuit. But, as discussed earlier, the legal system needs to be the very last resort. The financial and emotional costs are crushing—and the court will not resolve the problem. It will not necessarily exonerate innocent people. The best you can hope for is that guilt will not be proven, or that the case will be dropped. Meanwhile, you'll spend months, perhaps years, looking for every bit of evidence for the craziness or badness of your own child or accuser, just as she will be seeking all the worst possible information about you. It will probably cost most of your life savings for legal fees, and you'll end up worse off than before. Notoriety will ruin your reputation, even if you're innocent. Once the news media picks up the story, some people will assume your guilt, whatever the verdict is. Do anything possible to get the conflict out of the court and into the counseling office.

If there is no way to avoid a lawsuit, request mediation. That, at least, reduces the legal costs and time involved. Some children state that they just want to be heard and need to speak the truth. If this is the case, they will often agree to counseling or mediation with the commitment from the parents to listen. Remember that the first step is not resolution of the problems or even establishing the truth. The first step is to open the door of communication. Listening and reflecting with empathy and care will diffuse much of the anger. Your point of view must wait until your child is willing and able to listen.

Remain Positive

Remain positive, remembering God's love and wondrous works. In the rest of Psalm 26, David affirms his intent to sing songs of thanksgiving and to focus on all the wonders of God's love and his works. When we truly focus on God and allow him to fill those empty desperate places within us, we find comfort and peace and even joy. Paul and other first-century Christians were able to sing with joy from their jail cells. Joy did not depend upon their external circumstances, but upon the Spirit of the God of the Universe, who lived within them.

Carefully Choose Your Companions

In Psalm 26, David speaks of the importance of his company. When we are hurting or angry, we look for those who will support us and take our side. But David clearly chooses to avoid the company of deceivers or evildoers. At this time we need the company of spiritual people who will encourage and strengthen us to act in a manner that is kind, caring, open, and vulnerable. We will be tempted to act hard, cold, indifferent, and resentful, and to seek those friends who encourage such feelings and behavior. Resist that temptation by finding loving, generous, and kind friends.

Choose Forgiveness

After many years of living in caves and running away from King Saul's threats to his life, David had his chance for revenge. Saul was asleep and David had the chance to kill him. But he did not. Instead he cut off a piece of the king's robe, so that Saul could see that David spared his life (1 Sam. 24). In the same way, we need to give up our desire for revenge.

Until we do our part of the forgiveness process, we will remain bitter, revengeful, anxious, and withdrawn.[7] Our joy, peace, and enjoyment of life will be destroyed. No matter what is occurring around us, we are accountable for our own behavior and attitude.

You may have heard the phrase, "We will either grow bitter or better." Whatever the outcome of the false accusation, you can still be the person you would like to be. Maintain the hope that the outcome of all this will be restoration.

Building a bridge takes time and patience. The gulf between the sides may be enormous. The construction requires planning and careful, deliberate steps. Each bolt and each plank is essential. The joy at its completion is worth every cost and effort. Elicit the help of the most successful "bridge builders" available. The restoration of your family is not only possible, but essential.

Conclusion

How amazingly we are made. To consider that any of our memories from years ago can be stored in our brain relatively accurately is incredible to consider. To realize that we have an innate mechanism that allows us to "forget" or block awareness of traumatic events and the associated feelings that we could not have survived at the time, reminds us of our ability to endure. Yet even as a very young child, we continue to signal like a beacon seeking for rescue that something is wrong by behavior that mirrors central aspects of the trauma. And when help arrives, we can begin the process of recovery of memories and feelings, and arrive at the point where we can make sense of the chaotic world inside our mind. And finally, we can begin to complete the healing process, even when the damage has been severe. In whatever stage of the process we find ourselves today, there is hope. As a child we had no options, no choices. But as an adult, we can come to the place where we leave the past behind us, where we are free to live in the present with hope and plans for the future.

It is my hope that you have concluded that each memory is distinct and unique and must be considered individually. It is unusual for a memory to be totally true or totally false. There are many steps to take in evaluating the truth of each part of any significant memory; no easy answers exist. We do know aspects of a memory that are more likely to be accurate, such as the central features (as opposed to peripheral details), the initial occurrence of an event, those accompanied by strong emotion, situations that we see clearly with prolonged time to observe, events where we participate rather than just observe, and distinctive, unique features that are meaningful to us. To expect perfect recall of any event is unrealistic because of distorted perceptions.

Contamination can also occur in the storage process. We might be combining traumatic memories. We might be adding new information and be influenced by others, by books, by the media. We may have added missing pieces to flesh out the picture that we didn't understand as a child. We may have stored a memory that we have been told, but that did not actually occur. We might have imagined or seen an event into which we erroneously placed ourselves. We may have created a scenario that is symbolic of our feelings or interactions.

But probably even more errors occur in the retrieval process. We might be affected by our desired conclusion, thus selectively retrieving information. We might have used methods that caused distortion in the recovery of a memory.

Our internal needs as well as external influences can modify or contaminate our memories at each of the stages: perception, storage, and retrieval. We are capable of imagining events that never occurred to us, and accepting them as our reality. Children especially can be influenced by suggestions and even very subtle leading by most authority figures. This can include such mild forms as repeating questions, approval or disapproval for certain answers, anatomically correct dolls, or anything that causes a child to question or doubt their own perceptions or beliefs. The greatest risk is with the youngest children, who are usually more suggestible, but also in need of specific questions to elicit the information of abuse that has occurred.

Despite all possibilities of error, many of our memories are mostly accurate. If we are truly willing to seek the truth, being open to all options, we can usually discover it. The most powerful support of our childhood trauma usually comes from our unusual childhood behavior, where we act out a part of the trauma in play, hobbies, fears, obsessive interests, or compulsive behavior or thoughts. We might "remember" the trauma in repetitive nightmares. Our fear of a repeat of a trauma is intense, unless we have totally disconnected from our feelings. This leaves us with pessimism about the present and future, feelings of helplessness and hopelessness, and many other symptoms. We often find ourselves in repeated situations where we are either the victim or the victimizer. Physical problems and addictions are also common.

There is a high cost for blocking out a trauma and/or the feelings associated with it. There is also a high cost for believing false memories. Seeking the truth and the willingness to face the pain and the results is not only courageous but essential to our emotional, physical, and spiritual health. God intends for us to be free from the past, and that includes the behaviors and the feelings that we may not have even known were connected to our unhappiness in the present.

As we discover the true parts of our memories, there are many steps to take for our healing and restoration. But it's well worth the resulting freedom and wholeness that we can come to experience. A therapist can assist us in both assessing the necessary steps for us to take and guiding us through the process.

As we discover the false parts of our memories, there are also important steps for restoration and healing. Our family is of great importance. We should not sacrifice our family or friends for "memories" that might be false or partially false. Our memories are not reliable enough to be the only evidence to convict someone. We must check them out. Without some external corroboration, accusations are cruel and destructive, and they might be wrong.

Even if our memories are accurate, they don't belong in our courts, unless the perpetrator is a pedophile who still has access to children. Nor should we cut off relationships, except in the case of extreme danger, because it leaves us feeling helpless. We need to persist in order to regain our strength and confidence that we can cope with even frightening and difficult people.

And for those who have been falsely accused, parents or therapists, my heart goes out to you. I have talked with both groups of the falsely accused, and the pain is overwhelming. One therapist revealed that the pain of the accusation of a former client, although false, was more painful and shaming than the abuse the therapist had suffered as a child. There is hope for healing for you and your accuser.

The attacks on parents or therapists are not in a client's best interests. Instead of dealing with their own feelings and issues, it's a way to blame someone else. By doing so, a client will either miss or delay the growth that would be occurring if the focus was on the internal issues.

From my perspective, the debate and conflict over memories is focusing on the wrong issues. Researchers need to acknowledge that they cannot replicate trauma in the laboratory and to begin to study people who have experienced an already documented trauma. Researchers have not had the exposure to what clinicians see frequently—the recovery of memories that are experienced by the client and therapist as if they are occurring at the present time, with the client inundated by all of the smells, physical sensations, sounds, details, and emotions of a current trauma.

As clinicians observe the same intensity as trauma victims who are having flashbacks, it is difficult to believe that these are "false," especially in the central feature of the event.

Furthermore, some brilliant, well-known, and respected researchers in neurophysiology are beginning to find a neurological basis for both repression of trauma and the subsequent recovery of the memories, even years later. Several excellent literature reviews of the biological aspects have been published in recent years, suggesting that trauma is a "psychobiological event that produces not only adverse psychological effects, but also potentially long-term neurobiological changes in the brain."[1]

Clients have been examining "repressed memories" for a century, yet the conflict began mostly in the 1980s. The reason appears to be that memories moved from the therapy office into confrontations and legal battles. They changed from feelings and perceptions to be resolved into "truth" and "facts" and reasons to eliminate relationships.

Childhood trauma leaves a lasting effect upon children, even if they build a wall of defense to keep it out of their conscious awareness. But it is essential for therapists to understand that we can combine memories that are similar, thus the central idea may have occurred, but the specific details may be inaccurate. The specific details may be more symbolic of the entire relationship with the identified perpetrator than a realistic picture of an actual event. Therapy has no perfect way to recover memory. Thus we must encourage the expression of doubts about the truth of all aspects of a memory, and allow the story to change. We cannot be invested in the truth of a memory. That is up to each client to determine, with as extensive research as possible. Nor can we encourage closed, circular thinking, which says that the lack of evidence is even more proof of the premeditation of the abuser, or the conspiracy of those involved.

Very few clinicians doubt that memories of childhood abuse can be repressed or dissociated. Many do question the techniques—especially hypnosis, truth serums, and guided imagery—because these leave the client open to suggestions from the therapist who they are anxious to please. Thus they might take vague recollections and add imaginary detail to come up with a "memory."

With our current understanding of trauma and memory, it is essential to realize the possible contamination by suggestions, expectations, and needs, both internal and external. Memories need to be understood along a continuum, with very few totally false or totally true, but most memories a combination of both. Traumatic memories can be imagined, suggested, or implanted, but in these cases they lack the history of symptoms or signs that are expected for the particular incidence of abuse.

We still have much to learn about memories, as we seek to find the balance between encouraging children to reveal any abuse that is occurring and at the same time protecting the innocent from false accusations. Because both of these are so extremely devastating, the stakes are very high. Research is generally indicating that children can be very accurate eye-witnesses, but they are often reluctant to expose any abuse, especially about someone they know or in instances where threats are made. Perpetrators rarely admit their guilt, and can be very convincing about their innocence. On the other hand, some children and adults can be led or influenced by suggestion and innocent people find it almost impossible to prove their innocence.

Let's prayerfully remain open to the truth about every memory. Let's seek to support each other, working together to convict the guilty and protect the innocent. Let's learn more about traumatized children, promoting internal healing and restoration of our families.

Notes

Introduction

1. Carol Ness and Stephanie Salter, "Bitter Debate over Recovered Memories: Growing Number of Claims Sparks Argument on Validity," *San Francisco Examiner,* Sunday, 26 December 1993, fifth edition, p. A-1.

2. Bruce Bower, "Sudden Recall: Adult Memories of Child Abuse Spark a Heated Debate," *Science News,* 144, no. 12 (18 September 1993): 184.

3. Tori De Angelis, "APA Panel Is Examining Memories of Child Abuse, Researchers, Practitioners Represented," *American Psychological Association Monitor,* 24, no. 11 (November 1993): 44.

4. Laurie Denton, "Interim Report Issued on Memories of Abuse," *APA Monitor,* 25, no. 12 (December 1994): 8.

5. Denton, "Interim Report Spells Out Five Conclusions," *APA Monitor* (December 1994): 9.

6. Associated Press, "Recovered Memory Not Reliable, AMA Says," *San Diego Union-Tribune,* 16 June 1994, p. A-12.

7. Ness and Salter, "Therapists Split: Are Recovered Memories of Abuse Real or False? Decisions Fall to the Courts," *Chicago Tribune,* 27 March 1994, Womanews section, p. 12.

Chapter 1: Should We Always Believe Our Memories?

1. D. D. Femina, C. A. Yeager, and D. O. Lewis, "Child Abuse: Adolescent Records vs. Adult Recall," *Child Abuse and Neglect,* 14 (1990): 227–31.

Parents can help protect their children from continuing abuse by assisting them to understand that everyone, even the most loving person, might do bad and hurtful things at times. We all fall short of perfection. We need to train our children that if they will tell us about anything that feels uncomfortable to them, then good people can get help, and may be able to stop the bad behavior. Parents can model this by telling our children when we do something wrong and asking for their forgiveness, reassuring them that they did not deserve it. Then we must also change our behavior, seeking counseling, if necessary.

Many children need freedom to still have a relationship with the abuser, but with protection, so there is no opportunity for further abuse. Some children will not tell the truth without this assurance. Some adults will never face the truth if it requires ending a valued relationship. Children don't want to lose a loving relationship. So if they realize the abuser may not be allowed to spend time with them if anyone finds out about the abuse, a secret appears to be the alternative. Children seem to intuitively know they might not keep a secret. Believing it never happened is a safe choice that allows the loving relationship to continue.

I rarely recommend ending relationships except with a pedophile or someone extremely dangerous. The ideal resolution involves learning to enjoy the good aspects of every relationship, to tolerate the individual idiosyncrasies that aren't morally wrong, and to protect ourselves from destructive or abusive behavior.

Children recover the quickest when the wrong is directly confronted, when it is admitted by the offender (if it is true), and when the child feels safe from future abuse. To avoid all further contact only validates helplessness. It also prevents the opportunity to assess and evaluate the truth, both about the accused and about ourselves.

Chapter 2: Could I Have Repressed Memories?

1. Marilyn Van Derbur Atler, "The Darkest Secret," *People* (June 10, 1991): 88–94.

2. Ibid.

3. Elizabeth Loftus, interview by Sonya Friedman, *Sonya Live,* Cable News Network, Transcript no. 341, 19 July 1993.

4. Charles R. Figley, *Trauma and Its Wake: The Study and Treatment of Post-Traumatic Stress Disorder* (New York: Brunner/Mazel, 1985), 231.

5. Elisabeth Kübler-Ross, *On Death and Dying* (New York: Macmillan, 1969).

6. E. Mark Stern, ed., *Psychotherapy and the Terrorized Patient* (New York: Haworth Press, 1985).

7. "Testimony of Child Victims in Sex Abuse Prosecutions: Two Legislative Innovations," *Harvard Law Review* 98 (1985): 806, 807.

8. Lenore Terr, *Too Scared to Cry: Psychic Trauma in Childhood* (New York: Harper & Row, 1990).

9. Arthur Green, "Children Traumatized by Physical Abuse," in Spencer Eth and Robert Pynoos, *Post-Traumatic Stress Disorder in Children* (Washington, D.C.: American Psychiatric Press, 1985), 137–38.

Chapter 3: How Does the Brain Remember?

1. Anastasia Toufexis, "When Can Memories Be Trusted?" *Time* 28 (October 1991): 86–88.

2. Barbara Graham and Christina Ferrari, "Unlock the Secrets of Your Past: Early Childhood Memories," *Redbook* (January 1993): 84, quoting Scott Wetzler.

3. F. Shapiro, "Efficacy of the Eye Movement Desensitization Method in the Treatment of Traumatic Memories," *Journal of Traumatic Stress,* 2 (1989): 199–223.

4. Robert Jay Lifton, quoted in Judith Herman, *Trauma and Recovery* (New York: Basic Books, 1992), 38.

5. Mortimer Mishkin and Tim Appenzeller, "The Anatomy of Memory," in *The Workings of the Brain: Development, Memory, and Perception,* ed. R. R. Llinas (New York: W. H. Freeman, 1990), 88–102.

6. Eric Kandel and Minouche Kandel, "Flights of Memory," *Discover* (May 1994): 32–38.

7. James Dobson, "Intelligence and Learning," *Focus on the Family,* KPRZ Radio, 28 July 1994.

8. J. R. Goldberg, "Lies of the Mind: The Person You Most Often Deceive Is Probably Yourself," *Health,* 18 (August 1986): 64–68.

9. S. D. Solomon, E. T. Gerrity, and A. M. Muff, "Efficacy of Treatments for Posttraumatic Stress Disorder: An Empirical Review," *JAMA (Journal of the American Medical Association)* 268, no. 5 (5 August 1992): 633.

10. John H. Krystal, quoted in Bower, "Sudden Recall," 184.

11. Henry Krystal, "Trauma and Affects," *Psychoanalytic Study of the Child,* 33 (1978): 90–92.

12. B. A. Van der Kolk, quoted in Mary Sykes Wylie, "Trauma and Memory," *The Family Therapy Networker* (September/October 1993): 42–43.

13. B. A. Van der Kolk and Onno Vander Hart, "The Intrusive Past: The Flexibility of Memory and the Engraving of Trauma," *American Imago,* 48, no. 4 (1991): 444.

14. Van der Kolk, quoted in Jason Berry, "Sudden Recall: Memories Delayed or Imagined? Cardinal Joseph Bernardin: Sex Abuse Accusations by Steven J. Cook," *National Catholic Reporter,* 30, no. 6 (December 3, 1993): 4.

15. All of the researchers mentioned in this chapter are well worth studying. Two articles by Dr. Bessel Van der Kolk are of particular interest: "The Trauma Spectrum: The Interaction of Biological and Social Events in the Genesis of the Trauma Response," *Journal of Traumatic Stress,* 1, no. 3 (July 1988): 273–90; and (by Dr. Van der Kolk et al.) "Nightmares and Trauma: A Comparison of Nightmares after Combat with Lifelong Nightmares in Veterans," *American Journal of Psychiatry,* 141, no. 2 (February 1984): 187–90.

An excellent summary of additional research is presented by John F. Kihlstrom in "The Cognitive Unconscious," (*Science,* 237 [September 18, 1987]: 1445–52). It provides a much better understanding of unconscious processing that operates outside of our awareness, but affects our thoughts, feelings, and actions.

In his work, Dr. Squire also presents excellent information and summarizes the research to date, as well as the areas requiring further research (L. R. Squire, B. Knowlton, and G. Musen, "The Structure and Organization of Memory," *Annual Review of Psychology,* 44 [January 1993]: 453; and Squire, *Memory and Brain* [New York: Oxford University Press, 1987]).

16. I. Nadel and S. Zola Morgan, "Infantile Amnesia: A Neurobiological Perspective," in *Infant Memory,* ed. M. Moskovitz (New York: Plenum, 1984).

17. Terr, *Too Scared to Cry,* 170.

18. Terr, *Unchained Memories: True Stories of Traumatic Memories, Lost and Found* (New York: Basic Books, 1994).

19. Michael J. Beaudine, "Growing Disenchantment with Hypnotic Means of Refreshing Witness Recall," *Vanderbilt Law Review,* 41 (March 1988): 379.

20. Loftus, "The Reality of Repressed Memories," *American Psychologist* (May 1993): 518–37.

21. Ibid.

22. Terr, *Unchained Memories,* 171–72.

23. Ibid., 28.

24. Stephen Kosslyn, quoted in Kandel and Kandel, "Flights of Memory," 38.

25. Ibid.

26. Graham and Ferrari, "Unlock the Secrets," 84.

27. Goldberg, "Lies of the Mind," 64.

28. Loftus, "The Reality of Repressed Memories," 530.

29. Graham and Ferrari, "Unlock the Secrets," quoting Nancy Meyers, 84.

Chapter 4: Is There a Case for Repressed Memory?

1. Miriam Horn, "Memories Lost and Found," *U.S. News and World Report* (November 29, 1993): 52–63.

2. Graham and Ferrari, "Unlock the Secrets," 84.

3. American Psychiatric Association, *Desk Reference to the Diagnostic Criteria from DSM-IV* (Washington, D.C.: American Psychiatric Association, May 1994), 209–10.

4. Figley, *Trauma and Its Wake,* 54.

5. Richard W. Jones and Linda W. Peterson, "Post-Traumatic Stress Disorder in a Child following an Automobile Accident," *Journal of Family Practice,* 36, no. 2 (February 1993): 223.

6. Figley, *Trauma and Its Wake,* 231.

7. American Psychiatric Association, *Diagnostic Criteria,* 211–12.

8. Ibid., 229–32.

9. W. H. Reid and M. G. Wise, *DSM-III-R Training Guide* (New York: Brunner/Mazel, 1989), 158.

10. Several books have examined the clinical evidence of dissociation. Dr. James Friesen is a psychologist, minister, and adjunct professor at Fuller Graduate School of Psychology. His books, *Uncovering the Mystery of Multiple Personality Disorder* (San Bernardino: Here's Life, 1991), and *More Than Survivors: Conversations with Multiple-Personality Clients* (1992), present the theory and examples of the dissociative disorders. Other books that thoroughly cover this topic have been written by Dr. Frank Putnam (*Diagnosis and Treatment of Multiple Personality Disorder* [New York: Guilford, 1989]) and Dr. Collin Ross. Dr. Richard Kluft is the editor of *Childhood Antecedents of Multiple Personality* (Washington, D.C.: American Psychiatric Press, 1985), examining childhood causes of dissociation.

11. Bruno Bettelheim, quoted in David Calof, "Facing the Truth about False Memory," *The Family Therapy Networker,* 17, no. 5 (September/October 1993): 39–45.

12. Helga Newmark, "Stolen Childhood," *McCall's* (August 1994): 100.

13. E. Jacobson, "Depersonalization," *Journal of the American Psychoanalytic Association,* 7 (1959): 581–610.

14. Judith Herman, *Trauma and Recovery* (New York: Basic Books, 1992), 20, 24–26. C. Fischer, "Amnestic States and the War Neuroses: The Psychogenesis of Fugues," *Psychoanalytic Quarterly,* 14 (1945): 437–68.

15. H. C. Archibald and R. D. Tuddenham, "Persistent Stress Reaction after Combat: A 20 Year Follow-up," *Archives of General Psychiatry,* 12 (1965): 475–81; J. L. Henderson and M. Moore, "The Psychoneuroses of War," *New England Journal of Medicine,* 230 (1994): 125–31.

16. Archibald and Tuddenham, "Persistent Stress Reaction after Combat."

17. Winnie Smith, *The American Daughter Gone to War,* quoted in Calof, "Facing the Truth," 42.

18. John Briere, *Child Abuse Trauma: Theory and Treatment of the Lasting Effects* (Newbury Park: SAGE, 1992), 40.

19. B. A. Van der Kolk, *Post-Traumatic Stress Disorders: Psychological and Biological Sequelae* (Washington, D.C.: American Psychiatric Press, 1984), 63–66.

20. Van der Kolk, quoted in Berry, "Memories Delayed or Imagined?" 4.

21. Herman, *Trauma and Recovery,* 31–32.

22. Toufexis, "When Can Memories Be Trusted?" 86–88.

23. Horn, "Memories Lost and Found," 52–63.

24. Berry, "Sudden Recall," 4.

25. Herman, *Trauma and Recovery,* 88.

26. Jill Smolowe, "Dubious Memories," *Time* (May 23, 1994).

27. Sylvia Fraser, *My Father's House: A Memoir of Incest and Healing* (New York: Ticknor & Fields, 1988).

28. "Memory Loss as a Survival Method: Childhood Sexual Abuse Includes Related Information," *Healthfacts,* 16, no. 150 (November 1991): 1.

29. L. M. Williams, "Recall of Childhood Trauma: A Perspective Study of Women's Memories of Child Sexual Abuse," *Journal of Consulting Clinical Psychology,* 62, no. 6 (1994): 1170.

30. Ibid., 1171.

31. Ibid., 1170.

32. Ibid., 1172.

33. Ibid., 1174.

34. Loftus, "The Reality of Repressed Memories," 521–22.

35. Ibid., 522.

36. John Briere and Jan Conte, "Self-Reported Amnesia for Abuse in Adults Molested as Children," *Journal of Traumatic Stress,* 6, no. 1 (January 1993): 21–31.

37. Nathan M. Szajnberg, "Recovering a Repressed Memory, and Representational Shift in an Adolescent," *Journal of the American Psychoanalytic Association,* 41, no. 3 (1993): 711–27.

38. F. H. Frankel, "Adult Reconstruction of Childhood Events in the Multiple Personality Literature," *American Journal of Psychiatry,* 150, no. 6 (June 1993): 954–58.

39. Terr, "What Happens to Early Memories of Trauma? A Study of 20 Children under Age Five at the Time of Documented Traumatic Events," *Journal of Child and Adolescent Psychiatry,* 27 (January 1988): 96–104.

40. Lenore Terr, "Childhood Traumas: An Outline and Overview," *American Journal of Psychiatry,* 148, no. 1 (January 1991): 10–20.

41. Herman, "The Long-Term Effects of Incestuous Abuse in Childhood," *American Journal of Psychiatry,* 143, no. 10 (1986): 1293–96.

42. Herman, *Trauma and Recovery,* 20.

43. Graham and Ferrari, "Unlock the Secrets," quoting Dr. Karen Hopenwasser, 84.

44. Jerome Singer, ed., *Repression and Dissociation: Implications for Personality Theory, Psychopathology, and Health* (Chicago: University of Chicago Press, 1990), 429.

45. Ibid.

46. Terr, *Unchained Memories,* 35–36.

47. Barbara Kantowitz and Nadine Joseph, "Forgetting to Remember," *Newsweek* (February 11, 1991): 58.

48. Terr, *Unchained Memories,* 24.

49. "Memory Loss as a Survival Method: Childhood Sexual Abuse Includes Related Information," *HealthFacts,* 16, no. 150 (November 1991): 1.

50. Bill Schackner, "Old Memory Leads to Arrest in Killing," Pittsburgh *Post-Gazette,* 26 May 1994, sec. State, p. D1.

51. Lana Lawrence, interview by Sonya Friedman, *Sonya Live,* transcript no. 154, 13 October 1992.

52. Patricia Zengerle, "Man Found Guilty in 'Total Recall' Murder Case," Reuters, January 28, 1992, Tuesday, AM cycle, Pittsburgh.

53. "'Total Recall' Decision Upheld," *The Legal Intelligencer* (Pittsburgh), 12 October 1993, sec. Local News, p. 7.

54. Peterson v. Bruen (1990): 106 Nevada, 271, 792 p. 2D 18.

55. Gary M. Ernsdorff and Elizabeth F. Loftus, "Let Sleeping Memories Lie? Words of Caution about Tolling the Statute of Limitations in Cases of Memory Repression," *Journal of Criminal Law and Criminology,* 84 (Spring 1993): 129.

56. Berry, "Memories Delayed or Imagined?" 4.

57. "Memories of Abuse," *Los Angeles Times,* 16 October 1991, Home Edition, part B, p. 6.

58. Briere, *Child Abuse Trauma,* 100.

Chapter 5: Can Memories Be Distorted by Outside Influences?

1. Lawrence Wright, "Remembering Satan (I)," *New Yorker,* 69 (May 17, 1993): 60–66; "Remembering Satan (II)," *New Yorker,* 69 (May 24, 1993): 54–66.

2. Loftus, "The Reality of Repressed Memories," 532.

3. Loftus, quoted in Goleman, "Miscoding Is Seen as the Root of False Memories," *New York Times*, 31 May 1994, sec. C, p. 1, col. 1.

4. Ellen Bass and Laura Davis, *Courage to Heal* (New York: Harper and Row, 1988), 22.

5. Ness, "Woman Sues Author over Self-Help Book," *Times Advocate* (Escondido, Calif.), 22 May 1994.

6. H. Wakefield and R. Underwager, "Recovered Memories of Alleged Sexual Abuse: Lawsuits against Parents," (Presentation to the American Psychological Society, San Diego, June 1992).

7. C. P. E. Ewing, "Judicial Notebook," *APA Monitor*, 25 (January 1994): 14.

8. Briere, *Child Abuse Trauma*, 4.

9. John Doris, ed., *The Suggestibility of Children's Recollections* (Washington, D.C.: American Psychological Association, 1991), ix.

10. M. D. Yapko, *Suggestions of Abuse* (New York: Simon & Schuster, 1994), 44–54.

11. A. Rosenfeld, C. C. Nadelson, and M. Krieger, "Fantasy and Reality in Patients' Reports of Incest," *Journal of Clinical Psychology*, 40 (1979): 159–64.

12. "Guilt by Memory," Cable News Network, 3 May 1993.

13. *Prime Time Live*, American Broadcasting Company, ABC News transcript, 2 April 1992.

14. Richard Cole, "Jury Rules for Father in Memory 'Rape,'" *San Diego Union-Tribune*, 14 May 1994, pp. A-1, A-6.

15. Andi Rierden, "When a Buried Truth Wants Out, Is It Real?" *New York Times*, 24 April 1994, final edition, sec. 14CN, p. 1.

16. Richard Gardner, *True and False Accusations of Child Sex Abuse* (Cresskill, N.J.: Creative Therapeutics, 1992), 133–85.

17. Ibid., 105.

18. Ibid., 185–230.

Chapter 6: Would *I* Ever Create False Memories?

1. Squire, *Memory and Brain* (New York: Oxford University Press, 1987).

2. Kandel and Kandel, "Flights of Memory," 38.

3. S. J. Ceci and M. Bruck, "Suggestibility of the Child Witness: A Historical Review and Synthesis," *Psychological Bulletin*, 113, no. 3 (1993): 432.

4. Ceci, quoted in Goleman, "Miscoding."

5. Ceci and Bruck, "Suggestibility of the Child Witness."

6. Marsel Mesulam, quoted in Goleman, "Miscoding."

7. Doris, *The Suggestibility of Children's Recollections*, 115.

8. Gail S. Goodman, "Understanding and Improving Children's Testimony in Child Abuse Cases," *Children Today*, 22, no. 1 (January 1993): 13.

9. Ibid.

10. Gail S. Goodman, Christine Aman, and Jodi Hirschman, "Child Sexual and Physical Abuse: Children's Testimony," 14–20.

11. Goodman, "Improving Children's Testimony," 13.

12. Terr, *Too Scared to Cry,* 180–83.

13. Ibid., 181.

14. Graham and Ferrari, "Unlock the Secrets."

15. David B. Pillermer and Sheldon H. White, "Childhood Events Recalled by Children and Adults," *Advances in Child Development and Behavior,* 21 (New York: Academic Press, 1989), 297–340.

16. Terr, *Too Scared to Cry,* 183.

17. Ceci and Bruck, "Suggestibility of the Child Witness," 418.

18. Ibid., 417.

19. J. E. Mack, "Psychoanalysis and Biography: Aspects of a Developing Affinity," *Journal of the American Psychoanalytic Association,* 28 (1980): 543–62.

20. Jean Goodwin, ed., *Sexual Abuse: Incest Victims and Their Families* (Chicago: Medical Publishers, 1989).

21. Ceci and Bruck, "Suggestibility of the Child Witness," 426.

Chapter 7: How Can I Know the Truth of My Memories?

1. Goleman, "Miscoding," 1.

2. Harville Hendrix, in *Getting the Love You Want: A Guide for Couples* (New York: Harper & Row, HarperPerennial [1988]), presents this concept as a core cause of marriage problems. His video series and workbook (Imago Productions [1993]) vividly portray the way we bring the pain from our childhood into our current relationships.

Chapter 8: Am I Ready for My Memories?

1. Jones and Peterson, "Post-Traumatic Stress Disorder," 223.

2. Herman, *Trauma and Recovery,* 86.

3. Terr, "Childhood Traumas," 12.

4. "Biological Aspects of PTSD: Laboratory and Clinical Research," *PTSD Research Quarterly,* 1, no. 2 (Summer 1990).

Dr. Bessel Van der Kolk discusses the research concerning the biologic basis of post-traumatic stress ("The Biological Basis of Post-Traumatic Stress," *Primary Care,* 20, no. 2 [June 1993]: 417–32). He mentions "numbing," the immediate reaction to trauma (especially repeated trauma), with three lines of research that provide the biological basis for numbing:

(1) Downregulation of both the adrenergic system and the HPA axis
(2) The endogenous opiod system
(3) The serotonin system

He also presents research that "survivors of severe trauma have repeatedly been described as continuing to react with extremes of underarousal and overarousal to even minor emotional stressors." (See Dr. Van der Kolk, Dr. J. C. Perry, Dr. Judith Herman, "Childhood Origins of Self-Destructive Behavior," *American Journal of Psychiatry,* 148, no. 12 [December 1991]: 1665–71.)

5. Anthony and Cohler, *The Invulnerable Child,* 180–82.

Chapter 9: How Reliable Are the Different Methods of Recovering Memories?

1. Terr, *Too Scared to Cry,* 210.
2. Briere, *Child Abuse Trauma,* 21.
3. Terr, *Too Scared to Cry,* 231.
4. Ibid., 217.
5. Council of Scientific Affairs, "Scientific Status of Refreshing Recollection by the Use of Hypnosis," *JAMA,* 253 (5 April 1985): 1919.
6. Council on Mental Health, "Medical Use of Hypnosis," *JAMA,* 168 (1958): 186–89.
7. Kihlstrom, "The Cognitive Unconscious," 1445.
8. Yapko, *Suggestions of Abuse,* 55–61.
9. David Spiegel, quoted in Goleman, "Miscoding," 1.
10. J. S. Gordon, "The UFO Experience," *Atlantic,* 268 (1991): 82–92.
11. Jacqueline Kanovitz, "Hypnotic Memories and Civil Sexual Abuse Trials," *Vanderbilt Law Review,* 45 (October 1992): 1185.
12. Ibid.
13. B. L. Diamond, "Inherent Problems in the Use of Pretrial Hypnosis on a Perspective Witness," *California Law Review,* 68 (1980): 313–48.
14. Council of Scientific Affairs, "Use of Hypnosis," 1920–22.
15. Beaudine, "Growing Disenchantment," 379.
16. Michael Nash, "What, if Anything, Is Regressed about Hypnotic Age Regression? A Review of the Empirical Literature," *Psychological Bulletin* 102, no. 1 (1987): 42–52.
17. August Piper, "Truth Serum and Recovered Memories of Sexual Abuse: A Review of the Evidence," *Journal of Psychiatry and Law* (Winter 1993): 448.
18. Ibid., 461.
19. Ibid., 465.
20. Ibid., 462.
21. Terr, *Too Scared to Cry,* 180–81.
22. Andrew Murray, *Waiting on God* (Chicago: Moody Press, 1990); Murray, *The Prayer Life* (Chicago, Moody Press, n.d.).
23. Donna Leonard, *Lord, I'm Listening* (Wheaton: Victor Books, 1979).
24. Shapiro, "Efficacy of Eye Movement Desensitization Method," and "Eye Movement Desensitization Method: A New Treatment for Post Traumatic Stress Disorder," *Journal of Behavior Therapy and Experimental Psychiatry,* 20, no. 2 (1989): 211–17.
25. Shapiro (report to the Advanced Training Conference in EMDR, Los Angeles, 5–6 August 1994).

Chapter 10: How Can I Re-create My Past?

1. Erik Erikson, *The Life Cycle Completed* (New York: W. W. Norton, 1982), 32–33.

Chapter 11: How Can I Check Out the Accuracy of My Memories?

1. Terr, *Too Scared to Cry,* 247.
2. Marilyn Murray, *Prisoner of Another War: A Remarkable Journey of Healing from Childhood Trauma* (Berkeley, Calif.: PageMill Press, 1991), 50–53.
3. Ibid., 73.
4. Ibid., 164–71.
5. Graham and Ferrari, "Unlock the Secrets," quoting Ceci, and Dr. Mark Epstein, 84.

Chapter 12: How Do I Recover from Traumatic Memories That Are True?

1. McCann and Pearlman, *Psychological Trauma,* 38–56.
2. Shapiro, "Efficacy of Eye Movement Desensitization," 199.
3. Wylie, "Trauma and Memory," 42–43.
4. Rierden, "When Buried Truth Wants Out," 1.
5. Ibid.
6. Augsburger, *Caring Enough to Forgive,* contents page.
7. Ibid.

Chapter 13: How Do I Recover If My Memories Are False?

1. Rich Buhler, *New Choices, New Boundaries* (Nashville: Thomas Nelson, 1991).
2. Gary Smalley and John Trent, *The Language of Love* (Colorado Springs: Focus on the Family, 1988), 13–15.
3. Larry G. Day, *By Design in God's Image* (Portland, Oreg.: Mt. Tabor, 1992).

Chapter 14: How Do I Survive a False Accusation?

1. Charles R. Swindoll, "How to Do Right When You've Been Done Wrong," *Insight for Living,* KPRZ Radio, June 13–14, 1994.
2. C. R. Snyder, *Excuses: Masquerades in Search of Grace,* quoted in Goldberg, "Lies of the Mind," 64–68.
3. G. Gudjonsson, *The Psychology of Interrogations, Confessions, and Testimony* (Chichester, England: Wiley, 1992).
4. Elizabeth Loftus and J. M. Doyle, *Eyewitness Testimony: Civil and Criminal* (New York: Kluwer Law Book Publishers, 1987), 71.
5. Lorie Hearn, "Father, Daughter Settle Lawsuit over Alleged Long-ago Sex Abuse," *San Diego Union-Tribune,* 22 April 1994, p. B-2.
6. For those who have difficulty understanding reflective listening, I recommend the video tapes *Getting the Love You Want,* by Dr. Harville Hendrix, which present clear instructions and interesting examples. See note 2, chapter 7, above.
7. Augsburger, *Caring Enough to Forgive,* ch. 10.

Conclusion

1. Solomon, Gerrity, and Muff, "Efficacy of Treatments," 633.